# RIDING HIGH

American Edition published in January 1998 by

Jupitalia Productions
25750 East Lane
Covelo, Ca 95428
Phone and fax: 1-800-593-2603
e-mail tsimon@mcn.org

First published by Viking, London, in 1984
under the title Riding Home
British paperback edition, by Penguin, in 1985
First German edition by Rohwolt, Hamburg, in 1983

ISBN: 0 - 9654785 - 1 - 9

Printed in the United States of America

Also by Ted Simon

GRAND PRIX YEAR
JUPITER'S TRAVELS
THE RIVER STOPS HERE
THE GYPSY IN ME

# Riding High

by

## Ted Simon

Jupitalia

Covelo
California

# The Journey

## A CALENDAR

### 1973
ENGLAND • FRANCE
ITALY • SICILY
TUNISIA • LIBYA
EGYPT • SUDAN
ETHIOPIA

### 1974
KENYA • TANZANIA
ZAMBIA • BOTSWANA
RHODESIA • SOUTH
AFRICA • SWAZILAND
MOZAMBIQUE
BRAZIL • ARGENTINA
CHILE

### 1975
BOLIVIA • PERU
ECUADOR •
COLOMBIA • PANAMA
NICARAGUA
COSTA RICA
HONDURAS
GUATEMALA
MEXICO • USA • FIJI
NEW ZEALAND
AUSTRALIA

### 1976
SINGAPORE
MALAYSIA
THAILAND • INDIA
SRI LANKA • NEPAL

### 1977
PAKISTAN
AFGHANISTAN • IRAN
TURKEY • GREECE
YUGOSLAVIA
AUSTRIA • GERMANY
SWITZERLAND
FRANCE • ENGLAND

# Prologue

Six years before my great adventure began I bought an ancient ruin deep in rural France where much of life was almost untouched by the modern age. In those days many people still cooked on wood fires and worked their vineyards with horses. The old stone houses, huddled together for protection, were shady and cool in summer, dark and frigid in winter, and a nineteenth-century grandmother sheathed in black seemed to haunt every hearth.

Parts of my building were six hundred years old, and the neighbours who sold it to me were scarcely any younger in their attitudes and beliefs. They were peasants as gnarled and knotted, as frugal and hardy as the vines they tended. There were four in the family; an old man, his elderly wife, his step daughter and her illegitimate son. They lived next door in conditions so rustic as to be considered old-fashioned even there. One light bulb, two beds, the kitchen tap, the hearth and the mucking-out shed provided for all their domestic needs.

The old man ruled this decrepit roost with a capricious and sometimes violent hand, but even so there was a comfortable and satisfying rhythm to their lives. They were rarely if ever sick, and they were limited more by ignorance than by material constraints. So much of life had survived unchanged across the centuries - the work they did, the tools they employed, the food they grew and ate - that it hardly seemed to matter in which century they chose to live. With one exception, the outside world of high technology impinged so little on the village; two telephones, the radio and a faltering electricity supply installed in the thirties were the extent of it.

The one exception was so extreme that it was almost impossible to comprehend. Our village happened to lie on the flight path chosen by technicians in Toulouse to prove the world's first supersonic airliner. Once a week at least an ear splitting boom rang through the stone walls and shattered the calm of the valley, and the villagers looked up from their toil to observe Concorde hurtling through the stratosphere like a shining bolt from the blue.

The old man sold me his building for one reason only. The roof had fallen in, and it did not take him long to find the reason why. He was convinced that a sonic boom had brought it down. Nor was this the first time he had blamed a personal disaster on intruders from the sky.

Some sixteen years earlier, when his step-daughter became mysteriously pregnant, he explained to the village at large that she had fallen victim to the passions of a 'passing aviator' who had parachuted down to the vineyard where she was working and taken his will of her. This touching version of the Greek myth failed to convince the neighbours. They thought it more likely that it was the old man himself, and no modern Zeus, who had seduced her among the burgeoning vines, and their scepticism appeared the more justified as the years passed and the boy, far from being a demi-god, showed signs of becoming a halfwit. There were no biological grounds for this misfortune because the old man and his step-daughter were not blood relations, but the moral judgement seemed conclusive.

So that when the old man's building collapsed, people were more inclined to attribute it to his neglect than to heavenly powers. The roof had fallen, most probably, because he had done nothing to prevent it falling. Rain and rodents had attacked it, and the gradual decay of centuries had reached to the heart of the thickest oak beam. At last, under the astonish astonishing weight of its huge stone slates, the whole central portion of the roof, thirty feet long and fifteen feet wide, had thundered down on to the flagstones beneath.

Nevertheless, the old man stuck to his story. I watched him one day amid the ruins as he described the event. He was a small, indestructible runt of a man, who took root wherever he stood, as immovable as the scrub oaks on the rugged hillsides about us. His blue working pants were hitched up high above his prominent buttocks which were still tough and resilient from a lifetime of bending double with his fingers in the soil. The waistband of his long rough woollen underpants was folded out over the heavy leather belt encompassing his jaunty pot belly. His small bald head, jutting forward on a wrinkled neck, reminded me of a tortoise.

With one arm he pointed dramatically upwards.

'There was a conflagration in the sky,' he shouted. 'It was Concorde. I wrote to the President demanding compensation. But I never received a reply. What do you think of that? Eh?'

Before the collapse, the old building had served as a shelter for a small flock of sheep which his wife had taken up the hillsides every day to graze. It was a miracle, he said, that the disaster had occurred during the day. He was a believer in miracles, and the family traveled annually to Lourdes in search of them.

He appeared to have forgotten the arm which was still pointing to the heavens, and with his other arm he indicated the doorway.

'Mercifully the sheep had already gone,' he shouted, 'or they would all have been killed.'

He remained with his two arms outstretched, one vertical, one horizontal, looking more than ever like a small tree.

'*Et alors*, I decided to sell.'

First he sold the sheep, and then, when the rains began to penetrate the smashed flagstones and run into his cellar below, he sold the building to me for a song, on the understanding that I would repair it and keep his cellars dry.

The old building and I came together as in a dream. I did not know I was looking for it. In its own curious way the building might have been looking for me. Others had seen it, had recognized its possibilities and then, after a few dizzy flights of fancy, had let it go, guided regretfully by sound common sense. They had been daunted by its extreme state of decay, by the fissured walls, the rotten roofs, the sheep dung that lay thickly over its punctured floors, but they had carried away with them a vivid impression of its special qualities. Some of them were friends of a friend of mine, and through them the building disseminated its presence and waited patiently for exactly the right person to fall under its spell. When I saw it, I had not a moment's hesitation in realizing that I was that person.

I arrived in that remote corner of south-west France quite by chance, with twenty-four hours to spare and no thought of buying anything, but my friends persuaded me to look around, and the old building waylaid me. In this strange way, the best way of all, my life was changed completely.

Ruined and degraded though it was, the building had known days of grandeur. It was a medieval gatehouse, spanning a narrow road into the beautiful unspoiled village it was built to defend. It stood on the side of a valley overlooking neat vegetable gardens and a burbling stream. Its big windows, finely carved during the Renaissance, were blocked with stone, giving it the appearance of a blinded giant still defying its enemies, unaware that time had long since buried and forgot ten them.

I saw it first on a hot afternoon in August and stood between its roofless and broken walls imagining the armed bands of marauders who might once have viewed it greedily from the mountains above. A golden light seemed to shine out of the bare sandstone blocks around me, and the sun, unbearably bright, penetrated every crevice and threw shadows of painful sharpness. Behind blank door frames lay areas of cavernous darkness as black as molasses.

In its denuded state, the building revealed all the details of its construction and I could see how the walls had risen and fallen and risen again through the centuries. There were interesting remnants of vaulting, and a most unusual carved stone object which I eventually identified as a medieval refrigerator. I found myself itching to lay hands on the blackened oak, to raise the roof again, to open those glorious windows. The impulse to become part of its history was irresistible. Within moments I had decided to abandon my city life, already in disarray, and to pick up the challenge which I heard as loudly and clearly as if the building had spoken to me.

Next morning I began the negotiations. Poor though I was, the price was too low to be a problem. I wanted to buy the cellars too but the old man refused to sell them, and with reasons I could not oppose. In one cellar he made his wine and in the other he stored fodder for his horse. The most I could do was to secure a written agreement that if and when they were sold I would have priority over any other purchaser.

As soon as I possibly could, I sold up what little was left to me in London, came to camp in my ruin and set about restoring it. For four years I worked on it, alone at first, and then with a girl friend, Jo. I grew calloused and strong and ingenious, and learned about the other half of the world that my schooling and urban experience had entirely ignored, and without which life would henceforth seem unthinkably shallow.

Life with the old man next door was a constant exasperation. His natural conceit, his stubborn refusal to concede a point, infuriated the other villagers too, and this obduracy, combined with the touch of scandal over the illegitimate grandson, had already isolated his family from the rest. They were often bitter and suspicious of the world, which they felt was out to rob them, and mock them, and they imagined conspiracies where none existed. Yet boastful and ignorant as he was, the old man had an undeniable sweetness in him too which he was too naive to exploit, and it was that quality, I suppose, which made me value him so highly despite everything.

Our relations with them were always uneasy, and waxed and waned with the moon and the seasons, but thanks to Jo they were rarely hostile, because the old man's indomitably cocky nature always responded to female flattery.

The building made tremendous demands on us. There was a great deal to do, with limited means. The work was very hard. Only a degree of fanaticism made it possible. Gradually the house became habitable, and even beautiful, but always primitive, and always needing more and more effort. Finally, during our fourth summer, we broke under the weight of it. As though the roof had once more come crashing down.

Out of our disillusionment, pain and separation the journey was born.

When people asked me, later, why I chose to ride a motorcycle round the world I had dozens of ingenious explanations. The question was usually put by interviewers and I was expected to entertain them. I talked about curiosity, about my interest in the nature of poverty, about the pursuit of self knowledge, and of my reluctance to leave the world without having seen a good deal of it. The honest answer was too short and uncomfortable. I did it because I felt like it. All else followed from that.

It had to be an inordinately strong feeling, better described as a passion, to survive for so long and through so many vicissitudes. Many people thought it very strange that a forty two-year-old man would commit himself to such a journey.

'Aren't you a bit old to go round the world?' asked a young radio executive. To him, and to others like him, I was a freak. I did not even have a nominal pretext, the sort of thing a person might drum up when he wants to do something peculiar and still keep his respectability. I wasn't an expedition, or a Fellow of the Royal Geographical Society. I wasn't proving a product, or making a movie, or breaking a record, or 'doing it for England'. I wasn't even a fanatic for motorcycles, never having ridden one before.

It was the sheer extravagance of the project that seemed to make it hard to assimilate. If I had confined my ambition to the first leg of the journey, say from London to Cape Town, it might have been easier to absorb. An adventure like that could be accomplished in a few months (in fact it took me five) and still be contained within the framework of a 'normal' life. That would have been enough to provide all the risks, to run through the whole range of emotions, to meet life in the raw, human as well as animal, and to break out of the pampered enclave of Western civilization into the wild world beyond.

A person could return from such an escapade and still expect to take up his place in society, get on with his career and resume his duties and obligations like a normal chap. And if I had been hungry for a notable achievement to comfort myself with on my deathbed, well, London to Cape Town by motor cycle would have been no mean feat in itself.

But to go on for another 50,000 miles, through the Americas, Australia and Asia? Surely that was excessive. Four years on the road was a different matter to five months. After four years you drop out of people's address books. Friendships can atrophy, acquaintanceships evaporate, people can change and disappear. I thought it disturbed my friends that I should want to go to such extremes. Yet I can say, when the question arises for the umpteenth time, that it always seemed utterly worthwhile, the very best thing I could do.

I think now that the feeling had its origins in the far distant driftings of my father's ancestors. It was intensified by his own, still mysterious wanderings over the face of Europe before he arrived in England. And in me it was probably conceived out of my own insatiable yearnings and many sporadic efforts to break away.

At first, riding towards Africa, fearfully uncertain of my strength and courage, I knew fits of terrible nostalgia and remorse. The differences which had separated me from Jo and the old building seemed trivial, and I felt it could be only a matter of time before we resumed our life together. Then, as the journey took hold of me and I began to find my place in the vastness of the African continent, the pangs subsided. I saw them as symptoms of withdrawal from an addiction to property and security which appeared as an obstacle to the larger vision of life now dawning upon me.

The further I traveled the greater my confidence grew, until it became inconceivable that I would ever again allow myself to be shackled into domesticity. And yet, finally, perhaps because I traveled too far, that was just what I did do.

The journey arose from the ashes of the other quite different and opposite dream I had been pursuing in my old building in France, the dream to which I eventually returned; so that my life swung like a pendulum between two vital and conflicting needs, to wander and to build. It is with the movements of the pendulum that this book is concerned.

The world's open markets are enough reason in themselves to travel. In Penang everything was sold off bicycles, and here they are going, through the wash outside the covered market area.
It was the sight of all those interesting looking fish that prompted me to get out my pole, and led me to my doom.

*Riding High*

# 1. Penang

I f life is a journey, then the best journeys should be like life, and life goes up and down. When I arrived in Penang, a beautiful island off the shores of Malaysia, I had no idea how far down my life would go, but if it had to happen, it couldn't have happened in a more interesting place. The island used often to be called the Pearl of the Orient. It comes complete with tropical beaches, fascinating vegetation and wildlife, and an old, bustling seaport capital called Georgetown.

My Triumph and I limped into Georgtown in May of '76, riding on the last drops of juice in my battery. The stator had burned out in my alternator, just north of Kuala Lumpur. Usually I accepted these difficulties with good grace, but this one irked me constantly. For three years I had been carrying a spare of that very same part, but it was heavy, and in Singapore, I decided I would never need it. I wrapped it up and mailed it home. A week later, I needed it, and of course it could only be got from England. The Lucas company, one of my sponsors, had a shop in Penang, and they arranged to have it sent, but it would take a couple of weeks. So, as I waited while my two stators passed each other somewhere in mid-air, I took up residence at the Choong Thean hotel on Rope Walk, and went fishing off the esplanade.

At first I caught only plastic bags, but then I caught a submerged log. It was rash of me to think I could pull a log out of the Bay of Bengal on the end of a fishing line, but I wanted to save my tackle. The line snapped and shot the lead sinker into my eye, and that should have been enough to qualify me for a patch and a parrot.

Mercifully the eyeball did not burst. It merely filled with blood. When I reached the hospital they peered into the murk and said they could see nothing and do nothing until the blood had cleared. They took the only course open to them and immobilized the eye. Unfortunately, the only way to immobilize an eye is to immobilize its owner, and since one eye won't stay still while the other moves I was blindfolded, laid on my back and forbidden all kinds of things, including biscuits.

It was my second taste of imprisonment. In Brazil the police had locked me in a room for two weeks and left me to struggle with fear and boredom, but although the loss of liberty was almost unbearable I was at least free to relieve my frustration by physical movement and outbursts of rage. I invented 'prisoner's squash' and kept my body functioning more or less, bouncing a matchbox off the wall and trying to catch it on its erratic returns. And, greatest of all boons, I was able to read and write. Even then, I failed miserably to arrive at the philosophical equanimity to which I aspired.

This time I was much more closely confined. I was locked effectively into my head, and what I found there was not reassuring. At first the shock of the accident helped me to sleep a good deal, and during the first waking hours I was preoccupied by the novelty of my situation, wondering whether my right eye would recover and what, alternatively, I would do without it. After twenty-four hours that subject was exhausted.

I told myself that nobody on earth should be better able to benefit from a few days of blindness than I, with three years of traveling experience to draw upon. Riding the motorcycle alone for hour after hour, sometimes for twelve or more hours in a day, through barely changing landscapes in Africa and South America, I had never had a moment of boredom. I moved along entranced by the mysteries of the world I had newly discovered. A huge cast of characters came dancing, limping and bustling across my mind's stage, and I speculated endlessly on their nature and significance, and what I was to make of them. Surely I could bring them to life again now, more vividly perhaps than ever!

Strangely, these resources all failed me. It seemed as though it was the act of traveling itself which gave life to those memories. In the darkness, without the engine drumming beneath me, without the trees, hedges, grassland, rivers, mountains, plains, cattle and people flowing past, without the sky, the weather and the wind in my face, my imagination became as moribund as my body stretched out on the hospital bed.

The boredom became oppressive, a positive weight bearing down on me. It became painful. It became intolerable. My mind fought desperately for something to take a hold on. I watched it as a living thing, like a wild bird caged in my skull, dashing itself madly against the walls of its cell. In the darkness I became divided into my component parts. There was I, the observer. There was I, the body. There was my mind. And there was my memory. And because my mind refused to lie down with the rest of us, we were thrown into agonizing confusion.

Perhaps the description sounds unduly melodramatic, but no active person should be too hasty to judge before putting on a blindfold and spending a day lying on a bed. Most people find it hard enough to close their eyes and remain calm for as little as an hour. The effect on me, at any rate, was devastating.

Of course, nobody was in any way to blame for my state of mind. I was lucky to be in a hospital at all, and Penang General was, as far as I could tell, a good one. I was admitted free, without the least resistance or fuss, and I was in a spacious, airy ward with nine other patients. The nurses were cheerful and kind, some Malay some Chinese, and I lived for their ministrations to break the monotony. One of them taught me a few words of Chinese. Another described life under the Japanese occupation, and surprised me by saying how she preferred it to when the British returned. It was so much safer, she said, because practically every crime was punishable by death.

The specialist, Dr Manocha, was a grave and gentle man who took the trouble to explain carefully what he was doing (or rather, in my case, not doing) and why, and I had faith in him. The only thing I lacked that a Western hospital would have provided was a radio, but I began to think that without one I might well go crazy. I tried to count my blessings to still the frantic ravings of my mind, but the results continued to be disappointing and I was shocked by my performance. If there is one quality a traveler needs in abundance it is the ability to suffer frustrations, solitude and the unexpected with stoicism and good humour. I had thought until that dark time in Penang that I had learned my lessons well, and that traveling had greatly increased my peace of mind. Yet here I was, at war with my mind as never before.

Even so, there were periods of quiet. I found that when my eyes had been covered for a long time patterns began to form in the darkness, patterns I had not seen before They were three-dimensional, and resembled the richly intricate carvings of a Gothic altar screen or a cathedral facade. Broad masses of tiny detail spread and shifted before me, and I read all kinds of things into them, as one does with clouds, fire and the stars.

A vision came quite unbidden on the afternoon of the second day there. I had noticed when I arrived that a young Chinese boy lay in a bed not far away on my left, and I saw him now in the dark cinema of my mind. One by one, I watched his ancestors arrive to sit in a wide arc round the end of his bed with their eyes fixed on him, patient but intense. They were distinct individuals of all ages, some of them well enough defined to be recognizable should I have seen them later in the street, and the tableau remained fixed for some time. Of course, I thought there might be something prophetic about it, and feared that the boy might be dying, but he left the hospital some months later and, as far as I know, recovered quite normally.

On the third day the blood had cleared enough to let some light into my eye. I saw it as a frosted blur because of the drops of atropine that had been put in to relax the pupil. Manocha shone his light on the retina and said he could see only very slight damage. The best treatment, he told me, was to continue as before and let the eye heal itself. Another week of darkness lay ahead and I became desperate, somehow or other, to get hold of a radio.

As luck would have it, my first and only visitor came that afternoon. He was quite unexpected. I knew nobody in Penang who could have been sufficiently interested in my predicament. The Chinese sister allowed me to slip the bandage off my good eye for a few minutes, and my heart warmed immediately to see T'an standing by my bed.

T'an worked and lived at the Choong Thean Hotel in Rope Walk where I had a room and where I had left all my belongings, including the motorcycle with its burned-out alternator. It was a small hotel and T'an was the only full-time employee. There was another man who operated the Mah Jong table at the back, but that was in the evenings only. There were maids who came and went and probably did many other jobs as well. And then there were the prostitutes, comfortable Indian ladies most of them, who waited patiently downstairs for customers at five dollars a time, of which a dollar and twenty cents went to the hotel for the use of the small room 'short time' at the back.

T'an's function at the Choong Thean was vague and his salary was minuscule. Occasionally I had seen him with a broom in his hand or shuffling along the pavement on some errand, but his usual position was slumped half asleep on a kitchen chair in the middle of the entrance area. He was a short, stocky man in middle age, with a body fallen into sorry disrepair. His stomach and chest sagged below rounded shoulders, his ankles were rough, swollen and bent, and he moved as though he bore a heavy burden. Invariably he wore sandals, beige cotton trousers and a loose yellow tee-shirt, and as he sat dozing in the chair the neck of the tee-shirt always slipped to one side to expose a plump, womanish shoulder.

In repose, which was his normal state, his face was not specially prepossessing either. It was the round and wrinkled face of an elderly Chinese, topped by a close-cropped bristle of grey hair. It was when he spoke that the miracle occurred, transforming it, to my eyes at least, into one of the most wonderfully expressive faces I had ever seen. For T'an had one peculiarity which distinguished him; he was partially tongue-tied. A lifelong effort to overcome the defect had given him an astonishing power to communicate feeling and conviction. It was a talent that the finest actor might envy. Each syllable had to be constructed by energetic use of his lips and cheek muscles. Moving carefully from word to word, moulding each one and pushing it out past his encumbered palate like successive sculptures in air, raising and lowering the pitch to maximum effect, he projected an extraordinary degree of sincerity. His face, attuned since childhood to assist him in this endeavour, was devoted wholly to conveying the spirit of the sentence that his mouth was so laboriously piecing together, and the combination was irresistibly convincing.

From the first moment I heard him I had been so struck by the quality of his voice that I had tried, privately, to contort my mouth in every possible way to imitate it. At last, by pushing my tongue hard against the roof of my mouth and keeping it there as I spoke, I caught the flavour of those remarkable sounds. The sybillants fell like soft waterfalls; the words 'to do' sounded like the cooing of doves.

The vowels were long and plaintive and the overall effect was to make all his words sound tender and thoughtful. A few words from T'an, on any subject whatever, whether to ask me for a cigarette or to recommend a particular chow stall, always touched me and made me feel better.

The magic was all the more powerful for issuing from such an unpromising figure. In silence he was virtually expendable, but in speech he commanded the respect due a great craftsman. T'an turned the old adage on its head: in speech he was golden, in silence dross.

He showed a natural sympathy and an anxiety to please which was unlike the rather hard-edged politenesses I was used to receiving from other Chinese in shops and offices. He seemed to be somewhat bewildered at finding himself in such poor circumstances, and there was a suggestion that he had fallen on these hard times from a much more comfortable background. He talked of having passed a profligate youth, of gambling, driving fast cars and spending money in night clubs. In a morose mood one day he had dwelt on his misfortunes in the years of 'seventy-three and 'seventy-four, when there had been no work, and he had had to sell his stamp and coin collections to get 'food to feed my stomach'. He referred to lucrative jobs he might have got if he had had the courage to be operated on for his speech defect, but he said he was too frightened to 'cut the string'.

Now of course it was too late, much too late. He dreamed of winning a lottery, a dream he shared with virtually every other Chinese citizen of Malaysia, and once there was some mention of a piece of land to which he thought he had a claim, but he knew that his fate, most probably, was to drift down the rest of his days on odd jobs and charity. He had already hinted, in a courteous and roundabout way, at the part I might play in his declining years, when he told me about an Australian he had once got to know.

"Often from his homeland he would send me some dollars in a letter. He was so good to me. I do not know the reason why . . ."

Then the gifts ceased.

"Afterwards I wrote many times, but I did not receive a reply. Then one time I learned that this man is dead."

It wrung my heart as it had wrung his. T'an spoke an unusually good, if quaint, English redolent of colonial class rooms and missionary teachers. Words like 'seldom' and 'therefore' dropped like ripe plums from his fruitful mouth. This made him useful in the hotel, for neither the owner nor his wife, nor even the man with the Mah Jong franchise, could speak a word of English. However, the persuasiveness of T'an's speech, which affected me so strongly, was probably not as effective in Chinese. His relations with the management were not good, judging by the tone of voice in which his boss urged him to get to his feet and do something or other

Although I knew that he was cultivating me as a potential patron I could not bring myself to feel offended. What else was he to do? If I had been a tin tycoon I would have employed him to sit and snooze on my front porch. As it was I could scarcely begrudge him the odd cigarette and the loan of a dollar or two which he always offered to repay but with such a pitiable show of honesty as to ensure that he kept them. For this I was his favourite guest and I revelled in it.

So that when he arrived at my bedside and said: "Good afternoon, Mr. Simon. I am sorry to hear of your accident," the formal, conventional greeting, spoken with tied tongue, was like music to my ears and I was particularly happy that he had come to visit me.

T'an was carrying a small package.

"The boss has sent this for you," he said. The parcel contained some fruit and cake, more than enough of each, and not the cheapest kind. I was surprised. The offer was evidently sincere and not merely a token. I had judged T'an's boss as being too hard and indifferent for such a gesture, and his generosity came as a great relief. I had been trying to suppress my concern for all the things I had left at the hotel. As if he were reading my thoughts, T'an added:

"Do not be anxious for your belongings. They are all collected safely. The boss has put them in a cupboard and he has locked the door with a key."

"Please T'an," I said, "will you take my fishing rod back with you, and can you please buy me a small radio? The cheapest radio you can find. How much will it be?"

"I do not know. I will get one very cheap," he said. "Maybe only eleven dollars." It was somehow characteristic of T'an that he would settle on such an odd amount. The dollars we were talking about were Malaysian dollars, and there were four to the American dollar at the time.

I kept my money in a leather pouch which, apart from the motorcycle itself, was easily the most valuable item I possessed, and the key to my whole journey. It held the two passports I was permitted to carry so that I could move between mutually hostile countries. There was a domestic driving license and the torn remains of an international one, the card recording my cholera, yellow-fever and small-pox immunizations, spare passport photographs for visas, a list of Lucas agents, a cable credit card and a correspondent's credentials from the *Sunday Times* (mainly for show). There were two miniature address books with details of all the friends I had made in three years of wandering around the globe and of other contacts I hoped to meet on the way back. There was a bundle of traveler's checks for a thousand US dollars, just forwarded to me in Penang, the final installment which I hoped would get me back to Europe. There was a ball-point pen and some cash.

The pouch itself had been made for me in the Souk at Cairo. It was a simple and inexpensive object made of rawhide. Strung on a broad leather belt, it sat neatly under my stomach as I rode or walked, and because its contents were so valuable my hand would often move to it to reassure myself that it was there. Over the years the gesture had become an automatic, self-comforting movement, repeated whenever some shadow of anxiety or doubt crossed my mind. I touched it the way a Catholic would cross himself to ward off evil and temptation, and it responded to the frequent caressing and the rubbing of my clothes by acquiring a deep and lustrous patina.

It had become by now the Ark of my Covenant and the badge of my immunity, an object of beauty and veneration scarcely separable from the journey itself, although at the time I would have laughed at such a description. In the hospital I had taken it off the belt in order to fit it more easily into the small bedside cupboard.

I reached over to it now to give T'an the money he wanted. The pouch was so tightly packed that, to get at the cash I had to empty the contents on to the bed and then repack it.

I gave T'an twelve dollars.

"Please try to bring the radio tomorrow," I begged him. All the desperation of my dark and silent hours in the hospital returned to me. "I need it badly."

I felt foolish making such a fuss about a radio, ashamed of my sudden dependence and aware of all the other silent and equally sightless figures lying in the ward, uncomplaining.

"If the boss can permit I will return tomorrow," he said.

A picture from better days, with the precious pouch that was stolen from me in Penang. In many parts of Latin America police thought I carried a gun there, but in Australia they thought I was delivering telegrams.

*Chapter 1: Penang* ————————▶ 17

I put the pouch back in the cupboard and asked T'an to thank his boss for the gifts and take special care of my motorcycle. A nurse gave him the fishing rod to carry back and firmly replaced the bandage over my left eye.

He came back two days later with a tiny transistor. He had been holding out, he said, for a special price from a friend. That's why he was a day longer. He asked if he could pay back the extra dollar at the end of the month.

"The boss is not a kind man to me. I have no money and he will not give me one dollar from my next month wage."

To me the boss was kinder. He had sent another food package as generous as the first. I thanked T'an profusely and told him to tell his boss that I would probably be back in the hotel in a few more days.

As soon as T'an had left the ward I switched on the radio It was exactly what I had hoped for but in the two days of waiting my fevered impatience had all but burnt itself out The music was either Chinese, or Western with Chinese orchestration. As background music it might have been tolerable, but as the sole focus of attention it was as maddening and repetitive as the torture of a thousand cuts. The only English language was reserved for shrill commercials and the reception was in any case, terrible.

After six days of the treatment my mind gave up its frantic efforts to escape and sank into a torpor. My body felt slack and jaded and failed to function properly. Both had been used to an unusual amount of exercise and stimulus, and went to seed all the faster without it, the way a retired fighter runs to fat. Although the ward was as cool as it could be without air conditioning, the summer was building up to the rains and the constant humid warmth added to my lassitude. I already foresaw that it would take a lot of effort and some time to recover the spirit and physical confidence to get back on the road. Depressing as that thought was, it was nothing compared with the shock of despair that hit me later in the day.

Some obscure nervous impulse made me fumble blindly in my locker for my pouch. It was not there. I could not believe it. I did not dare to believe it. I ripped the bandage off my left eye and searched everywhere. It was gone. Even as I looked, I began to think how incomprehensible it was that I should have left such a valuable thing in an unlocked cupboard while I, myself, was blindly unable to protect it. And yet how monstrous, I thought, to be betrayed and robbed in a hospital where faith and trust were of the essence, and in the blind ward of a hospital at that, where the patient was doubly helpless.

I simply did not have the energy to be furious. For a while I toyed with the hope that the thief might simply steal the money and leave the rest to be found somewhere, as had happened years before once in Libya. But neither the pouch nor any of its contents were ever seen again, and feeling quite incapable of facing the consequences I sank into fatalistic apathy.

During the weeks that followed I paid the penalty for becoming the hero of my own myth. For a long time, without realizing it, I had gloried in the role of someone chosen by the gods, whom the gods would protect so long as I, for my part, remained true to the exploit which first drew me to their attention. I felt I had been riding the continents of the world in an aura as bright and invulnerable as the shining of legendary knights, an aura which reserved me for a particular destiny, immune from the petty injuries and humiliations that beset an ordinary tourist.

I had grown used to observing Westerners trapped in their various forms of misery. I had seen them sick, languishing in their dysentery and hepatitis. I had met them destitute after robbery, besieging their unsympathetic embassies. I watched them pass mournful days and weeks at the counters of banks, waiting for stolen traveler's checks to be refunded. And wherever they met, I had heard the unceasing laments for lost cameras, watches, jewellery, passports, wallets, all the bright and precious things that stream from the rooms and persons of tourists to nourish the parasitic underworld that feeds off tourism, just as the dockland, Conrad's 'border of filth and infamy', feeds off sailors.

I had become rather heartless about it, thinking of all that vice and all that innocence as somehow deserving each other in a mutually fulfilling symbiosis. There might be something salutary in the experience of a white Westerner, with three weeks to visit the Orient, expecting to see some sights, take some pictures, eat some spicy food, finding himself laid low, stripped of his belongings, forced into some sleazy hole through lack of funds and made to identify just for a moment with the realities of the world whose glossier aspects he had hoped to carry home on his colour slides.

The view from my window in Room 6 at the Choong Thean hotel.
Over the fish scale tiles, the domes of the mosque glimmer gold.

I had to learn that the immunity I had apparently enjoyed for
some time was not a magical gift bestowed on me (and somehow
enshrined in a leather pouch) but a habit of vigilance formed in earlier days at the expense of much effort and anxiety, and some bitter
experience as well, which needed to be constantly revitalized. I had
been blind in more ways than one. What happier hunting ground
could a sneak thief hope for than a blind ward? Bitterly I wondered
whose eye had gleamed when I spread my wealth out on the bed
that day. But I had fallen too far, physically and mentally, to draw
strength from philosophical speculations. I regarded myself simply
with contempt, as someone who had let himself be injured, ripped off
and humiliated – just another foolish tourist feeling sick and queu-
ing at the bank.

I came out of hospital and took a bus into town hoping that the bustle of the streets would bring me to life. I walked up Campbell Street to Rope Walk looking for something, anything, that would catch my imagination and release me from my numbness. Campbell Street is lined with jewellers' shops where the Chinese invest in gold the money they fail to lose in gambling. Before the accident I had always marvelled at the number of these shops, at the amount of business they did, at the extraordinary aroma of reverence that emanated from the mouth of each of these carpeted Aladdin's caves. But this time there was no spark.

I rounded the corner to the Choong Thean Hotel, almost the first building on the left-hand side. The high green wooden shutters were folded back, and the ground-floor front was completely open to the street. On the left of the cement floor one of the 'girls', wrapped in her sari, sat knitting alone on the long wooden settee. The settee was made of a fine hard wood and richly carved. In an antique shop in London it would have sold for enough money to release its occupant from her profession for life. Any other time this ironic twist to the old joke of 'sitting on a fortune' might have cheered me up, but not that day.

T'an sat on his chair as usual with his head lolling and his mouth open. Behind him, alongside the staircase that rose to the two floors above, stood my Triumph. Just looking at it made me feel nervous and weary. It was not a glamorous machine in the modern style. The frame was black; the tank and mudguard maroon. All the painted surfaces were so dented, scratched and worn that they absorbed light rather than reflecting it. The aluminum crankcase was dulled and pitted by sand and seawater, and the underside, with its handmade iron sump shield, was clogged with mud. The simple, classical lines were even more obscured by bars and brackets to carry the heavy bags and boxes now locked away in the boss's cupboard.

On the road, all these bumps and blemishes had delighted me. This was no plaything for urban cowboys and café racers, but a scarred veteran of deserts and creekbeds and impossible peaks. Every scrape and deformity, from the slightly twisted forks to the battered wheel-rims, told of some remembered encounter with the hard edges of a world I had already explored for some 40,000 miles. This was my spaceship and time machine. With my life-support system packed tightly round its frame, I had ridden it through the looking-glass to a head-on collision with my dreams. We had penetrated the fantasy of Arabia, the black tribal nights of Africa, the South American pageant of gunpowder and guitars, the sap-sweet, drug-lit trip of California, the crude laconic crust of Australia and the swarming shores of the Asian hive. In each case I had known the intense thrill of expectation as I conjured up a lifetime's imaginings for the last time, before my fantasies bowed finally to the irresistible and even more satisfying truth of the place itself.

With all these remembered glories evoked by the sight of the motorcycle, I was dreadfully downcast by my weakness and sense of inadequacy. I felt scarcely capable of wheeling the machine off its stand without dropping it. The dread vista of bureaucratic obstacles ahead of me as I tried to replace my passports, licenses, certificates, all that paper paraphernalia, was too depressing, and I deliberately looked away and told myself: "Some other time. Not now."

The woman on the settee interrupted her knitting to give me an uncommonly sweet smile, and said, "Hello. You are feeling better now, is it?"

T'an raised his drooping eyelids, and his face came to life.

"Mister Simon. You are back so soon? You see your motorcycle is safe? It is so heavy. Yesterday I was obliged to move it in the street. We were three persons to move it." He climbed slowly to his feet and the boss's wife waddled in from the kitchen at the back and smiled at me as well. They spoke in Chinese and T'an told me:

"You can have your same room again. Number six is free. She will open the cupboard."

It felt like coming home. I gathered up some things from the cupboard beneath the stairs, and began to carry them up to my room on the second floor. T'an picked up one small bag and followed, hanging on the green wooden banisters as he climbed the purple-painted steps. At the first-floor landing I heard the remembered clacking sound of the abacus in the room below mine, where the same two men seemed to spend all their days calculating amid books, bales and boxes. The friendliness and familiarity of the Choong Thean began to sweeten my bitter frame of mind. I opened the thickly encrusted green-louvered shutters of my room, causing some lethargic pigeons to totter a few paces along the ledge of crumbling masonry that ran below the windows. Once again I experienced a sharp pang of nostalgia for my boyhood, evoked by high windows, flaking paint and pigeons on a ledge. Across the road was a lovely roof of speckled orange tiles, packed together as tightly as fish scales, and above that but some way distant rose the gleaming gold cupola of the mosque.

T'an raised my spirits another notch with his elegant references to the dollar he would regretfully be unable to return for another few weeks, and the cigarette which his lamentable penury drove him to request. Then he left me. I sat for a moment with a cigarette in my hand on the edge of the cane and mahogany opium couch, thinking about the past, about hotel rooms I had lived in long, long ago in Paris, about the pleasure I once used to get from smoking cigarettes; searching anywhere among my memories for a key with which to begin the slow, hard job of winding myself up again. Then I went out to the coffee shop.

A person bereft of purpose or direction needs a dependable point of attachment to the earth, as much as a ship without crew or rudder needs a safe anchorage. Rope Walk was my harbour. At night I anchored thankfully at the Choong Thean for a mere five Malaysian dollars a night. During the day I shifted my moorings to the Kedai Kopi, a coffee shop at the other end of the short road, near the corner with Chulia Street.

Like most shops in the tropics, the Kedai Kopi was entirely open to the street, without windows or doors, only a single large shutter which was closed during the night. The floor, I think, was tiled and the walls painted, though it could have been the other way round. Simple wooden tables and chairs took up most of the space, but there was a counter and an ice chest at the back.

In the morning I came for coffee and fingers of hot buttered toast. The toast was made from slices of traditional English white bread, which were called tin loaves, with the crust trimmed away and the slices cut in strips. It was always done like this in Malaysia, a throw-back to colonial times and, as it happened, another link to some unresolved childhood memory.

I pampered myself with mug after mug of sweet instant coffee made from whole milk. Sometimes I ate one or two of the hot suety pastries stuffed with meat or jam called dim sum which cooked in a stack of steaming cane baskets near the entrance. This was always an adventure. I never was able to remember the Chinese words to distinguish between pork, prawns and jam, and would just point at random, say 'one piece', and wait to see what my tongue encountered inside.

Less useful to my convalescence was the ginger beer. When I discovered bottle upon bottle in the ice chest I quickly developed a craving for it. All around the world, in Africa, the Americas, Australia, I had fought against the awful American colas and their sickly orange and lemon cousins. They have become such immense industry that they have almost succeeded in replacing water as a drink, even in the most remote rural shanties. The discovery that even African tribesmen and South American Indians were tempted to waste their tiny resources on these dreadful drinks was so offensive to me that I resisted them as best I could.

But ginger beer stood for something pure and natural out of my childhood. Every day the heat and humidity seemed to increase, and I knew better than to bloat my stomach with sugary fizz, but the mere idea of ginger beer was so refreshing that I drank one after another. It was fortunate that my cravings didn't extend to alcohol. There were cans of Guinness to be had too, brewed under license in Singapore. The custom at the Kedai Kopi was to drink it off the shelf, where it got considerably warmer than body temperature. The effect of hot Guinness exploding in the mouth was curious and worth a try, but I did not find it addictive.

During the day, when I didn't have to tussle with some bureaucrat or other, I sat and tried to restore from memory the addresses I had lost and to pull myself together. The phrase describes quite accurately what I needed to do. During my time in hospital the different parts of me seemed to have come adrift. My legs felt shaky, my vision was still uncertain and my body felt like a sack of uncoordinated organs alternately sulking and bickering among themselves.

On top of that I had to get checks refunded, to get vaccinated and inoculated, to replace the driving license and at least one passport, to renew my visa, and to swear out affidavits with the police, in Malaysian of course. In a temperate climate and in good health it would have been an irksome prospect. In the tropics, feeling as I did, the task sometimes seemed beyond me. Then I would have another ginger beer and feel the worse for it.

Enough of this maudlin self-pity. Think of the millions who would envy you, would give anything to holiday in Penang, Pearl of the Orient. Just look around you. It's enough to make your senses sing. Well, isn't it? At the chow stall across the road, the cook spins the flywheel fan with his foot, forcing air into the charcoal blaze, sending up a blast of flame and sparks as he shovels the ingredients round the hot sides of the wok with furious energy.

How many kinds of noodle does he have piled against the inner wall of his glass case? How many different herbs and sauces? The odours of soy and prawn drift down the street, to mingle with incense from the Chinese undertakers and the smell of fish being carried past in wide baskets. Three Indian bakers on bicycles sail past in stately procession. They lean back in their saddles, ringing their bells to attract attention to the large glass cabinets balanced impossibly over their rear wheels. They are all selling the same buns and loaves. Why on earth do they ride together, then, if they are in competition? Why do the Indians here always lean backwards, even when they're walking, at such a precarious angle that it seems they must fall?

On the pavements of Chulia Street there are carpenters. basketmakers and mechanics, sawing, weaving and hammering, surrounded by a tangle of merchandise. Grocery and hardware shops, furnished in the old-fashioned way with shelves and jars and counters, display a bewildering variety of things so strange to the Western eye that they seem to belong more to the age of alchemy and the witch's cauldron. There are roots and barks and leaves, and slimy things in bottles. There are all kinds of grains, beans and peculiar powders heaped in sacks and sold off old brass scales in expertly twirled cornets of rough grey paper.

Everywhere what you see is the thing itself, not the package or the advertising display. Here is a world of reality. Here you buy the sugar, not the brand name. You buy the biscuits, not the graphics. Heavy ropelike coils of glistening black chewing tobacco lie on the floor. Dense blocks of prawn paste squat by the abacus. There are drums and barrels and carboys and crates, and incense sticks as thick as an elephant's leg.

In the streets the car has not yet taken over. On small Japanese motorcycles, waves of neat Chinese in white shirts and gaudy helmets rip into the atmosphere with the racket of unfettered exhaust. Rickshaws and bicycles swarm too. The rickshaw drivers clang and shout for custom, and pursue tourists with offers of hotels and heroin.

"Hey, Johnny," they yell, "want smack?"

Well, thank goodness, I didn't fancy smack, because I was ideally placed to succumb. The wonderful confidence I had taken so much for granted was gone. That powerful feeling, the sense of conviction which had launched me on my journey and kept me going so long, had drained away. And I felt that if I persisted without it I would be in grave danger. It was that feeling which had protected me and kept me alert. Without it I had no faith in my judgement or purpose. In its absence, observing with despair the aching space inside me where it had been, I saw the strangeness of it for myself, and glimpsed for a while what is the hardest thing for a person to see, which is his oddness to others.

That particular passion which caused me to pursue for years on end a journey that others would scarcely contemplate, that many regarded as an act of folly or arrogance, arose out of my own peculiarity. I saw that it would make me a difficult person to live with, just as I knew that without it I could hardly live with myself.

I liked the Kedai Kopi because they didn't speak English, and were far from fashionable. The clientele was purely local, either Chinese or Malay, shopkeepers, rickshaw drivers or artisans who brought their workshops out on the pavements of Chulia Street every morning. The owner played Chinese pop on the radio and patrons read their newspapers from top to bottom instead of from left to right. Because the customers were so thoroughly ethnic and poor the advertisements on the wall gave me endless amusement. There were two calendars, in particular, which in this context looked sublimely futile and ridiculous.

One showed a young, blond and very English racing driver of the witless type who invariably gets himself killed halfway through the first season. He was smoking a Rothman's, and the legend read: 'When you know what you're doing. . .' You had only to look at him to know he didn't have a clue.

Another showed an almost identical nitwit pretending to be a boat designer and demonstrating to his client the plans for his revolutionary new sure-to-sink hydrofoil. He was smoking State Express, 'The successful man's cigarette'.

Beneath this second calendar one day a skinny brown man came and sat. His feet were bare and blackened by dirt. He wore only a brown singlet and ragged khaki shorts, the habitual dress of the men whose swollen calf muscles pumped the pedals of the bicycle rickshaws around town. It was his face and manner which drew my attention and held it. He came in and sat with rapid, jerky movements and a great show of impatience. From under beetled brows he peppered the room with brief angry glances, warning us all not to waste his valuable time with our idle chatter and nonsense. He behaved, in fact, like a man who knew he was the center of attention, a man of power whose every whim could spell ruin or reward for those around him, like a choleric general coming to shake up his slovenly staff on the eve of a great battle. I watched breathlessly to see what grim business he was about to settle.

With lips compressed and every feature of his face under tension, he brought from his pocket an empty, pristine yellow State Express packet and two creased paper packs of cheap national cigarettes. Then he set about transferring the cheap cigarettes into the prestigious box. I was quite transfixed by the sense of importance he gave

Why Indians should have a monopoly on the baked goods business in Penang I never discovered. Perhaps they have a better sense of balance. It would need that to pedal these big showcases around town. Not so the fruit vendor, below. He's a Malay and needs three wheels to stay upright.

to himself and his task. No great leader at a moment of crisis could have assumed more gravity. On him, of course, it was as absurd and incongruous as was the fatuous man in the calendar hanging above his head.

When he dropped the empty wrappers on the floor, there was a scream of rage from the other end of the cafe, and I waited to see my ragged King Lear's composure crumble, but he picked up his pieces of paper as though they were medals and, with a final reprimanding sweep of the assembled company, he turned his back and stalked away, 'the successful man' to the last. Yet he did not even aspire to the status of a rickshaw. Outside stood an outsize sack and a big basket. He swung the sack over his shoulder, then grasped the basket by the rim and dragged it away defiantly down the road.

This fine piece of madness did something to bring me to life again. On my dreary visits to the police station, the immigration office, the hospital, the bank, the post office and the inoculation center, I tried to see people for the diverse and fascinating individuals they were, rather than as a tiresome crowd competing with me at counters and blocking my way on buses. There is always a choice between these two attitudes and there is no doubt about which is the better one to take. If you can't see the people for the crowds, you have no business to be traveling at all, but it takes some energy, imagination, and detachment. As my strength gradually returned, the faces around me reminded me of why I was there.

Why do the faces of the poor seem so much more expressive and interesting than those of affluent societies? Deprivation and hardship make deeper imprints, of course. And then physical marks and mutilations are more common. Birth itself is more haphazard, producing more distortions than we the privileged would permit. Childhood ailments and other diseases can ravage the skin, bend the bones, rot the teeth, leave a milky glaze over one eye or put a squint in another. Hard labour may crook the neck, pull down one shoulder, leave a permanent grimace or a lopsided walk. All the exaggerated physiognomies of nineteenth-century London that Dickens described so vividly are still on display now in the poor world. But if that were all, it would have only the repellent novelty value of a freak show at the circus.

In the cities of the underprivileged world it is the range of character and emotion that strikes the eye more even than the physical oddities and deformities. Vitality, intelligence and cunning are so much easier to recognize where the struggle is fiercer. Those who want to win against the odds have to become more truly themselves, stamped by their strongest emotions. Generosity, kindness and wit become more remarkable too. It seems to be that much easier to see people for what they are. Life in the streets of Penang cannot help but be more exciting than it is in London or New York, provided always that one has the strength and resilience to stand up to it.

During those first few days when I was trying so hard to recover my belief in myself and my purpose it was T'an who knew best how to nourish my shrunken ego. Drawing on a tradition of sycophancy practiced for 5,000 years as an honourable art, he flattered me with the sure touch of a master. At least once a day he seized on some aspect of my journey and puffed it fondly into heroic dimensions.

"In Africa I suppose you were often passing through the jungle," he suggested, in the tones of hushed awe which came so easily to him.

"Well, yes," I admitted, modestly.

"And you were meeting, I think so, many wild animals."

"Yes, I suppose I did," I said, remembering how benign those encounters had been.

"Oh you must be a very brave man. If I would go in the jungle or the desert I think I must die."

He shuddered, deftly evoking scenes of desperate combat with lions and venomous snakes. In mournful humility he expressed his sense of the dreadful loss he might have sustained if my bones had been left to decorate some beast's lair, and of the superhuman qualities I must have displayed to escape that fate.

I of course knew better and I was never so infatuated by his version as to want to refurbish my own memories, but he did remind me that I had once anticipated my journey through Africa with the same fearful imaginings, and I felt better for knowing I had overcome them.

On other days he thrilled at my seeming immunity from the bandits who, he felt certain, must have infested every one of the forty-five thousand miles I had come thus far. He marvelled at my mechanical ingenuity in keeping the motorcycle going, at the strength of my arms (which I considered puny) for having wrestled with the handlebars over rocks and riverbeds, at the genius I had shown in assembling the myriad bits of equipment which he had seen on their way down to the cupboard under the stairs and then back up to my room again.

I always left him feeling a bit stronger, wiser and more important, and if the therapy cost me a few cigarettes or a couple of Malaysian dollars at the end of the month then I think, as therapy goes, it was about the cheapest and most effective I could have received anywhere on this earth.

T'an was also my link with the boss. Through him I was often invited to a midday or evening meal with the boss, his wife, and the Mah Jong supervisor, though T'an himself was never so lucky. The table was set in a cavern of a room at the back, opening on to a covered well. That whole part of the hotel was dark, moist and cool, with grey stone-paved floors and encrusted walls of no recognizable colour. The cooking was done in the well area, sometimes by the boss, sometimes by his wife. She was a fat woman with indolent features who waddled about in her black pajamas, while he favoured blue and white stripes to his pajama trousers and a tough expression on his face. The gossip, according to T'an, was that she was the real owner and he the manager, and that she used this leverage to keep him in line.

The cooking interested me as much as the food. There was no kitchen as we in the West would understand it, modern kitchens having become largely showplaces for designers. At the Choong Thean there were no symmetrical rows of self-important jars and bottles. There were no racks of shining pans, no cutlery, no plastic surfaces and stainless-steel hobs. There was not a gleam or a glint in sight anywhere. A few large blackened woks and cauldrons, some wickerwork baskets and strainers, a chopper, a cold tap and a bucket were all I noticed. There were some ingredients in containers to be sure, but the tins and pots were so nondescript and used that they seemed to vanish as soon as their lids were replaced.

I found that eating with Chinese people the meals they had prepared for themselves was very different from my experience of Chinese restaurants. The food appeared on the table in large bowls, generally swimming in liquid. Much of it was unrecognizable and some looked like the contents of a weed-choked fishpond brought to the boil, but most of what I could bring myself to try tasted very good, and I was convinced, without knowing why, that it was nutritious and health-giving.

The fact that I could only communicate with them by grunts and signs and the very few words I had learned in hospital (probably wrongly) made the experience all the more exotic. I knew it was as close as I could hope to get to the real China, which was still in those days shut tight as a clam.

After a while I took to wandering round the town, trying to rekindle my pleasure and interest in life. I spent hours in the fish and vegetable market. I ranged along the waterfront, and browsed for an afternoon through the stock of a carpet salesman. I took the Ayer Itam bus to the botanical gardens and passed a day among the lawns and wooded ways watching the monkeys skittering through the trees and bouncing their babies on the grass. I drank cocktails in the revolving restaurant on top of the Meridian Hotel, watching Penang spin slowly into the dusk beneath me and renewing my contempt for the sterile pretenses of international hotels and their occupants.

One day, in a fit of sudden resolution, I went into a little leather-goods shop and bought a square foot of supple tan leather. With a fine Victorian stitching tool given to me by a friend in Buenos Aires I made a copy of the pouch I had lost. It took me most of one day to make, and it was a first big step towards recovering my belief in the future. Almost immediately afterwards I learned that the spare part for my motorcycle alternator had arrived from England. The next morning, gingerly, holding my breath and shaking inwardly, I wheeled the Triumph out of the hotel into Rope Walk.

T'an, the boss, and the downstairs ladies watched with varying degrees of admiration and amusement. There was enough of a charge still in the battery to get me to the Lucas workshop. I kicked the engine over and it started faultlessly. I rode out into Campbell Street and, with all the panache of a middle-aged gentleman on a penny-farthing, made my way through the streets of Penang

For almost a week after that I was immersed in motorcycle maintenance. Dr Manocha had warned me not to ride very far for two weeks, in case the vibration shook the retina loose in my eye again. I was glad to follow his advice, feeling still too decrepit to want to get on my bike in a hurry. All the same I was beginning to make some sort of cautious plan. It was already the end of May and I had been in Penang for almost a month. An Indian passenger ship called the *Chidambaram* was due to sail for Madras on 26 June and I booked myself a passage.

As soon as I dared, with the bike in good order again and my retina firmly buttoned back into my eye, I rode the five hundred miles to Kuala Lumpur and back to collect my new passport, grudgingly given, from the British embassy. That left me with enough time to make some sort of a trip into Thailand. I bought myself an ornate and expensive visa from the Thai consulate and reassembled all my bits and pieces, from tools to teapot, in their respective bags and boxes. On the morning of Friday, 11 June, I waved the Choong Thean goodbye, promising to be back in ten days.

In some parts of the world people have a genius for  bringing beauty  to the most mundane objects. And the soaring canopy on this ox cart in Malaysia is a fine example.

The last town before the border on the trunk road to Thailand was
Alor Star. I arrived mid-morning and saw a dreary collection of
small stores attended by a gas station and a bus depot, all dis-
coloured and sodden by a recent burst of hot rain. Following a sign
for Padang Besar, I rode up a muddy dirt road to the guard room of
an army post and asked for Captain Dylan, far from sure that I wanted to find him.

This curious and rather appalling man had appeared in my life six
weeks earlier, before I ever arrived in Penang. I was then traveling
north from Singapore on the West coast of Malaysia, and at that time
I had Carol on the bike with me. We had been traveling through
Australia together for almost half a year. We were still very close, but
enveloped in sadness because we knew that we would soon have to
separate. The sadness was bitter as well as sweet, and the fault was
mine. My journey had become an all-consuming mission which I
found I could not share. During the last months I had been eaten by
the secret knowledge that it wasn't working for me, that I would have
to go on alone. Some miserable but defiant part of me would keep crying 'Mine, mine, all mine'. I knew I had been guilty of a gross error,
and the weight of it bowed me down. At last, on the ship from Perth
to Singapore, among the monsoon rainstorms and not far from the
misty remains of Krakatoa, our own personal storm broke.

After much misery and some recrimination Carol decided to leave
me somewhere north of Kuala Lumpur and make her own way
through Indonesia. I was thankful but deeply distressed by what I
had done, for she had come a long way and made sacrifices to be with

me. The pressure of the guilt stayed on me a long time. One blow after another hit me as soon as we parted, and I could not help feeling, lying in hospital in Penang, that I had brought these misfortunes down on my own head and that there was no knowing when the retribution would end.

But on that day in April, north of Singapore, when we came to the small town of Pontian Kechil, we still had a few more days left together. The road ran close to the coast of the Straits of Malacca. Pontian was just two rows of houses on either side of the road, wood-frame houses mostly, painted blue, green and grey. As we rode through I noticed a small hotel on our right with cheerful red paint round the entrance and a nice hand-painted sign which read 'Hotel Jaya'.

I would have liked to stop there but we had to go on to the government tourist lodge because we had no Malaysian money. It was too late for the banks, the next day was a national holiday and then came the weekend. In Johore a woman tourist official with lips like the roof of a red pagoda had told us that the government lodge in Pontian was our only hope for changing money. A room there was supposed to cost twelve dollars, which was expensive but not impossible. We found the place just beyond the town, off the road by the seashore. It was built of concrete and roofed with tiles, a modern building by Malaysian standards. A Morris Minor was parked outside and some laundry fluttered on a line. Between the washing line and the building, partially concealed by the flapping clothes and a low wall I saw a man turn with an odd, erratic movement to stare at us.

He was an Indian with the square features, light complexion and soft nose of a Punjabi, and he had a wet towel wrapped round his forehead. I saw his mouth open and he seemed to be shouting something, but the motorcycle engine drowned his words. I cut the engine just as he emerged from behind the wall and revealed himself to be dressed in jodhpurs, khaki socks and slippers. His voice blared out in mid-sentence with parade-ground strength as the engine died.

'. . . Brandy, what! I say, topping good show. Damn good. Let's have a drink. What's your fancy?"

He was desperately drunk and his breath preceded him in waves as he engineered his way towards us. Although his language was decked out in the full idiomatic regalia of an Edwardian officers' mess, the accent was blatantly false. The multiple fraudulence of an Indian trying to imitate Colonel Blimp and sounding instead like a Cockney barrow-boy made me uneasy. We had had a hard day and come a long way and I was too tired to tangle with the riddle of the Raj. I excused us with vague promises of future drunkenness, and we went to find a room.

The cheapest room was fifteen dollars, not twelve. The extra three dollars were for an air-conditioner which wheezed and roared in its cage like an asthmatic lion, and we quickly switched it off. The management said they could not change our checks but would be happy to wait for the money. That meant we would have to stay there four nights. It was not what we wanted to do. The room was furnished and decorated to cheap American motel-chain standards. It was all right, but it was not what we had come to Asia for. Its best feature was a lovely view of the sea, and of a small island and a neatly built wooden jetty that snaked out over the flat, darkening water. A fiery sunset broke through the rain clouds on the horizon, flashing pink and purple off the surface of the sea. The view made us all the more eager to get out of the room.

"Let's try and make it back into town tomorrow," Carol said.

"Okay. Maybe we could check out that little hotel we passed. Perhaps we could eat there tonight."

"I don't want to meet that drunk downstairs," she said. "Say, that's a sweet-looking jetty."

We walked out on the jetty and after sundown, at about six thirty, we went into Pontian to the Jaya Hotel. There was a small restaurant on the ground floor, with a few simple wooden tables and chairs and a big curving counter with a broad top just inside the entrance. It was clean and there were a few touches here and there which showed that the owner cared, a lick of paint, a nice poster on the wall and so forth. A pleasantly alert boy brought a fizzy orange, a beer and a menu card. The menu was in Malaysian but it's a simple language and by then we could read most of it. We ordered some Chinese dishes. When I asked for an explanation of one item the owner was quick to come over himself. He had been joking with a few other men across the room, but his eye had been on us most of the time. He was a short, broad-chested man in a shirt and a coloured sarong; a Malay with some Chinese in him, I thought. He laughed – 'Ha ha' – after every phrase and sentence, and there was a piratical glint in his black eyes. His good humour was convincing and infectious. I liked him immediately.

He told us what we wanted to know, and a bit more.

"This durian fruit, ha, ha, you are asking about, isn't it, ha, ha. It is a very fine fruit all right, from my own garden, ha, ha, but if you do not know the taste, better not to order without trying first, ha, ha. Some people do not like durian at all, ha, ha. Say it taste like bad cheese." And he laughed very merrily.

We both said we would have some another time and asked him about a room in his hotel. He had a nice one, he said, for six dollars. We explained our problem over the checks.

"No problem," he laughed. "Tomorrow you can change at bank."

"But isn't the bank shut tomorrow?"

"Maybe. Then I will open it myself," he roared. "Tomorrow morning you come early. I fix it."

The food was good. We saw the room and liked it. Within two hours he had told us that his name was Ambak Jaya, that he had been a policeman in Singapore, that he had worked and drunk and gambled so much of the time that he became ill and his wife had refused to stay with him unless he moved with his family to a quieter life. Now he was happy. He had the hotel. He had his garden outside the town, and he had his family. His wife, the heroine of this simple tale, we had already met. She had come out of the kitchen to show us the room, and it was she who made his story credible.

I have never anywhere met a person who conveyed, at first sight and consistently thereafter, a greater degree of warm-hearted sincerity. She had a good strong body, a little heavy but still pleasing, and she went about her work with uncomplaining ease. Her black hair, tied smoothly behind her head, was streaked with white, and neither she nor Ambak were young but they were both vigorous. Where his energy was released in erratic, extrovert bursts, hers had a calm, steadying nature and promised to run on unabated for ever. Her face was the expression and reward of her disposition; clear and unruffled, sometimes smiling, sometimes serious, but always lively and beautiful. For a woman like that, I thought, a man might forswear many vices.

We arranged to return next morning for breakfast. Ambak would get our money sorted out and then, he said, we were invited to go with him to his garden and see for ourselves the tropical fruits he grew there.

We walked back to the lodge through a night so black that once past the edge of town we had almost to feel our way. From the overgrown garden of an isolated house we were serenaded by an orchestra of bullfrogs, booming through the darkness, unnaturally loud, raising in the imagination a monstrous caricature of their actual puny selves. The lodge was all but asleep. Only the bar was lit and through the open door, alone with the barman, we saw and heard our Indian acquaintance booming his own unchanging song, for much the same reason, I thought, as the frogs in the night. We crept quietly past the door and went to our room.

"I guess I should feel sorry for that guy," Carol said later, "but it's hard."

At eight next morning the heat was already gathering strength, but the red shutters of the Hotel Jaya were firmly shut. We knocked a few times and waited. Across the road the bank was shut and barred as though for ever and the street was deserted. I knocked again, feeling the disappointment, even deprivation, as I realized how much I had been attracted to the Jaya family atmosphere. We were about to walk off when we heard shuffling sounds. The shutters scraped open. Ambak peered at us from beneath sagging eyelids, pulling his sarong up and around his substantial waist. He appeared to have been lying on the counter top just inside the doors. His face, still half asleep, was like a mask of tragedy, all his features drooping in despair, as though he had just seen his whole life wasted. Then, with a perceptible jolt, he brought himself up, the mask broke into a brave grin and the fire lit in his eyes.

From then on the day continued exactly as he had forecast. We breakfasted on coffee and spicy vegetable pasties. At nine, miraculously, the bank opened for an hour and we did our business. Ambak hired two bicycle rickshaws and we set off in convoy with Ambak, his two school-aged children and ourselves, down a long dirt road to the garden which he had now elevated to the rank of 'estate'.

In fact there were several acres of orchard and vegetable beds. We met the mango, mangostin, pineapple, coconut, banana, cashew and custard apple. There was the big knobbly jack fruit, the even bigger breadfruit, and the redoubtable durian which Ambak supported in a truss of woven rushes, like a herniated testicle, to prevent it from falling off the tree when it was ripe.

Ambak's most valuable crop came off the limon trees he had imported from Ipoh. The fruit, he told us, smelled like lemon but grew to the size of a melon, and was indispensable to the Chinese New Year ceremony which made it so profitable to grow. Becoming familiar with the peculiarities of these exotic fruits was a great help to us. It made us feel that we had gained a foothold on the land instead of merely flying through it on the bike.

We lunched happily on dim sums, beer and blistering coffee, and feeling unusually euphoric and courageous I insisted on pedalling the rickshaw back to town myself. In Singapore, when Carol saw her first rickshaw she was outraged. She declared with great passion that the sight of poor, half-starved men labouring to transport fat rich men around town was disgusting to her. She would never be a party to such exploitation. My own attitude was more pompous than passionate. I thought it was better to take as many rickshaws as possible and overpay the drivers rather than to honour their dignity and leave them without work. On the other hand, I was curious to know just how tough the work was.

The rickshaw we had come in consisted of a bicycle with a rudimentary sidecar attached to the left. The driver and Ambak (who was no lightweight) sat crammed into the little bench seat and giggled anxiously as I set off down the stony path. I found the pedalling, on flat ground at least, much easier than I expected and we rattled along at a good pace. The problem was steering. The path was straight but narrow. The vehicle was quite wide and seemed to be rather loosely put together. As I gathered speed we wove wildly from one side to another before I began to get the hang of it. We had only been going a short while when I saw another rickshaw advancing towards us. I was too engrossed in my own performance to pay it much attention and it was a specially loud burst of nervous laughter on my left that made me look ahead again. The other rickshaw had stopped and one of the passengers was changing places with the driver. He was close enough to be plainly recognizable, and not only by the white towel wrapped round his forehead. I saw that he was wearing cavalry boots with his jodhpurs, and he began to charge towards us with much zest. We were approaching each other quite rapidly now and it seemed wise to slow down and get out of the way. The Indian, mad or drunk or both, was holding the handlebars with one hand and whipping himself along with the other which held a glittering object not unlike a brandy flask. He seemed to think he was Lord Cardigan, because as he came upon us I heard him cry:

'Charge, the Light Brigade!'

It was then that my other problem came to light. The rickshaw had no brakes. What followed all happened rather swiftly. I swung out of the way, oversteering hopelessly. The Indian swept past with his brandy bottle raised up high, shouting, "Hurrah! Jolly good show. Have one on me, old boy. . ." and so on. Our rickshaw plunged off the path and careered along a row of vegetables until the third wheel fetched up against the base of a chicken coop, spinning me round and all but tossing Ambak and the driver in among the hens.

We stood up and watched the marauders disappear down the road. Our other rickshaw was prudently parked on the verge, and Carol was laughing her silly head off.

"You'd think he would have stopped,"I said, ruefully.

"Did you see the other fellow in the rickshaw?" asked Ambak, who seemed to think it was all very funny too. "He was the Police Inspector. Why should he stop?"

We pushed the rickshaw, which seemed none the worse, back on the road and the driver cautiously resumed his saddle.

"And the Indian," I asked. "Who is he?"

"Some soldier fellow, I think, ha, ha. Maybe he is in love."

I recovered my humour very quickly when I saw that no harm had come to the rickshaw, and we laughed all the way to the hotel. Ambak's unfailing merriment and enthusiasm changed the whole tone of our experience, raising my spirits and sharpening my curiosity. We settled our affairs with the lodge, took our things back to the

Jaya, and then rode the bike south along the coast to a fishing village called Kukup. We ate fresh seafood in a restaurant perched, like the houses, above the water on piles. A soft-spoken Scots rubber planter, lunching there with his doll-like Chinese girl friend, advanced our education in tropical crops. Below the deck where we ate, a man stood up to his shoulders in water, scrubbing the sides of his boat, the sunlight glistening on his wet muscled arms.

So much of our sadness and weariness seemed to have fallen away, and the world was pleasant and exciting again. We trundled slowly back to Pontian and on the way investigated a curious building by the roadside, drawn to it by the big revolving tube sticking out of its side. A man was splitting up sections of tree trunk and feeding them into the mouth of the tube. The tree, I saw, had a strange pithy texture, and the man explained that he was milling sago, adding to the day's discoveries the remarkable fact that sago comes out of trees. There were teeth inside the tube to mash up the pulp and a constant flow of water washed the starch out from the fibres into a series of tanks, where the sago settled in tiny pellets. Every now and again a customer cycled up with a piece of tree trunk or left with a bag of sago. What a world of surprises.

We spent the evening with the Jaya family. They continued to delight us, and seemed to take real pleasure in our company. It happened that the following day, a Saturday, would be my forty-fifth birthday, something which up until then I had not wanted to think about. Now it came as a happy pretext for a party. I asked Ambak's wife whether she would cook us all a birthday lunch if I bought the ingredients, and she fell in with the idea very readily.

We came very close to the Jaya family in that short time. The children too treated us with familiarity, though respectfully, in a way which somehow intensified the relationship. There were two boys and a girl, between the ages of six and ten, and the respect they showed us affected us strongly, as we were not used to it.

The next morning all of us except Ambak went to the market together. It was a fine way to have a birthday, I thought, walking to market with such good, easy people, looking forward to good food and even better feelings. Open markets are among the world's great joys. To be surrounded by a profusion of produce fresh out of the earth and

Sago was what puddings were made from in my childhood, but I never dreamed that it came out of tree trunks. Here is a sago mill in Malaysia. People bring their own sections of tree – they are quite light - and have them milled through the revolving tube, which has internal teeth. The slurry that emerges is settled in tanks.

the sea, to be able to buy directly from the stalls of farmers and fishermen, is a vital part, it seems to me, of a good life. There is something obscene about the way food is shunted hundreds and thousands of miles around our industrialized countries before it arrives, often sterile, frozen and exhausted, in the consumer's hands. Just as bad is the fact that many of the best kinds of food never arrive at all, simply because they are less well suited to shipping and storage. In the big country markets of Africa, Latin America and Asia, these limitations don't apply. Whatever can be grown or caught in the area is there for sale, and the rarer or more delicate varieties are often the tastiest and best.

The market at Pontian, small but good, had many kinds of fish I had never seen. Huge, plump pink fish with coarse scales, heaps of long thin silvery fish like sword blades with forked tails, and small fish with unusual marking, curious shapes and exotic fins. Ambak's wife was determined to get a fish she called *ikan bower,* that she swore was the best. I left them and wandered off among the more ramshackle stalls set up for the day beyond the official marketplace. A cloud burst open above the town and I took shelter for a while under a tin roof, enthralled by the operation of a chicken-plucking machine; a drum lined with rubber knobs which whirled round like a spin-dryer, cranked by hand. Such simple devices, used as a matter of course a few decades ago and now forgotten in the West, always fascinated me. Then I returned alone, through the downpour, skipping between awnings and overhanging balconies, and dawdling around shop windows.

The lunch was ready at two o'clock. The children had set up a table on the landing outside our room, and laid a pretty cotton tablecloth over it. Then they brought up one dish after another, in a never-ending stream. There were noodles, vegetables, cucumber salad, roast chicken, goat and eventually three beautiful diamond-shaped fish in a sweet-and-sour sauce.

Ambak and the children came up to eat with us. It had not occurred to me that they would bring presents too, and I was overwhelmed by the gaily wrapped packages they carried with them. The smallest boy gave me a box of pretzels. The daughter brought two small towels. The older son gave me a sarong. All were presented very correctly, with solemn greetings. Ambak had a big carton which he handed over last with a broad grin. I looked inside and pulled out a stuffed monkey. The monkey sat on the table, about eighteen inches high, and watched with mild surprise as we drank and laughed and ate too much. Then we slept through the afternoon, with the rain streaming down outside.

When we woke it was dark and the rain had stopped. Carol said we should go out and she'd buy me a birthday drink. I was feeling relaxed and happy and I wanted to meet the Indian face to face just once before we left so I suggested that we walk to the lodge. She grimaced only slightly, and agreed.

"I'll take the Indian, I guess, but can we give the frogs a miss ?"

"Why?"

"They make me think of the foghorns in the Bay."

There had been some very good times in San Francisco, but I didn't want to get sentimental thinking about them.

"They sound more like people to me," I said. "I've met a lot of frogs in my time. I think the Indian is a frog. Or a toad. Like Toad of Toad Hall. 'Toot, toot! Charge, the Light Brigade!' You know. I'm sure Mr Toad had a drinking problem, discreetly overlooked in the book, of course."

"Then that makes Ambak an affable lizard," she said, getting into it, "and you, baby, are a chameleon. Oh boy, but aren't you ?"

I didn't like that too much, and dropped the game before it became nasty. Outside the air was delicious and fresh. The rain had washed the heat away, and some stars shone brightly between patches of hurrying cloud. We walked down the path between the road and the lodge. The frogs, unaccountably, were silent. A ghostly figure in a phosphorescent bubble of light drifted slowly along the shore, a space intruder which resolved itself into a prawn fisherman working the shallow waters with a candle strapped to his forehead and his net extended before him as he walked.

The Indian was in the bar when we arrived. He had to be. He was facing the barman across the counter as we walked in and turned round as though he were expecting us.

"Ah, there you are. What's it to be, eh? Better start with a brandy. Karim, two large brandies, chop chop." Then he swallowed what was left of his own drink and added, "Make it three. And we'd better have three beers while you're about it. What!"

I was waving my hand in a futile gesture to refuse the brandy when he went on to order the beer, which was what we wanted anyhow, so I gave up the struggle then and there. He seemed to be relatively sober, and had exchanged his jodhpurs for a safari suit. His speech and his accent were as outrageous as ever, and he continued in full spate.

"So! You're from England. Well, that's a jolly fine place. I was at Sandhurst myself. Got a brother in Southall. I say, old boy, should have stopped my rickshaw yesterday, but d'ye know what? No damn brakes. Bloody shame. We could have had a drink. Actually, though, my cousin wasn't frightfully keen. He's a police inspector, you know. That chap you were with – shady character – in trouble. Cases pending. That kind of thing. Wouldn't do.

"I say, you've got to damn well drink up. Karim! Another of the same, and make it snappy." And he actually snapped his fingers.

Karim didn't mind. He seemed to enjoy being ordered about. He was a tall, gangling Malayan Moslem with fine mobile features and lustrous black eyes. His wide mouth widened even further whenever he was addressed, and as the evening wore on it became obvious that he was flying on some kind of dope.

The Indian insisted on ordering round after round. It emerged that he was, or said he was, an army captain stationed on the Thai border. He made some reference to sorties into the jungle and horrible times being shot at by 'the Reds'.

"So I'm down here to bloody well drink up and forget. Time for another. Karim! On the double."

"Are you anywhere near Alor Star?" I asked.

"That's right. Padang Besar."

"Because I'll be going through there in a few weeks."

"Well, jolly well look me up at Padang Besar. Just ask for Dylan. Everybody knows me."

"Like the poet?" I asked, surprised by the name, but he looked blank.

"What?" he said.

"The poet, Dylan Thomas. He could drink too. You'd have met your match there, boyo!"

He had a wary look about him, and it took a beer to wash it away. Occasionally he directed some elaborate courtesy at Carol, whom he addressed as 'my dear lady', but she said virtually nothing and, I guessed, found the scene rather detestable.

I would have liked to find out more about Ambak's supposed crimes, in order to defend him, but I found it hard to keep the Captain's attention focused where I wanted it. Indeed, my own attention was not at its sharpest any more. I always resented people who were forever ordering drinks, because I had never yet found out how to refuse them. The Captain fascinated me. He seemed as phony as ever, and yet he was also extremely real, and I couldn't put my finger on the fraud. I had hoped to catch him out *in flagrante delicto* but my perception dissolved in the alcohol, as did the differences between us, and by midnight we were as jolly a band of revellers as one could meet.

It was then Karim remembered that they were showing the Cup Final on TV. In Malaysia the sport that gets all the headlines, that draws the fans from one end of the country to the other, inspiring fanatical team loyalty, furious street-corner argument and heavy gambling, is badminton. My delight in badminton was limited by my upbringing. Childhood prejudice made it difficult for me to take seriously any sport involving feathers. Politely I asked which teams were playing, hoping to move the conversation on to other fields.

"Manchester is playing with Southampton," he said. "Manchester United I think, isn't it?"

"Oh, *that* Cup Final. Come on then, let's get it."

We rushed into a small room behind the kitchen, where Karim had his bed and a small black-and-white TV set, to watch the most important event in the English football calendar relayed live from Wembley Stadium in London. It was 10,000 miles away as the satellite flies, but I had traveled 55,000 miles through thirty-two countries and England seemed as distant from me as the moon. If the Queen had dropped through the roof and knighted me I could not have found it stranger than this minor miracle of communications. Karim pressed the button, a clear picture of the game appeared instantly, and within seconds I watched Stokes score the only goal of the match to win the Cup for Southampton. Five minutes later the whistle blew and the game was over.

Karim somehow attributed this masterpiece of timing to me, and decided that a man of such astounding good fortune must also be rich in practical wisdom.

"I am in love," he declared. "Oh, my heart is aching so. What can I do? You must tell me. Too much it is hurting."

His huge deliquescent eyes were full to bursting with romantic melancholy.

"Attention!" the Captain barked. "You are being mawkish. Enough of this mawking. Drink up! Let's have another. It's my last damn night and there'll be no damn mawking in the mess."

I wanted to hear more of Karim's story. In my drunkenness I was feeling mawkish enough myself to believe that I had the power to treat his lovesickness.

"What is so painful about it?" I asked him.

"My heart is too full of love, I cannot speak." He patted his heart to make sure it was still intact.

"You are speaking too damn much already," said the Captain. I noticed then that he was actually angry. He had moved along the bar a few feet and was staring with apoplectic eyes at Karim who, just as surprisingly after playing the dutiful barman all night, was now ignoring him, or pretending to.

Still I blundered on.

"What do you mean, Karim?" I asked.

"She is too beautiful. I cannot tell her. Every day I am seeing her, but what to say, what to do?"

The incensed Captain burst out: "You know damn well what to do. You can jolly well shut up and bring some brandies."

The tension between them was acute and embarrassing. I was trying to think of something to do or say to lower the temperature when the Captain raised his empty glass, opened his mouth, and dropped unconscious to the floor. He sat down first, then fell backwards with his feet still at the bar and his glass clutched upright over his stomach.

Karim came round to look at him with a curiously mixed expression of repugnance and tenderness.

"What shall we do with him?" I asked. "Shall we put him on the couch?"

"No, I will put him on the bed if you will help me."

He raised the Indian by the armpits and I took his feet. He was not heavy and we carried him easily to Karim's room. By the time he was laid on the bed he was snoring gently.

"Would you like another brandy?" Karim asked us. "The Captain will pay."

We refused the offer and walked back to the hotel.

The frogs were booming their sonorous reminders again.

"Why the hell did we do that?" Carol exclaimed hotly. "What a weird scene."

I was too drunk to comment, dreading the hangover that was already tapping at my skull, and we went on in silence.

Next morning, devastated by alcohol poisoning and sickened by the sense of waste and despair that lingered from the night before, I trudged down to the bike with our bags and boxes. Only Ambak was there to see us off. His wife was still at market and the children were at school. We missed them dreadfully, and I felt that I had wantonly dissipated and lost something of great value. We left Pontian finally at noon with subdued and inadequate farewells. There was nowhere to pack the monkey, so I wrapped it in plastic and tied it on the back over the number plate.

Some days later, up in the mountains, Carol packed her meagre belongings in the red rucksack to go her own way. As for me, I rode off as quickly as I dared, with only the stuffed monkey riding behind me, feeling relieved and guilty as sin.

When I got to Alor Star six weeks later I had forgotten about the Captain. Then the sign for Padang Besar reminded me, and I followed it as a duty to unfinished business. It never does any harm, I told myself, to have friends in the army, especially at borders.

The entrance to the army camp was unimpressive, a small shack beside a wooden barrier and a muddy track leading apparently to nowhere. A glum soldier in a green waterproof cape stared at me while I manoeuvred the motorcycle so that I could talk to him. There was often this odd hiatus when I stopped to talk to strangers, getting the bike into position, taking off the helmet so that they could see who they were talking to. It was prolonged this time because I couldn't find neutral on the gearbox. Eventually I had to stall the engine in first gear, which irritated me a little and perhaps put a sharpness in my voice I had not intended.

"I'm looking for Dylan," I said. "Captain Dylan."

It meant nothing to him.

"Dylan," I repeated. "He said everybody knew him."

"I don't know him. What company?"

"I don't know," I said, beginning to feel foolish. "He said I would find him here, that's all."

I stopped at the sound of laughter from inside the hut. A voice called: "Tell him he's too late. They took him away already."

"Took him away ?'"

"He was shot."

A smooth brown face appeared round the doorway and, on seeing me, stopped laughing and became stern.

"Who are you?" it demanded.

This is a question I have always had difficulty answering; earlier in life because I genuinely didn't know, and later because I knew too well.

"My name is Simon," I said. "I . . ."

"Are you family?"

"Well, no. I'm a friend of his . . ."

"A friend!" The laughter almost returned. "What kind of friend are you and what . . . ?"

"Look here," I interrupted. "You said he was shot? What do you mean? How was he shot? Is he all right, or . . ."

Again the voice broke in, peremptorily. "If you are not family I can tell you nothing. You should write to GHQ. You can go now."

And the head disappeared.

I waited a moment wondering what to do. The episode was quite out of character with army behaviour, but smelled strongly of police. It was hard to leave the riddle of Captain Dylan unsolved, but I told myself that it did no good to make enemies in the army, even less among the police, and particularly not at a border. I put on my helmet and retired with the better part of valour to enter Thailand.

**4**

The journey I had set myself that first day out of Penang could not have been simpler. From the border to Haad Yai was only thirty miles or so on a good flat road. There was no need to change money. American dollars were acceptable everywhere at a generally agreed rate of 20 *baht* to the dollar. In any case there was nothing I needed to buy before I arrived.

I tried to settle down on the bike and recover my old easy rhythm, but it would not come. Some of this I could put down to the nature of the excursion itself. It felt strange and somehow offensive to be making a circular tour limited to a few days and to know that I would be coming back on this same road. I could not hope to see more than a small southern patch of the country and the thought was depressing. Compared with the grand, sweeping journeys I was accustomed to making across countries and continents it seemed like a mean little trip.

I knew it was foolish thinking. It meant that I had lost touch with the real excitement of travel, which is a thing of each day, each hour, each moment. Instead I was trying to rebuild my confidence on an abstract image of myself as the great circumnavigator, forever pressing on into the unknown. Realizing this, and without T'an to feed me my daily dose of flattery, my morale slumped even further.

It was a vicious circle. To be worth making at all a journey has to be made in the mind as much as in the world of objects and dimensions. What value can there be in seeing or experiencing anything for the first time unless it comes as a revelation? And for that to happen, some previously held thought or belief must be confounded, or enhanced, or even transcended. What difference can it make otherwise to see a redwood tree, a tiger, or a humming bird?

Happily it is beyond the capacity of human beings to anticipate things exactly. How one would laugh at someone who, shown an elephant for the first time, said "Ah, yes, just as I expected." But there certainly are people for whom the first experience of an elephant would be no special event.

Everything depends on the elephant in the mind and the amount of imaginative effort that has been lavished on it. If it is a mere sketch or outline, then as long as the real thing roughly resembles it, that will do. There is no reason, after all, for being more fascinated by real elephants than by imaginary ones. If, on the other hand, you have spent years doting on the idea of elephants; if you have fired your imagination to divine what it must be like to touch its hide, to feel its breath, to hear it snorting and trumpeting, to climb up like Sabu and ride in majesty on its back, then the real experience when it comes is a source of lasting wonder and interest.

An army may march on its stomach, driven by orders, but a traveler must fly on the wings of imagination, like Quixote, fuelled by the fantasies of a lifetime. What I suffered, as I came into Thailand, was a collapse of the imagination. I went along staring about me in dull discomfort, hoping that something would happen soon to get me flying again.

I had heard nothing about Haad Yai to recommend it except as a stopping place on the way. As I rode through it I saw only shops, houses and small businesses. King's Hotel caught my eye first, with its expensive modern facade proclaiming that it would cost too much for me. Then, next door, squatting in the shadow of its neighbour, I noticed a small restaurant with a dingy hotel sign added as an afterthought.

I parked the bike outside the door where I would be able to see it, stuffed my keys and gloves into my helmet, and looked inside the restaurant. It was a grubby fly-blown place and I would have left to try elsewhere if a voice had not called out to me.

"Hello. Come and sit down."

The invitation came from a tall, thin European with lank blond hair who was twisted around in his chair to see me. Opposite him sat another man, shorter, heavier, with a carefully trimmed black beard, who stared at me with a stony expression. I sat next to the darker man to keep my eye on the bike. There were two smeared Coca Cola bottles between them.

"Are you staying here?" I asked. They said they were, and that it was cheap. The blond man with an obviously Scandinavian accent said he was Norwegian. His companion was Swiss. We exchanged the usual details, where we were going, where we had come from. They had both just arrived from Bangkok. The Norwegian had no particular plans except, he said, "to look for a girl". He appeared gloomy and quite nervous, and talked about getting a girl as someone who, feeling the flu coming on, might talk of getting some aspirin.

The Swiss was going on to Malaysia, and was full of complaints about the arrogance and deceitfulness of the Thais. He had been cheated and his camera had been stolen.

"Everyone here loses his camera," he said, bitterly. "You must watch your stuff like an eagle. The Americans have spoiled this country completely. It is all corrupted. One time it was not like this. There was another tradition. Wherever you went, people were always giving freely what they had. Now they are just taking all they can."

"You are quite right. . ." said the Norwegian. He spoke an efficient but mechanical English which he drove out of his mouth in lurches of fluency, like a tank turning a corner.

"You are quite right" - grind - "Thailand was full of Americans" - judder - "the people were dependent on them" - clank - "now they are gone . . ."

His theory was that the Thais had become greedy and obstreperous because the Americans, having spent freely during the Viet Nam war, had now abandoned them in the grip of a habit they could not afford.

The Swiss listened with an air of disapproval which seemed habitual. A man came through from a door behind the counter and I asked him for a room. He took me up to the first floor. It had been divided into boxes with flimsy hardboard partitions, and for 35 *baht* I got one of these with two narrow beds, a fan and a gauze-covered hatch escaping onto the narrow space between the hotels. I took all my things off the bike and humped them up the wooden stairs, locking them into my cubicle with the padlock provided. The management consented to bring the bike into the restaurant at night when they locked up.

It was still only mid-afternoon. I went back to my seat downstairs and was wondering what to do when two Thais came in from the street, smiling softly in an ingratiating but businesslike way. One, with a wispy black moustache and wearing an American sport coat, said:

"We are ready now. You can come along, please."

The Norwegian turned his blanched blue eyes on me.

"We are going to some houses to see the girls. You should come too. Maybe you can find one you like."

"Sure, mister," said the Thai. "You come for the ride."

I overcame my distaste and agreed to go "for the ride". We walked outside and climbed into the back of a miniature Japanese bus. There were two short wooden benches, with room perhaps for a party of six or eight. I wondered whether we were going to pick up other passengers for the tour. It seemed like a peculiar way to proceed to the temples of Eros. I had always imagined that one would be slightly drunk in a taxi, rather than burping soda water in a minibus. Also it seemed like the wrong time of day.

Perhaps I showed my bewilderment.

"You don't worry for anything," said the driver. "I live here twenty-five years. You take number of car, and you can tell police."

He smiled again, sure that everything had now been happily taken care of. We drove away and stopped after a few minutes outside a shop.

Curtains were drawn across the window on the inside. On the outside a sliding steel grille, used to lock up the shop from wall to wall, was almost closed, barely leaving access to the narrow door. We trooped silently into a stark square room with painted cement walls and ceiling, lit by a fluorescent tube. The shock made me wonder what I had been expecting. Plush? Piano music? Bawdy songs? Chandeliers? A deep-bosomed madam in a ballgown? The collection of tawdry old images, left to gather the dust of decades in my mind's attic, was suddenly and cruelly exposed by the demolition squad.

In front of the curtain, on a stand, a television set was yattering quietly in Thai, showing pictures of a refrigerator and a proud housewife. On rows of hard chairs ranged against two of the walls the girls sat in silence watching the TV. Our escort waved us to an empty wooden bench against the remaining wall. The center of the room was bare. We might have been waiting for the dentist.

The girls looked quite lifeless, though they turned their heads as if to prove that they were, in fact, alive. They were all very young. I could not have said how young, and it may be that they had no idea either. The Swiss and I said not a word. The Norwegian jerked his head from one end of the row to the other and ground out some meaningless jokes which served rather to deepen the silence. The girls wore ordinary working clothes. Only the make-up on their puffy faces conceded anything to the kind of work they might be called upon to do.

The Swiss glowered at them. I fidgeted in embarrassment. Then the Norwegian stood up, cleared his throat, muttered something negative, and we followed him out to the bus. We drove to two more such places. They were almost identical, as were the girls, except that there were shelves on the walls crammed with cuddly toys. In these scenes of fearful boredom, my sense of revulsion and pity struggled to survive but finally succumbed. At the last stop, where the Norwegian was clearly determined to give the goods an even longer and more detailed scrutiny, I borrowed his copy of *Newsweek* and distracted myself thankfully from the miserable business.

The US primaries were dragging on and I skipped past them to read about a conference being held somewhere where delegates were meeting to improve the world's drinking water. People were forever meeting, at great expense, to provide for others what they would not touch themselves. Who ever heard of delegates drinking water? In any case, the plan was quite improbable. It would compete with the soft-drinks industry, and the cola corporations would never allow it.

I read on. A British cabinet minister was in Vancouver fulminating about slum clearance and expensive new housing projects. He said, quite rightly, that it would be wiser and cheaper to rehabilitate the houses that already existed rather than sweep everything old away. I remembered Singapore's proud boast – a new high rise apartment built and finished every fifteen minutes. The first blocks, built only six years before, already looked like slums. Yet they couldn't tear down the handsome old colonnaded houses fast enough. Impossible to stop. What would the bright Chinese entrepreneurs do without these projects to pay for their Mercedes and their hi-fi lifestyles?

Peculiar contemplations to pursue in a brothel, but not so irrelevant perhaps. My own sexual impulses were frozen and shrivelled in this morgue of emotions, where all human warmth had fled and the living dead attempted their quasi-necrophagous deals among the debris of fallen empires. In this negative state I saw behind me a world of moral chaos and abuse where great cultures sagged and collapsed like wax temples tossed into a melting pot, rendered down by the greedy heat of progress. A world of half-crazed individuals clinging to the sticks and tatters of half-remembered beliefs, administered by the fully crazy with their insane dreams of world domination, and driven by the butcher centurions, the 'anything for a buck' boys, the asset-strippers, the demolition men, the multinational cocaine-cola salesmen, the arms dealers, all the assorted pimps and purveyors of pulp.

A world debased by commerce, defaced by advertisements, degraded by mass production, defiled by petroleum products, desecrated by concrete, demeaned by squalor, deflowered by reason, deluded by politicians, depraved by propaganda, debauched by credit, devastated by war and on the verge of destruction.

I looked up from the magazine, and noticed one girl who was prettier than the others. She might have been any age from twelve to sixteen. She was fondling a toy chicken in her lap, her eyes withdrawn and dreamy. For a moment I played with the old brothel-reformer's fantasy of paying the fee and offering my services as a platonic confidant and counsellor, but caught myself out instantly, having plumped for the pretty one.

She was not pretty enough for the Norwegian, evidently. Nor were the others. With a sigh, he gave up. The girl of tonight's dreams was not there. Our guides, forever solicitous, said we must visit 'The Bungalow'. That was where the best girls were: "Very expensive."

By now I had become genuinely curious to see what, if anything, would satisfy the Norwegian's yearnings. When he asked what I thought, did I want to go, I said, "Sure. Why not. If it's not too far."

"No. No. Not too far," said the Thai. "Just on edge of town."

The Swiss nodded assent silently, allowing no hint of emotion to escape him, as though he were some kind of government inspector going wearily but doggedly about his duties. I wondered what he was so carefully concealing.

The Norwegian spoke sternly, almost harshly, to the Thai.

"Very well, we will go to The Bungalow. . . If you find me a nice girl . . . and I don't think it is very likely . . . I will stay with her for maybe one week. "

He seemed to be becoming more nervous all the time, and his body vibrated with a thousand tiny spasms of movement, like tremors arising from deep, unbearable tension.

We climbed back into the bus for the fourth time. The Norwegian went on talking, as if to me, but loudly enough for everyone to hear.

"My girl has left me . . . I sent her money. . . I have given her 10,000 *baht* from Norway. . . But she is sick. . ." He coughed in illustration. "She has gone away . . . I offered to take her to a doctor. . . She has bronchitis and gonorrhoea . . . For an injection . . . she won't go . 'Is too painful' she says. 'Too pain-fool' . . . I am heartbroken . . . I must have a girl to forget."

I murmured my sympathies, waiting for something more to emerge. He asked me how I paid for my journey and I explained that I wrote for a London newspaper. He became instantly enthusiastic.

"Ah, yes. I too worked for a newspaper. . . In Norway, but it was not enough money . . . so I became a radio operator to travel . . . I worked on a ship for two years between Malaysia and China . . . never got off the ship. It was a hell of a life. I nearly got a breakdown."

I thought he was being a bit shy. He had had his 'breakdown', I felt sure, and would have another. I remembered hearing that for marine radio operators it was the main occupational hazard. Some went crazy and jumped over the side.

The 'bungalow' was a modern two-storey villa in a suburban garden. As we walked into the lounge, the Thai pimp told us that his star attraction had not yet come home from school. I asked why she was doing this work. He explained politely that she needed the money to buy her schoolbooks. I felt free to believe whatever I liked.

She came in soon afterwards from the kitchen and sat down on a sofa, demurely folding her hands on her pleated navy blue skirt. She had white-skinned clean features, a faint moustache and a dazzling smile. The Norwegian looked at her uneasily. I thought his resistance was remarkable. There were two other women in the kitchen, and one of them came through to walk upstairs.

"That one I like," said the Norwegian. "How much is she for one night?"

She was obviously older, perhaps nineteen or twenty, and her skin was a more natural colour for a Thai. Next to her, all the 'little girls' we had seen seemed to belong to a world of sickly fantasy which presumably satisfied the Thai philanderer's erotic ideal. I had to grant the Norwegian some grudging and limited respect for holding out. He struck a bargain quite quickly, at twenty dollars, and she got into the bus with us.

She seemed an ordinarily nice person, with little English and therefore little to say to us. The Norwegian tried his strangely fractured conversation on her and I tried to speak to the Swiss, but he could not take his eyes off the girl. I left the three of them in the restaurant and went upstairs to wash. When I came down they had disappeared.

I was not tempted to eat in that place, and went out to look for my supper. I did not look far. The expensive hotel next door housed a restaurant on the ground floor and displayed a menu in the window. The prices, when I translated them into dollars, did not seem too high. Feeling feebly unadventurous I went in.

The floor was crowded with Thai couples, four to a table. On a small stage some musicians were playing selections from ancient Hollywood musicals. A suave young man took me round to one side of the room and gave me a table raised slightly above the dance floor with a good view of the crowd. They were all carefully dressed, the men in business suits and ties, the women in cocktail or party clothes, but beyond that there was a uniformity in their manner which made me think that they belonged to some group or profession. The waiter spoke just enough English to let me know that they were all policemen, presumably with their wives. I guessed that they must be well above the lowest rank, and I watched them with increasing curiosity.

I had hardly begun on my salad when the musicians gave way to a speaker who had made his way from one of the tables. He spoke with unselfconscious ease and, as far as I could tell, with humour. Oddly enough, his audience seemed to be paying him no attention. The couples went on chatting and giggling as though he were merely testing the microphone. This seemed not to affect him in the slightest, and when he finished and introduced another speaker there was vigorous applause.

The new speaker appeared to have more serious and telling points to make, but the diners continued as before to talk and laugh among themselves. The effect was all the more surreal because of the utter normality in which, taken separately, they were behaving. It was as if an invisible mirror stood between the speaker and the floor, reflecting on one side a rapt and appreciative audience, and on the other a pianist playing background music.

I felt like Gulliver cast into some Swiftian land.

As a crass Westerner I always had a tendency, when some bizarre behaviour bewildered me, to credit Orientals with subtleties I could not hope to fathom. Was it possible that the Thais had reached such a level of sophistication that they could distinguish openly between the necessary rituals of a convention and the concomitant nonsense? Naturally there would have to be a speaker. It was equally natural that he would have nothing to say. To listen with insincere attention to his banalities could only cause embarrassment to both sides. Better to honour him by enthusiastic applause when he rose and sat down, and by taking evident pleasure in the occasion.

My theory seemed too crude to deal with all the nuances.

It was also possible, of course, that they were a bunch of bad-mannered louts. They did not look like louts, but with policemen I had found one could not always tell.

The second speaker ended his speech to a tumult of clapping. Three girls came on the stage wearing the costume, jewellery and make-up of the traditional Siamese dance. The musicians played and the girls danced, hips swaying and arms waving with the languid and sinuous movement of underwater plants. For this the diners interrupted their conversation. They watched the dancing with evident pleasure, and applauded the girls enthusiastically, betraying no loutishness whatsoever. Then the band returned to playing Western dance music.

Some couples got up from their tables and took to the dance floor. To my utter astonishment, in their conservative suits and chic dresses, they faced each other and began to dance with the same slow stylized movements of the temple dancers who had just disappeared. If a band of naked cannibals had danced the fox-trot around a boiling missionary I would not have been more surprised. It was such an anachronism, combined with such an incongruity of dress, that made me know I was really in a very foreign country.

During the course of my dinner, the young man serving me had been trying to tell me something. His English was a great deal worse than he imagined it to be, but he was proud of it and, to avoid disappointing him, I followed his facial expressions and nodded or grunted where it seemed appropriate, occasionally even risking an ironic chuckle which might be taken any way he chose. Gradually I realized that he was not just dispensing generalities, but was proposing a plan of action to which I had apparently agreed. I felt too tired and withdrawn to admit that I had not understood a word of it. In one of those curious lulls that sometimes fall on the noisiest assembly I heard him say, in friendly, confiding tones:

"Nine is open. Then you go."

I grunted again and finished my dinner. It was just nine o'clock. I wanted to linger with a beer and write in my notebook. He came back, nodding happily.

"Now is nine. Now you go."

I stared back blankly at him, and asked for another beer.

"You can go," he insisted, looking at his watch. "Now is . . ." and his English dissolved once more.

When he saw that I meant to stay, he became suddenly remote and very correct. I could see he was hurt and humiliated. He brought my bill later without a word. No doubt he was thinking how incomprehensibly foreign I was. I wondered whether he was crediting me with subtleties beyond his understanding.

"What the hell," I said to myself as I left. "It was probably just another brothel . . ." But I felt sad and defeated, and not really up to traveling as I understood it.

The night was unpleasantly hot, and the room full of mosquitoes and dank odours from the alley. I dreamed a great deal, woke frequently and wondered about the Norwegian and his girl. When I heard sounds on the landing I got up, impelled partly by curiosity and partly by the need to relieve myself. I came out just in time to see the girl slip back through a door into one of the rooms.

I woke up early, anxious to get away. Should I say goodbye? As I paid my bill, I asked where the Norwegian was.

"Upstair. Sleeping.""

"Ah," I said. "And the Swiss?"

"Same thing."

"Which room?"

"Same room."

"Oh," I said, and left.

**5**

It had so often happened on my journey that after an unpleasant or disturbed night, instead of feeling tired and reluctant to face the day I was all the more confident and eager to get going. It was as though the purpose of the night was less to refresh the body than to give the mind its chance to flush out contradictions and frustrations. In the mornings after those long, dark hours of restlessness and vivid dreams, I had the clear impression that in some obscure chamber of the mind a loud debate had taken place, with heated argument, manoeuvring and mudslinging and that at the eleventh hour the different sides had triumphantly hammered out an agreement. I took my dreams to be the evidence presented by the parties to the dispute. They were different from the dreams I had had in earlier life, in which I was left powerless in the face of some predicament. I still found myself in dangerous situations and awful figures from my past still loomed up to threaten me, but I was able to overcome the dangers, and the dreaded 'authorities' either crumbled or became benign.

This busy and encouraging nightlife had continued, as a vigorous counterpoint to all the excitement of the days, since my journey had begun. It filled me with the hopeful belief that while I was traveling with such exhilaration around the physical globe I was also journeying much more freely through my own past and its buried memories, and perhaps even reconstructing my own history to accord more usefully to the realities of the world as I registered them day by day. In fact, I deliberately let the events of the night influence my progress directly, by trying as far as possible to make my practical decisions in the morning according to how I felt, rather than to a preconceived plan. This was an extraordinary luxury, denied to all but the most privileged and the most primitive. I knew it and revelled in it. This exceptional chance to lead a completely integrated life in which waking and sleeping, the conscious and the unconscious, were so closely joined, gave me a great incentive to keep going.

The mental ferment began to subside in Australia, when I tried to share my journey with another person, and it collapsed altogether in Penang. Now as I rode away from Haad Yai in the fresh morning air I felt the first faint bubbling of that familiar excitement. Nothing like the full-blooded rush of joy I had been used to, but a taste and a hope.

In all the events at Haad Yai I had been nothing more than a voyeur, a passive and, I thought, rather disreputable observer of other people's peculiarities on the seedy fringes of a decaying culture. Yet I had come away with pages of jottings in my notebook, and a mind too busy with speculation to dwell on its own miseries. I realized that since my accident I had made hardly any notes, and this new beginning gave me added encouragement.

The world around me, as always, answered to my mood. Where the previous day the road had seemed dull and repetitive, today it blossomed with interest. The landscape and its people came alive for me, and I absorbed the changes since Malaysia. The painted wooden houses of Malaya, with their mouldings, decorations and other refinements, were gone. Here the village houses were bamboo wattle and daub with thatched roofs, long simple structures with their own natural beauty.

The roads were quieter. Ox carts, water buffalo, the paddy fields all around, indicated farming on a smaller scale, and the peasant's frugal concern with every square foot of productive soil gave the landscape the neat, jewelled appearance of a painting in miniature.

There were few cars, some trucks, many bicycles and quite a number of small motorcycles. These last amazed me by the use they were put to. It became common to see an entire family squeezed on to one little Honda or Yamaha; two adults with a child on the tank; the same with another child clinging at the back; the same with yet another child perched on the handle bars; and finally, my personal best sighting, three adults and two children glued together like Siamese quins on top of a hardly visible machine.

My aim that day was to get to Phuket on the West coast and then to find a place called Kata beach. A mild-mannered young German traveler called Hans-Georg had first told me about it in Penang. I had formed an instant and instinctive liking for him and trusted his judgement. Phuket was an island some 150 miles north of Haad Yai, connected by bridge to the mainland, with many beaches, some busy, some almost deserted. Kata beach, he said, was quiet and beautiful, and I imagined myself recovering there the wholeness that I had lost.

Some of the physical queasiness was already leaving me. I had the motorcycle to thank for that. One would not suppose that sitting on the saddle in a fixed position for hours on end would offer much in the way of exercise. It might even be thought a rather constricting and constipating form of inactivity, inclined to shake one's blood into one's boots, and rattle the vertebrae in an unhealthy manner, but curiously enough it has the opposite effect. All the muscles are in constant, if imperceptible, use to relieve the discomfort, and the vibration always seemed to have a good effect on my digestion. Those were the physical benefits of riding, but it also had the great negative virtue of removing me from the temptations of ginger beer and other sops craved by an idle and discontented mind.

In the afternoon I passed among some rock formations unlike anything I had seen before. They rose up abruptly from the undulating fields, pillars of stone as tall as a house, as though each one had been punched out of the earth's crust from below by one mighty blow still with its cap of topsoil and vegetation intact. The trees, bushes and grasses burgeoning on their crowns and dangling over their sides in such thick green luxuriance looked, from a distance, like immense wigs on supporting pedestals and conjured up images of some ancient race of giants. As they became more numerous and closer together the road rose and cavorted among them in ever-tightening curls. These gyrations tested the handling of the Triumph to the limit and I finally realized that my uneasiness on the bike was not just a subjective phenomenon, as I had imagined, but that there really was something wrong.

When I found that the alignment of the rear wheel was hopelessly out and corrected it, the bike seemed to jump forward like an animal released from a snare, and my confidence leaped forward with it.

So I arrived in Phuket stronger and happier than I had felt in weeks. Kata beach was not easy to find. The road signs were in Thai, and my questions were met with polite incomprehension. Whichever way I tried to pronounce Kata it meant nothing to anyone, but I guessed my way and was lucky and found the dirt track which led me five miles across the island to the far shore just before dusk.

The first sight of Kata delighted me. From the brow of the last hill I saw the beach below me in the shape of a broad smile between two promontories. The sand was bright and clean; the sea, green in its shallows, blue in its depths, was on fire from the setting sun. Coconut palms clustered above the high tide mark, shading a broad strip of flat ground between the beach and the hills.

I followed the track down to the beach. Where it turned off to the left stood a rudimentary cafe or bar; a few tables on an earthen floor enclosed by a low wooden balustrade and sheltered by thatch. I stood the bike against the trunk of a palm and as soon as the engine noise stopped I felt at peace.

One of three men sitting in the cafe rose to welcome me in modest English.

"How do you do? Would you like a drink?" he asked.

I could not tell whether he was the proprietor, or whether it was a friendly invitation from a guest. I settled for a glass of tea which would not be of sufficient consequence to matter either way.

We sat at a table and exchanged a few questions and answers, diffidently, as the twilight gathered about us and the lamps were lit. I knew two things about Kata. At one end of the beach, Hans-Georg had said, lived a schoolmaster, a nice man who spoke English and had a little hut to rent. At the other end of the beach lived a French woman called Adrienne who was worth knowing. I had already guessed that I was sitting with the schoolmaster, and before asking him about his hut I said:

"Do you know someone called Adrienne?"

He looked out into the night and, quite innocent of the theatrical effect, pointed and said:

"There she is coming now."

I looked up, startled to see two headlights approaching through the palms. I walked out of the hut and waved my hand at the Datsun pick-up as it appeared. There were four people in it, two women in the front and a couple in the back.

A woman with coppery gold hair and strong regular features was driving. She stopped beside me and examined me with a pleasant, expectant look.

"Excuse me," I said. "Are you Adrienne?"

"Yes. Can I help you?"

Her question was deliberate, not perfunctory, and warmly put with a slight French accent. Instead of the neutral or defensive tone I expected, and which would have seemed natural, her voice implied an actual interest in my circumstances. Her initiative surprised me, heightened my senses, and left me a little flustered and awkward.

"Well, a friend of mine told me, er, suggested that I might try to get in touch. Hans Georg? Do you remember? A German? He was here a few weeks ago?"

It was obvious that the name meant nothing to her. I stumbled to a halt, and my awkwardness increased.

"Never mind," she said. "Tell me, are you staying here?"

"Well, I would like to stay a few days. I haven't seen anything yet . . . I mean, I've only just arrived and . . ." Really, I thought, this has got to stop. I'm behaving like an adolescent on his first trip abroad.

She took me off the hook very easily.

"We are just going to eat some fish on the beach. Would you like to come?"

"That would be wonderful. Gosh. Are you sure . . . ?"

"Yes. Of course."

The reassurance was calm, and unequivocal. My own dithering responses embarrassed me but, more than that, they revealed how far I had drifted into confusion. Then I felt a sudden and profound sense of relief.

"Is it far?" I asked. "Shall I follow you? I'm on a motorcycle."

"You can leave it here and get in with us. It will be all right."

To leave the bike and everything on it was something I never normally did without a great deal of thought. It was my tribute to this woman and the occasion that I believed her and climbed unhesitatingly into the back of the Datsun. She introduced me to her son, Dan, a heavy young man who acknowledged me in an offhand way, and his girl friend Karen, an American in her late teens.

They had little to say to me as we bounced along the rough track. It was a lovely, warm night. I leaned back, gripping the side of the pick-up and watched a big moon sail among dramatic bars of cloud, brushed by the black silhouettes of palm fronds. I had the pleasant feeling that everything was happily settled and I was content to keep to myself for a while. There would be plenty of time for talking later.

The only one of us who spoke much was the girl, Karen. Or rather she did not so much speak as utter. She had evidently been complimented on the beauty and sensitivity of her utterances, because she produced them with an assurance that was quite unnatural for her age and completely unjustified by what she said. She had also dressed to suit the part, but her make-up and her elaborate ethnic clothes were out of place, and the prominent Indian head band was an overstated affectation of a 'hippy' idea I was sure she could not understand.

All the way, she strained after her verbal butterflies, but caught only bats.

"The sky," she announced, "is like Beethoven's Fifth Symphony. "

And you, I wanted to say, are like Herb Alpert playing it.

She buzzed and crackled on through the evening as disturbing as a faulty generator that produces no light.

Dan cheered her on, appearing to marvel. For him she was Donovan in drag.

We arrived eventually at a small restaurant, and sat around a wooden table embedded in the sand to order shrimps, fish, rice and vegetables. The third woman, who had been sitting next to Adrienne in the cab, was introduced to me as Alice. She was a blonde Jewish girl of about thirty, and she responded to my few polite questions with suspicion and a touch of hostility. I gathered that she was Australian and had run away from her family to live and study in Israel. Her manner provoked me into saying that I had been twice to Israel and had found the people too harsh for my taste, a remark which confirmed her in her poor opinion of me. She turned to Adrienne and engaged her with a loud monologue about Hong Kong and the fashion industry, praising and condemning everything and everyone in the most lavish terms.

Adrienne smiled gently and after a while took advantage of a pause to ask me where I had come from on my bike. I said I had come from England.

Alice pointed her forceful jaws at me and cried:

"*What* did you think of Nepal? Wasn't it the *most?* I mean, didn't it just *freak you out?*"

"I haven't been there yet."

"Oh, but you *must.* It's the most *incredible* thing."

"Yes. I. . ."

"And you *must* go trekking, because that is *totally and completely amazing.* Go on the Annapurna route, and you *must* fly up to Namche Bazaar if you can afford it and visit the *genuine* Tibetan communities."

"Well, I. . ."

"Oh, and you should *absolutely* go to Kopan, you know, the monastery? It's a Mahayana monastery. You could stay there a few days. Ask for Nick. He's a *really amazingly wonderful person.*"

"Nick?"

"He's a Mahayana monk."

"Nick the monk. What's there to do?"

"The best thing to do is meditation. It's *really outstanding.* You know. The quiet. I mean. It'll *really freak you out. Totally.*"

This last, delivered at almost screaming pitch, was a bit too much to take. The moon dived behind the cloud, and I couldn't hear the waves any more.

"Is that what you did up there?"

I didn't try too hard to hide my incredulity. She was noisy, almost hysterical, but she was sharp too.

"Yes," she said shortly. "Have you finished with the fish?"

Karen was gazing rapturously to sea.

"I think I see George Harrison walking in on the waves," she murmured. "I mean I can almost see it, can't you?"

"Yay," said Dan. "Right on."

Adrienne asked me what kind of journey I was making and I had to say that I was 'going round the world on a motorcycle'. I hated the phrase. It always sounded supremely silly to my ears.

"Then which way have you come so far?"

I explained in as few words as possible. I found I could hardly bear to talk about my own adventures because of the sense of disgrace I still carried with me from Penang. It was like being asked to recall the sweetness of a honeymoon during the bitterness of a divorce. I felt terrible pangs of loss and regret for the first lyrical years of my journey, and feared that such joy could never be recovered. To the others I must have seemed a recalcitrant, rather arrogant man for withholding so much.

"Down through Africa," I said, "then round South America and up to California. Then round Australia and up from Singapore. "

"How long has that taken you?"

"Well, it's nearly three years now."

"And how many kilometres is that?"

Adrienne was softly persistent, and I began to feel better about it.

"In miles it's just over forty-four thousand, on the bike that is. So that would be about seventy thousand kilometres."

"A long way," she said. "You must have learned a lot."

"It's impossible not to," I said, though I did not really believe that. There were blind travelers, and stupid ones too.

"You must sometimes have wished you could just stop and go home. No?"

"No," I said. "Never. I have never wanted to stop, even at the worst moments."

I surprised myself with my own vehemence. *It's true,* I thought, *nothing will make me stop. So it must be all right, if I believe in it that much. Really, I already owe this woman a lot.*

Alice was fidgeting belligerently, and burst out:

"Where were you in California? I mean, you must have passed right by Esalen. Did you go?"

"No, I didn't go. I've heard a lot about it. Encounter groups, stuff like that?"

Alice of course had been there. She had, in fact, submitted herself to an impressive array of healing influences. She had visited ashrams, monasteries, shrines and temples of counter culture. She had rubbed shoulders with gurus, monks and the acknowledged heroes of alternative medicine, Feldenkreis and Govinda among them. She adulated them. She spoke of them with shrill awe. She heaped her praise upon them all. 'Hallelujah,' she shouted, 'for they are all totally amazing and incredible and completely powerful high-energy people,' and 'Glory be,' she sighed, 'for I am freaked out.'

Unhappily, they must have missed Alice with their high-energy beams of enlightenment as she prostrated herself before them. She had succumbed, while traveling, to a combination of sickness and heartbreak, and it was Adrienne who had gathered her up from the wayside like a stricken bird. She had been convalescing at Kata for several weeks and had already recovered most of her vitality, which was of a high order but of the kind that is self-consuming. Behind her square, intelligent and somewhat greedy face I imagined a girl who believed that unless she shouted very loudly she would cease to exist.

We continued talking for some time, Alice with more pugnacious accounts of miracles she had perceived and charismatic geniuses she had befriended, Karen with ever more painful failures to grasp the muse, I with increasingly acerbic judgements and refusals and Dan with occasional ponderous betrayals of ignorance. It struck me that, with the exception of Adrienne, we were a pretty disagreeable and unsatisfactory lot. Yet, oddly enough, we coexisted and, for all our antipathies, we were even enjoying ourselves. This triumph of mediation was achieved by Adrienne. Throughout our displays of belligerence, pomposity, sulking and affectation, she gazed with equal and unmistakable fondness on all of us and radiated a peaceful glow that had some authority too. The calming influence of the sea and the stars seemed to flow through her, and the great warm night above our little lamp-lit table drew out our silly fears and spites and soaked them away.

I envied Adrienne her composure. She had that combination of sensitivity and detachment which I was so anxious to recover and I was very glad when she asked if I would like to stay with them. I was curious to know the source of her strength, since it was obvious to me that it had come as the result of prolonged effort and determination.

I found the motorcycle just as I had left it, and I followed the others to the far end of the beach. Between the palms we passed more huts, some lit by fluorescent tubes, some by oil lamps. Through the shadows figures in sarongs moved softly about and among them I saw the quiescent mass of a water buffalo, sleeping.

**6**

Adrienne's house stood on a rise above the bay, and was big enough to hold us all in comfort. I woke up in sunshine with a glorious view of the sea. From that time on until I left four days later I was left entirely in peace to do as I wished. Most of that time I had the house to myself. Adrienne ran a small handicraft and jewellery shop at a resort on the other side of the island, and the others were usually away during the day. It was the first time in many months that I had enjoyed the combined comforts of space, shelter and solitude.

To be able to move from room to room, from sofa to armchair, from bedroom to bathroom to kitchen, to live for a while with carefully made objects in well-designed spaces, to enjoy the patterns of light and shade on polished wooden surfaces, to be cool, quiet and undisturbed for as long as I liked, these were luxuries that I appreciated as never before. Despite the allure of the beach and the sea I found I wanted nothing more than to stay in the house and dream, doze, think, write and, above all, read.

There were books in French and English. Many of them were by Buddhists and about Buddhism, and I leafed through them superficially at first, and then with ever greater curiosity and a kind of inner laughter. Just to read the texts was like leaving the twentieth century behind as a bad dream.

I found an immediate affinity with the ideas and images that jumped out of the pages before me. My reading was quite unmethodical. I hopped from book to book, reading odd paragraphs and then wandering off into my own thoughts in contradiction, I felt, of the dedication and discipline that the texts seemed to demand. No doubt true disciples of the Buddha (or bikkhus, as it appeared they were known) would have regarded my butterfly approach with some disapproval, and yet those random samples seemed to come together quite coherently to form a picture which surprised me by its familiarity, as though it had already existed subconsciously and was simply being developed in a conscious way.

I read from the Buddha's Discourse on the Arousing of Mindfulness:

'A *bikkhu,* gone to the forest, to the foot of a tree or to an empty place, sits down, bends his legs crosswise on his lap, keeps his body erect and arouses mindfulness in the object of meditation, namely the breath which is in front of him, and he lives independent and clings to naught in the world.'

There was enough in this simple prescription to keep me thinking happily for the rest of the day, It was so easy to imagine the forest, the tree, the disciple in his saffron robe, the lithe elasticity of his limbs as he slots his feet under his hips and stretches his spine in a movement which separates his life from mine by one inimitable act. Why to a forest? Why to the foot of a tree? What a relief to be a disciple and not to have to ask such silly questions. Must one really adapt one's body to such an excruciating position in order to 'live independent and cling to naught in the world'? But what an admirable state to aspire to. How difficult would it be to arouse mindfulness in the breath which was in front of me?

I wrenched my legs into the closest approximation I could manage to the lotus position – which no *bikkhu,* I'm sure, would have recognized – and tried to concentrate on my breath. It went well for about four seconds. Then my back began to ache, my knees itched, a fly tickled my neck, I found my mind wandering like a mongrel dog to the four corners of the room, and though I tugged furiously on the lead I could never keep it to heel for more than a few seconds at a time.

I read on, looking for clues, fascinated by a preoccupation with the simplest acts, such as *Mindfulness on the Modes of Deportment:* 'When standing, lying, or however the body is disposed internally and externally... his mindfulness is established with the thought: "The body exists" to the extent necessary for just knowledge and remembrance, and he lives independent and clings to naught in the world.'

Or 'In going forwards and backwards, in looking straight on and away from the front, in bending and stretching, in wearing the shoulder cloak, the robes and the bowl, in regard to what is eaten, drunk, chewed and savoured, in defecating, urinating, in sitting, sleeping, walking, speaking and keeping silence . . . '

Sometimes the language made me hoot with laughter, by the way it recalled the ludicrous terminology of military manuals and parade-ground procedures ordering the disposition of the parts of the human body into precisely ordained configurations – 'thumbs along the seams of the trousers, feet at an angle of forty-five degrees' and so on.

I fell to ruminating on my first traumatic months of military service, on the pulverizing effect of being ordered at every moment of the waking day to conform to rules that seemed as nonsensical as they were stringent, and I remembered having to admit, at the end of it all, even as I was marching to nowhere through deep snow, that I felt a lot better for having been deprived of the time or the need to think about anything more complex than putting one foot in front of another.

How much better though to achieve the same sense of calm well-being without having to march to someone else's orders; to be able to do it, even, sitting under a tree, or in the harmless act of putting on a robe.

From a philosophical point of view I was ripe for Buddhism. All my experience in the world had prepared me for it. The things I admired were always those things conceived in humility and discipline, things derived from the bounty of this earth and bent patiently and modestly to the uses of man: small, sensible (though often beautiful) buildings; good vegetable gardens; useful objects made with care; things made in proportion to human needs and to a human scale.

The trend I saw was in the opposite direction. In the rush for product, profit and power there was little room, and even less respect, for personal virtues. The animal aspect of human behaviour was in the ascendency everywhere, disguised maybe as triumphs of technology, revolutions in agriculture, architectural enormities, miracles of medicine, and revealed in bigger slums, bigger famines and bigger weapons. The contrast was brought home to me by my personal experience. Individuals received me everywhere with generosity and showed great interest in what I was doing. More often than not they shared my hopes for a simple, natural life and my fears of uncontrolled mechanization, but whatever their feelings about the way things were going, nobody imagined for a moment that he or she could do anything about it. And as for those who were supposedly in control of events, cynicism about them, their powers and their motives, was absolute.

Any ambitions I had ever had about trying to exert some political influence over events began to seem utterly foolish. Human activity in general, I had come to realize, was as frantic and automatic as the foraging of rodents and the coupling of cats in the night. Most social behaviour was clearly prompted by fear and greed, and societies were too obviously dominated by a minority with a particular talent for translating their greed into power and wealth. The existence of this class, and its impact on the face of the planet, was becoming more evident all the time. These were the people, energetic, ingenious, clever and above all greedy, who were the engine of material advancement in the world. Through battling with their own fears in order to satisfy their appetites they acquired a gut-felt intuition for knowing how hard to squeeze others. If there was a way to make money they would always take it. For them, feasibility was the acid test of acceptability. If they appeared sometimes to turn aside from some particular piece of exploitation or chicanery, pleading moral scruples, it would always be in reality that they did not see their way clear to making a profit in the long run. Any society which wanted to make rapid progress would have to learn to harness their energy, to lure them into paths profitable to all, and to bribe them with honours and position.

Some of them, of course, would always be criminals, but the majority were highly respectable; leaders in commerce and industry, bankers, brokers, dealers and the like. They were an unstoppable force in the world. If thwarted of legitimacy by some ideological quirk such as Communism, or some religious aberration like the Holy Islamic State, they would burrow in and make their way by corruption from the root to the flower, as avaricious as any termite. And not a single one of them would recognize himself by that description. They were the embodiment of what people meant when they said 'You can't change human nature.'

Most of the abominations I had witnessed in the world were their work. The dumping of trashy goods on the Third World, the disruption of healthy rural life, the spread of drugs and corruption, the growth of crime, the collapse of cultural values, and all those travesties symbolized by the crass, modern bank buildings leering contemptuously over the miserable hovels of Africa and South America.

Oppressed by this vision of the world, and preoccupied by the question of what to do about it, what kind of life to lead, I fell back inevitably on the power of personal example. The only thing to do, I thought, was to lead, as best one could, the life one thought was right, and let others decide whether it answered their needs also. As Pope said: 'When vice prevails, and impious men hold sway, the post of honour is a private station.'

The ideas of Buddhism responded very well to that sentiment. Yet I was hardly appropriate material for a *bikkhu*. For one thing, I enjoyed life too much. The Buddhists, I read, insisted that fear and craving govern all earthly behaviour, and that satisfaction can only be had by complete detachment from earthly things. Yet even *bikkhus* had to eat. Was it wrong for them to enjoy their food? Some aspects of Buddhism seemed fanatical in their complete denial of any degree of value to earthly experience. 'The futility of life and the world' was constantly reiterated. But why could the world not be taken for what it was, an inferior garden perhaps of limited value, but a garden nonetheless. Anyone who insists that the penny whistle in his hand should be a violin would soon find it futile, though it can play a pretty tune.

I talked these things over with Adrienne occasionally in the evenings. She was not impressed by my criticisms.

"It is a personal matter," she said. "There is no dogma. Everybody must find his own way in the end. However much you read, it will all be changed by practice. The key to it all is meditation."

Even so, I went on reading and absorbing what I could, with the thought that somewhere along the way, later on, I might find myself in a better frame of mind to pursue it. One section had me staring at the page for a long time; partly because of the lurid images it evoked, partly because of the window it opened on forgotten aspects of life in an earlier age, and partly because I could see its great value and importance. I found it among the discourses on *The Noble Eight-fold Path,* and it was entitled *Cemetery Contemplations,* with the rather eerie footnote that 'only a corpse of one's own sex is suitable'.

The *bikkhu* is instructed to go to a cemetery, or charnel ground as it was in those days, where bodies were simply thrown out and left. On the first day 'he contemplates a body, dead one, two or three days, swollen, blue and festering', and he thinks of his own body thus.

On the second day he observes a body being eaten by crows, hawks, vultures, dogs, jackals or by different kinds of worm, and he thinks of his own body thus.

On the third day he finds a body reduced to a skeleton together with flesh and blood held in by tendons, and he thinks of his own body thus.

On the fourth day he finds a body reduced to a blood-besmirched skeleton without flesh but held in by the tendons, and he thinks of his own body thus.

On the fifth day he finds a skeleton without flesh or blood but held in by the tendons and he thinks of his own body thus.

On the sixth day he finds a body reduced to bones scattered in all directions and he thinks of his own body thus.

On the seventh day he finds bones white in colour like a conch and he thinks of his own body thus.

On the eighth day he finds bones more than a year old heaped together, and he thinks of his own body thus.

On the ninth day he finds bones gone rotten and become dust and he thinks of his own body thus.

Apart from wondering how a twentieth-century bikkhu would manage, I was overwhelmed by what this discourse reveals about the change that has taken place in our perceptions of life and death. It was the detail, right down to the 'different kinds of worm', which brought it home. It began to seem quite extraordinary to me that in the Western world a person could, and probably would, go through life without ever witnessing death, let alone viewing a naked corpse. And as for putrefaction, such horrors were associated only with fears of a holocaust, or the final sporing of the nuclear mushroom.

I could not bring myself to believe that this was healthy. In life we were amidst death and it would be better for us to have that fact brought home in ways more natural and less sensational than news stories and pictures of remote violence. I had already begun to appreciate how far removed we were, in our modern ways, from the climate, from the origins of our foodstuffs, from the construction of the simplest house, from the distinction even between needs and wants. We were dangerously detached from the basic facts of existence, and surely that would make us very vulnerable to fantasies, and far too obedient to those who could threaten us with the loss of our customary comforts.

In fact it began to emerge much more clearly that the cosseted lifestyle of the West depended on a multitude of fears quite as much as on greed. And perhaps the real purpose of all those little fears was just to distract us from the one big one, the fear of death. How many people, I wondered, would continue to go to the office every morning if they had to pass through a charnel ground on the way?

As the days passed at Kata my admiration for what Adrienne had achieved in herself increased, and her influence on the rest of us continued to surprise me. We others were all, in our various ways, crippled by a sense of inadequacy (although mine, I hoped, was temporary). We would normally have bristled in each other's company, but in that forgiving atmosphere we got along fairly well. In Dan I discovered a pleasant and well-meaning young man, and it was impossible to dislike him or his girl friend. Alice remained as overwrought as ever, but we also managed to talk quite easily about many things, and she did finally scrawl her Nepalese trekking instructions into my notebook, including the words 'most incredible thing', in a chaotic and childish hand.

Adrienne attributed her benevolent effect on us to her work with Buddhism, but I saw it more and more as something in her own personality which had been happily released. Thinking about this, and about my own experience, I was thrown back into believing that the power of personal example was always more fruitful than any religion or philosophy. Indeed, what was best in all those systems, Buddhism, Christianity. even Marxism, seemed to stem directly from the best personal qualities of their founders, while what was worst in them was brought about by the later efforts of zealous disciples to abstract and codify their teachings.

The wonderful warmth, compassion and serenity emitted by good people was what worked miracles on this earth, either at the homely level of Adrienne and the Jaya family, or at the incandescent heights of a Buddha or a Christ. The teachings were surely secondary, instruments to fasten the attention of lesser mortals and hold them closer to the benign influence.

It was so easy, I thought, for a troubled soul to drift into wasteful and destructive ways, and my own recent history, including the episode with the baleful captain, began to read like a parable. On the other hand I knew, from other times, how my own clarity and confidence could seem to summon up all that was best around me, as though by choosing good over bad one could remake the world.

But the power was not in the words. It was in the feelings.

Things began to fall into place.

On the fourth day, quite suddenly, I felt whole and well again. Everything took on a new dimension. I wanted to swim, and run, and do things. I wanted to write rather than read. It was like a rebirth. On that same day Adrienne and Alice decided to take the bus to Bangkok, running the risk of being robbed by the bandits who had held up several buses on that route in recent weeks.

I stayed on with Dan and Karen for two more days, glorying in my recovery. On my last afternoon in Kata I walked up the hill behind the house and over the brow to look down on another bay, smaller than Kata and, as far as I could tell, uninhabited. I could encompass the whole picture in one glance: the long gentle slope of the beach, utterly smooth; an audience of palms respectfully inclined towards the sea, quite still in the hot afternoon lull; and the pale green water washing the sand and fading, with hypnotic regularity, to lay white lace ruffles of foam in unbroken arcs from one end of the beach to the other. It was an image of perfection, renewing itself with every fresh impulse from the sea.

A Thai prince, according to Adrienne, was planning to build a hotel at Kata. Soon all this would change. I stood and watched for a long time, wishing I could stand there for ever, miserably aware of the fickleness of my attention, feeling the sense of wonder and beauty slowly diminish as my mind began to fidget with irrelevant thoughts and sensations. I turned away, sadly, knowing that unless I left I would risk losing it all.

On the crest of the spur dividing the two bays stood a hut, enclosed with its small vegetable patch within a low stockade. Just inside the gate three boys and a dog were happily tumbling over each other. I passed them again on my return. The eldest boy stood up and called 'You.' A short, sharp vowel sound, 'Yu.' The smaller boys stood behind him, chorusing 'Yu, Yu.' He held his two hands in front of him, fingers outstretched in an attitude of supplication, and pushed them towards me in a series of jabbing movements. 'Yu. Yu.' Between the palms was a small green mango.

I walked up smiling to accept the gift. Then one of the smaller boys shouted: 'One *baht.*' I stopped. My smile must have vanished in surprise. A shock wave of emotion jolted the small group, and I saw the little boy's expression change from bravado to dread.

'No, no,' he cried, apparently overwhelmed by guilt. I took the fruit, reflecting that it would probably be my last chance to accept an unsolicited offering. Tomorrow there would be no free mangoes in Thailand.

The Thais were renowned through many centuries for their spontaneous small acts of giving to strangers. Wasn't that what the Swiss had said at Haad Yai? How extraordinary that I should arrive just as this ancient tradition was crumbling away! No, not at all extraordinary. It was we who had brought it about. I felt a spasm of disgust, as I saw myself lumped in with the craven Swiss, the cracked Norwegian, and all the other limping misfits come to suck at the husk and complain that it was dry.

The Thai prince would build his hotel. The boys would become bolder and learn to worship the dollar while we played games with Buddhism. Then we could all blame it on the Americans. I tried the mango then let it fall from my fingers with regret. It was too hard and bitter to eat.

The journey back to Penang was full of irritations. A soggy looking sky promised rain and later delivered it in unpredictable showers. I missed signs and took wrong turnings. I lost my rainjacket at a gas station. Two dogs and a kid goat came within inches of my front wheel and a lorry forced me on to a patch of newly laid tar and stones.

The hotel at Trang, where I spent the night, seemed to be a lucky find compared with the dismal hovel at Haad Yai. It had real rooms in it and a pleasant reception area downstairs. They let me wheel the bike in straight away where it could be seen and supervised from the bar, so that I didn't have the job of taking everything off it. I went for a walk round the town and bought a Hong Kong umbrella for 54 *baht,* having wanted the traditional lacquered paper ones but not liking the bits of green plastic that were now used to protect the crown. I wandered about in the rain for a while looking at shop windows and markets until I found a nice place to eat. I had fried chicken noodles with fat shrimps, beer and coffee. It should have amounted to 39 *baht,* but when the bill came all the prices on the menu had been reduced by a third. This had never happened to me in my life before, and it cheered me up immensely. Although it was still early, I found the hotel already locked up, and the night man let me in. The bike seemed safe enough, and I went to bed very tired.

Something woke me in the night, and I could not get back to sleep. Two people in neighbouring rooms were snoring, with loud honking noises, but I had the impression that something else had woken me. I wrote for a while in my diary about the day's ride from Kata. I had seen a man pick up my jacket at the Esso station and drive off with it before I could get back to stop him. He had driven right past me, in a green car. The number, of course, was in Thai script. I described the small rubber plantations grouped around attractive mud-and wattle cottages at the roadside, and the thick mats of latex hanging over wooden rails in front of them. I recorded my regret at missing the temples and the cave at Phangna. It seemed that, from a conventional point of view, I had seen virtually nothing of Thailand, and yet I felt as though I had absorbed a great deal, perhaps because I had gone through so much myself.

At seven I was up and dressed to take coffee and dim sums downstairs. The weather was dry and bright, and the day seemed to be starting well until I saw that the tank-bag on the bike was sagging miserably on one side. It was normally plump and tightly packed, and the hostile emptiness where something should have been was matched by the sudden hollow in my stomach. I knew instantly that the camera had been stolen, and realized in the same flash of thought how doltish I had been to suppose that the thieves would all be outside the hotel. And it was that, more than the loss itself, which almost dragged me right down. Would I never get it right again?

It was a mere formality to put my hand in the bag and confirm the theft. There was no chance, I knew, of recovering the camera. So why bother to mention it? I asked myself. Why not just wheel the bike out on to the street with a satisfied smile? Why let them all know that yet another improvident idiot had fallen victim to the national sport? First my documents and my money. Now the camera. Truly, I had joined the ranks of the despised.

I scanned the Thai faces around me, looking for an averted eye, any sign of unnatural indifference. I might as well have hoped to see a stone Buddha shed tears. My rage and bitterness were too strong to be contained. Stiffly at first, then with gathering force I announced my loss. I complained, accused, attacked, railed and stormed to a crescendo. The faces smiled, grew solemn, displayed astonishment, disbelief, sorrow, anxiety and outrage. At every moment in the development of the drama they supported my performance beautifully. Then they brought on their own finest player, the manager, an actor of towering talents.

Addressing each of his men in turn, he upbraided them severely, and one by one they withered visibly and became abject. Then, with his company gathered around him, he brought the show to a close with breathtaking virtuosity. He held out his hands in that same prayerful clasp from which I had recently plucked an unripe mango, and bowing his body towards me he raised his face from the level of my waist. Drawing his lips tightly across his teeth he contrived an expression which combined the deepest desolation with a smile that spoke of his abiding faith in my ability to rise, godlike, above adversity.

'Sorry, sorry,' was all he said. Then, straightening up, he repeated the whole astonishing movement, as though impelled to an encore by irresistible applause. His mime, done without benefit of make-up or stage lighting, and only inches away from me, was superb. The smile with the corners of the mouth drawn down was, to hotel management, what the pianissimo with open throat is to operatic singing. A *tour de force.* I never saw anything so good again in a hotel or a theatre. It was probably worth the price of the camera, and I tried valiantly to make myself believe it as I rode away. Anyway I had another camera, and the true significance of the incident was that my systems were still full of holes.

The Thai border official was the same one who had ushered me in ten days earlier. His pot belly, his broad, swarthy face and flower-patterned shirt were immediately recognizable. I filled out another set of forms in quintuplet and paid 30 *baht* for stamps. Because Saturday was a Thai holiday, he explained in silky tones, there was another 50 *baht* to pay for overtime. As he spoke he reached under his shirt to pull out a pistol, and tossed it into the drawer of his desk. I paid up without a murmur, and stuffed my four dollars' worth of pink paper into my pocket. At the Malaysian checkpoint I asked a man rather acidly whether he charged overtime as well. His smug reply was quite irritating.

'My dear sir,' he said. 'This is Malaysia, not Thailand.'

It was shortly after this, glancing at my map, that I happened to see Padang Besar marked on it. I had not noticed it before because it was not where I had expected to find it. In fact it was twenty miles farther along the road from the camp where the unfortunate Captain Dylan had supposedly been shot. I had clearly never been anywhere near Padang Besar, and the whole incident began to feel like the figment of somebody's imagination.

Some people, I reflected, took potent drugs to give their experiences that extra surreal dimension, but I seemed to manage quite well without them.

An ordinary day on Chulia Street in Georgtown, Penang, and below, here comes the juice-mobile. A mill for crushing sugar cane.

There was a new employee at the Choong Thean when I returned. He was a burly Indian with bandy legs which sprang outwards from his khaki shorts. I had become used to T'an's heavy indolence, and the Indian seemed to me to be everywhere at once, poking into corners with his broom and grinning with a garish display of golden molars. His English had a slippery ease which I found a little shocking after the slow succulence of T'an's speech, and I felt that his presence robbed the hotel of much of its former appeal.

I got the same room, number six, for the third time, and the Indian helped me take my things up with a show of energy I found inappropriate and distasteful. T'an himself remained more somnolent than ever in his chair downstairs. On that first day we hardly exchanged a word.

I was sitting on the bed thinking about how to use the days before my ship sailed for Madras when there was a knock on the door and a thin blond man of about twenty-five came in.

"How d'ye do," he said, with a New Zealander's stifled drawl. "I'm Jack. The Indian bloke told me you were just in from Thailand. I'm in number seven next door."

He gave me a bony hand and I shook it a bit reluctantly at first and asked him to sit down. He wanted to know about taking trains to Bangkok and I could not help him, but he had an interesting manner and I began to like him. He told me how it felt to leave New Zealand for the first time and arrive in Asia. His natural reticence was bursting at the seams. "It was like I'd never been alive before, y'know? . . . Like coming out of the womb."

After a little while he asked me if I'd like to smoke some opium.
"Where?" I asked. "Here?"

"Nah," he said. "There's a den round the corner. The trishaw
Johnny here can fix it. It's okay. I've been once."

He shamed me. Only nine days out of the Antipodes and he was
already taking in his stride an experience I had been hesitating over
for weeks. I was always nervous about drugs, for fear of accidental
brushes with officialdom which could easily put an end to my journey. Also, I hated doing deals with hustlers like the 'trishaw Johnny',
a Malay who actually called himself Jimmy and who had been pes-
tering the occupants of number seven for as long as I had been at the
hotel. He seemed to go with the room. I had sometimes wondered
whether the Chinese, with their special sympathy for numbers, allot-
ted room numbers according to their reading of the client's personality. My own number, six, had a tediously rectangular feel to it. If I
were a runner for an opium den I would not waste my time on a six
when there was a prime and racy seven next door. Well, anyway . . .

"All right," I said. "What's the damage?"

"Four dollars a packet – Malay dollars, of course. You pay the driver when you come out. I had one packet last time. I might try two
tonight."

I could not visualize a packet of opium, let alone the inside of an
opium den. My impressions on the subject were formed, even before
my baroque notions of what a whorehouse should be, through childhood reading of Edgar Wallace and lurid accounts of the Boxer rebel-
lion. I imagined slumped bodies, vacant faces, a fetid smoky haze and
dim dragons with ruby eyes.

We went out in the late-afternoon twilight, with the heat of the
day still bearing down heavily. The den was in Aik Seng Bazaar,
which ran alongside Rope Walk behind the hotel. It was a rather
formless, intriguing area, a jumble of stalls, huts and cheap eating
places. Most of the asphalt had broken up and given way to earth
and stones. Big trees still stood here and there offering shade. It
might have been a last remnant of old George Town, a fit subject for
an engraving. It was also a haunt of the more villainous-looking
trishaw drivers who rested there at crude benches under the trees,
where I imagined they did their business and extracted their com-
missions from the heroin dealers. I had long ago christened it Smack
Alley.

In the darkness, long angular faces, glittering eyes and bare skin swam in pools of lamplight, with just a hint of danger, enough at any rate to satisfy my expectations. Jimmy stopped the trishaw and pointed to one of several board shacks with flat tar-paper roofs. We went inside.

The interior was all in shades of cream and brown: the bare wooden walls, a small darker wooden table, the even darker floor, a solitary candle flame in an unusually thick glass lamp, and the creamy torso of the man who stood behind the table beaming at us. He was short, plump and Chinese, and wore only striped pajama trousers with pockets, and sandals. A pair of small gold-rimmed spectacles was embedded in his fat cheeks, and his eyes literally twinkled through them with all the merry benevolence of a Pickwick.

He seemed to speak very little English, and contented himself with the barest essentials – 'Come-ha, please. Sit down-ha. How many packet you like-ha?' – but through his manner and his gestures he managed to convey an extraordinary courteousness and respect. I felt I had been given an effusive and elaborate welcome, all the more remarkable given his primitive conditions.

He waved us to the bunks that filled the back half of the shack. They were two double bunks, set at right angles to each other, and so broad that a man could lie crosswise on them. There would have been room for a dozen or more people, but we were alone and the brown-printed linoleum with which they were covered was bare.

We lay down facing each other, about a yard apart, and watched the preparations. He bent down to reach for a shoe under his desk, and from this he extracted two packets of opium. From a drawer he took out a pipe, and then brought these objects over to us, carrying the candle as well, so that strange shadows moved around the den emphasizing our intimacy. He knelt between us and, with deft deliberation, assembled the pipe. It was a most beautiful object: a dark wooden tube bound by silver rings like a flute. The wood's deep lustre glowed in the candlelight. The pipe was blocked at one end and had a mouthpiece at the other. Into a hole near the blocked end he fitted the bowl, which was another piece of polished wood shaped somewhat like a mushroom with a small cavity in the top. Then he picked up a packet.

It was made from a single leaf, folded once across the middle and then once along each side. He opened it to show us the button of dark brown tarry matter it contained. We lay with our heads resting on shaped wooden blocks, and his hands and the candle were between us, though a bit farther from the wall, so that our faces and his hands made a triangle with the candle in the center. The world beyond the edges of the triangle faded from sight and everything within it became very intense, charged with a calm excitement such as the best rituals always produce.

He scraped up some of the dark resin on the end of a long needle and held it over the candle flame. I became aware of the extreme thickness of the glass which was itself shaped like a candle flame with just a narrow opening at the top. The glass had been cracked at some time and repaired with a thin wire. Over the heat of the candle the opium softened, coalesced, became shiny and threatened to fall. Expertly, the den-keeper kept the opium dancing on the end of the needle as it began to swell and bubble and make fantastic shapes. In this hot, almost liquid state he thrust it into the bowl, forming it into a plug, pushing the needle through it to form a channel for air and then twisting it out to leave the plug in place.

He gave the pipe to Jack who held it with the bowl inverted over the flame. As the opium burned he drew the vapour into his lungs.

"One big breath-ah," the keeper coaxed. "Ah. Good. Very good."

There were four pipefuls in Jack's packet. Then we started on mine. The trick was to draw all the opium into the empty lungs in one long, smooth pull, and on the second pipe I managed it quite well. Entranced by the ceremony, I could have lain in the den all night, sheathed in its amber glow. I certainly expected to lie there for a while and experience the effect of the opium, but when Jack's second packet was gone it became clear that we were expected to leave.

Full of the experience but with nothing to say, we let Jimmy carry us back to Rope Walk and paid him off. Jack was beginning to feel a little remote and wanted to go to his room. I walked to the Kedai Kopi and sat for a while with a glass of tea, looking across the road at the Kung Fu rehearsal rooms and feeling peacefully perplexed. Perhaps the world did seem a shade more distant than usual, but one packet of low-grade opium was obviously not enough to tilt my perceptions very far. My sense of intoxication, my feeling of satisfaction and well-being as I slumped in the chair and stretched my legs, was not the effect of the drug at all. It came directly from the ceremony itself, from the excitement of having penetrated another of life's mysteries.

With something of a shock I realized that the opium was irrelevant to my experience – it might as well have been chewing gum or marshmallow. But why? Why should a little fat stranger in pajama pants fussing with a pipe and a candle in an outsize packing case have induced in me such a state of bliss?

Well, that was a deliberate falsification. He did not fuss. Quite the contrary, his skilful hands were a joy to watch, and the dignified and thoughtful way he practiced his craft made him no more a stranger than would be the priest giving Communion. In fact, it was this sense of communion with others, in silence and utter simplicity, which stirred me, and which could happen as well in an opium den as in a church. or for that matter in a Turkish bath, in a barber's chair or on a masseur's table. The joy of it was that it allowed people to come together, to participate in something, in a way to know each other, without the use of words – those words which we abuse so terribly to create suspicion and fear, to bully, to condemn, to judge and to alienate others.

That was part of it then, that easy complicity in a ritual, soothed by the murmur of a prayer, the sucking of a pipe, the hissing of steam, the barber's hand on the scalp, everything functional, nothing spurious, all challenge and anxiety removed. But added to this, what made the moment unique was the intensity of revelation.

I remembered a tea-house halfway across the Atbara Desert in Sudan, where every moment seemed to stretch to eternity.

And the workshop of Delio Quiroz in Argentina, an aromatic treasure-house of saddles, boots, hides and harnesses, where I worked for two days under that genial old leather-aproned craftsman, cutting and stitching a new saddle cover on machinery more venerable even than he.

And being invited, one big black night, to dance with Turkana tribesmen and emulate the stiff shuffle of the ostrich and the soaring leap of the giraffe.

What united all these moments was an absolute authenticity of environment, a sense of the past in the present, a complete identification between people and place, and a sense of mystery partially disclosed within me. In the excitement of such initiations there was cause for a joy as heady as any drug induced ecstasy.

What did that make of me, then? Some sort of cultural Luddite? Maybe. But I knew I could only be satisfied by the real thing, and the more I saw of the world, the more I realized that the real thing was running out. Some people, younger people, would explode with contemptuous mirth and claim that the real thing is being born fresh every minute, but they delude themselves. Things take time to become real, to absorb the mystery. Homes, for example. Who is making real homes any more?

The slow plodding drumbeat from the rehearsal room became louder as though a wind had veered into the mouth of the cafe. They were practicing the Lion Dance for a big parade. I crossed over and peered round the screen that stood just inside the open doorway. The huge dragon's head, its fiery eyes popping and rolling, its jaws lolling open and snapping shut, was only a few feet away, jerking to the rhythm, with the long silk body rippling behind it. It was the spasmodic movement of the dancers which brought the beast to life, lending it a terrible energy and presence. It writhed, darted from side to side, even rolled over on its back, and although the dancers, their bodies and feet, were plainly visible all the time, the creature overcame them completely and absorbed their life force into its ritual existence.

Rope Walk, I realized, was devoted almost entirely to ceremonies and rituals of one sort or another, for the living or the dead. It was a street of funeral undertakers, musicians, sword-swallowers, firedancers, and manufacturers of ceremonial artefacts and incense. I began to wonder how foolish I might have been to despise rituals, to dismiss religions as so much mumbo-jumbo, as the 'opiate' indeed of the people. But it is one thing, I thought, to enter freely into a ritual, and quite another to be enslaved by it from childhood, remembering the deadening weight of the school services and chapels I had had to endure. No doubt it was other people's unfamiliar rituals which promised fulfilment, and I blessed the good fortune that allowed me to dip into them as I buzzed, like a bee, across the honeyed cultures of the world.

I walked past the Choong Thean to Cintra Street and the Tai

Tung, the best affordable restaurant I had yet found in Penang. Goldschmidt, the fat Austrian, was there alone at a marble topped table. I hadn't seen him since my accident and I sat down with him and ordered pig's trotters in ginger. While he was eating I began to tell him where I'd been and what I'd been thinking about.

"I don't know what you mean about real homes," he said, wiping his greasy chin on a paper napkin. "It sounds too romantic. "

Being Viennese, Goldschmidt professed himself naturally to be a cynic, though he was far too passionate for the part.

"Well partly, I suppose, I mean a house that your father and grandfather lived in. I can only imagine what it would be like to live with things that were made or marked by my own ancestors – old fruit trees, a summer house, carved initials that sort of thing."

"Pretty horrible. You wouldn't like it. You'd rip it all out. If they were my ancestors you would."

"But even then you'd be forced to think about it – about them and their lives. You'd get some kind of perspective."

"Maybe, but it's impossible. It's always been impossible. Look, in three generations the house would have to be the size of a village."

I wouldn't give up. I was intoxicated by my vision of old wood and stone, of surfaces dented and dignified by use and age, of home-grown food, home-baked bread, children playing with their grand-mothers, geese grazing in the orchard and sheets flapping in the wind. My ideal home was a cornucopia, producing not only a flood of good things to eat and drink but a living source of ideas, attitudes and beliefs.

Goldschmidt was not immune to the allure of it, but went on opposing it on principle.

"The State does not allow you to make home-baked children any more. They have to be baked in schools. Then afterwards they run away to become pop stars and scientists."

"Well, who wouldn't run away from the sort of homes we have now?"

Western life seemed immeasurably bleak to me, the very reverse of my ideal, a sort of vacuum cleaner that sucked up everything indiscriminately, useful and useless alike, and then farted and shat in a bag for the garbage collector to take away. To bring up a child in such an atmosphere would be a crime.

We went on talking, wandering down the old, familiar tracks of rural life, its potential and isolation, of communes and their notorious instability, of self-sufficiency and its undeniable hardships . . .

"But you've got to start somewhere," I protested.

"No I haven't. You have," he said, grinning.

"All right. I have, and I will. I've seen too much now to let it go. We're filling the world with our rubbish. Every culture in the world is getting polluted. The Arabs, the Africans, the Thais — they don't know who they are any more."

I told him about the policemen dancing like Salome and dressed like IBM executives, and the squalor of my trip around the brothels.

"All the sick Westerners are out here now, rooting around. Some go to brothels, some to monasteries. It's all the same to me. They don't get cured but they spread their sickness everywhere. The forests are shrinking, the deserts are growing, the dirt is spreading, and people don't know what to believe any more. That's what I mean when I say that the real thing is getting harder and harder to find."

I wandered back to Rope Walk happier than I had been for a long time. At least I had made some sort of sense for myself out of these recent fragments of experience. Overheated though my arguments may have been, I felt I had got some grip on life again. The journey began to seem real once more.

"You're cured," I said to myself aloud, and laughed at the simultaneous notion that others might well see me as having suffered a severe, and possibly fatal, relapse.

The doors of the Choong Thean were closed, but T'an let me in. He was in his usual chair in the center of the floor, in front of the motorcycle. I sat on the carved bench, brought out my cigarettes and offered him one.

"The day after tomorrow," I said, "I am going. On the *Chidambaram*. To India."

"I am so sorry," he said. "I wish you could stay longer. It will be a bad time for me. At the end of this month I will have no more job."

I stared at him in horror.

"But T'an, that's terrible. What happened?"

It struck me as a tragedy because I thought of him as quite helpless.

"The Indian is a bad man. I have found for him this job because I believed he was a good man. But he is a bad man. Now the boss has given me the sack."

"But what will you do?" I asked.

"I do not know. Perhaps I will be lucky."

If I could have spoken to the boss in his own language I would have tried hard to persuade him to change his mind. From the point of view of attracting foreigners like myself, I thought T'an was a genuine asset. At the same time, I could not help the slight suspicion that there might be more to the story than T'an had given me. He was quite the most modest and harmless beggar I had ever known, but he was a beggar none the less. Did he beg from everyone ? Did he do more than beg? And deep down there was a last, lingering, inadmissible suspicion that maybe, on his second visit to the hospital, T'an might have had something to do with the disappearance of my pouch. It was such an unworthy doubt that I did my best to disown it, but it was enough to taint the well.

During the next day, as I was packing some things to send to England, the stuffed monkey among them, I talked to T'an several times, trying to make up my mind about what role I should play in his salvation. With my newly recovered strength and self-confidence I should have had energy and compassion to spare but, in fact, my feelings took me away from him. As I prepared myself for India, T'an and his predicament became, by slight degrees, more remote, and I dismissed my more grandiose schemes of patronage as impractical and foolish.

On my last morning he told me that he had got a bed with The Little Sisters of the Poor, and that his name there would be Albert T'an, no doubt to make him that much more palatable to the Christian order. I left him some money in the form of further unpaid debts, and later sent him more notes which I had been unable to change. For a long time afterwards his memory troubled me, as if I had abandoned an elderly relative. He had been important to me at a difficult time, and I had failed somehow to discover the right way to express my obligation.

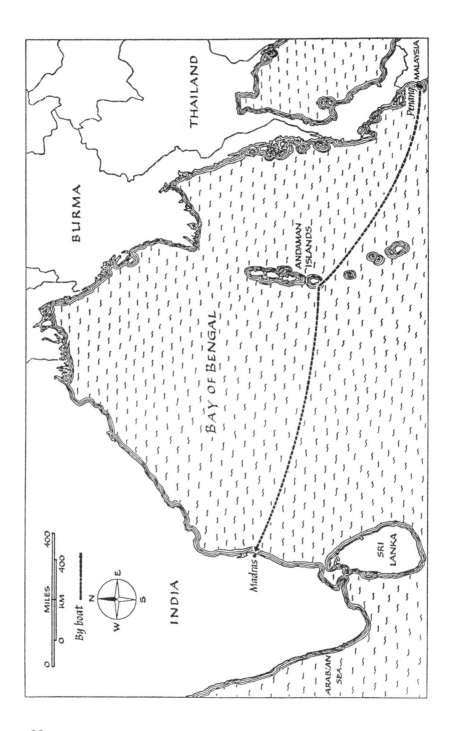

MILES
0          400

KM
0          400

By boat ▬▬▬▬▬

N
W ✦ E
S

THAILAND

BURMA

Penang MALAYSIA

ANDAMAN
ISLANDS

BAY OF BENGAL

INDIA

Madras

SRI
LANKA

ARABIAN
SEA

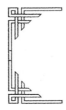

# 8. India

*C*hidambaram, Chidumbrrrum, oh, how I loved to say ChiDUMbrrRUM, the syllables resonating and reverberating between my lips. The *Chidambaram* was a big white ship on a big blue sea, bound from Penang across the Bay of Bengal to Madras, the last of the big ships for me on my meandering trail around the globe. For four days and three nights she would cosset me in careless indolence before the great adventure of India, and the long ride home.

She was a fallen aristocrat. Once she had been called the *Pasteur,* when she was a luxury liner on the North Atlantic route. In those days she pandered to wealthy gamblers who liked to while away their days and their fortunes between Le Havre and New York at roulette and chemin de fer.

She still carried her haughty nose in the air. The large stairways and lavish saloons were all intact, carpeted and embellished with engraved glass and crystal, furnished with grand pianos and softly submissive sofas.

All this grandeur was devoted to a mere sprinkling of first class passengers, and I was not strictly speaking one of them. In Singapore, when I first inquired about the crossing, I was told that all Europeans were obliged to travel first class, lest they should find it too distasteful to share cheaper accommodation with Indians. In Penang, however, the agent confided that the policy was subject to mutation, and sold me a dormitory berth, saving me a hundred dollars.

I soon found that my nationality and the colour of my skin were more potent first-class credentials than any mere ticket, and I roamed the ship at will. At night I shared a cabin with three Indians and found nothing too distasteful in that. Not even the cockroaches upset me. They were small, black and relatively unobtrusive. I ate spicy Indian food and liked it a lot better than the dull European meals served 'upstairs' which I also sampled when visiting the crème de la crème.

Generally I spent the day observing the antics of the second class Indians. Most of them seemed to be students going home from somewhere for the summer vacations. They were the noisiest and most aggressive people I had seen. To call them high-spirited would be like calling Hitler enthusiastic.

They devoted the larger part of their time to what they called 'ragging'. In the gangway outside my cabin I saw a miserable young man on his hands and knees surrounded by a yelling and jeering mob. He was fiddling with something on the carpet while behind him another man was making weird cranking motions with his arm, as though winding a starting handle. I found out that the victim was being forced to measure the length of the passage with half a matchstick

"They are calling him a donkey and winding his tail," said one of my roommates. It went on for hours and sounded very nasty. The poor fellow was not as badly off as the Jews who were made to scrub streets with toothbrushes – at least at the end of the day he would survive – but I learned that 'ragging' in India had often led to injuries and even death, and was forbidden by law. During the voyage the purser several times broadcast warnings over the ship's PA system that 'ragging' must stop and offenders would be punished.

The second-class bar was a scene of further enlightenment. It was strewn with empty beer cans, paper rubbish and patches of vomit. The barman glowered from behind a small hatch, part prisoner, part warder. He was a giant of a man, with a maniacal face deeply marked by fear, melancholy and sheer hate. The patrons crowded around him like medieval bear baiters, taunting, prodding and shouting demands. It was a bizarre and dreadful place which dealt another rude blow at my preconception of Indians as a courteous, soft-spoken people.

It was only on the second day that I discovered by chance the existence of a third class. With the thrill of descending into an ancient and unsuspected cellar I found my way into what must once have been the ship's holds. I was amazed by what I saw. It was like being in a battery for hens, but with the cages enlarged to human proportions. In these wire-mesh structures large numbers of the very poorest Indians were bedded down with their belongings.

Their circumstances were probably not as bad as the impression they made. Ventilation was good and they could get out on to one of the forward decks. Their normal living conditions might well have been worse, but it was my first experience of seeing people organized into spaces and structures I associated only with domestic animals; and India hit me there, for the first time, between the eyes.

The *Chidambaram* became my earliest crude model of Indian society. I saw her, in my mind's eye, sliced down the middle from stem to stern. In her hold beneath the sea, crammed into their cages as ballast, were the teeming masses, in an indistinguishable jumble of dhotis and saris, all contributing their iotas which separately entitled them to their daily pittance of rice and dahl, but collectively kept the whole ship afloat.

In the middle stratum a layer of loud, arrogant, bad mannered men with their heads only just above water, wearing foreign clothes, speaking a foreign language, over-indulging in foreign habits, and pretending to a superiority which was in no way apparent.

And in the lofty upper reaches, occupying half the ship's accommodation, a handful of Olympian figures so far out of touch with the rest as not even to question their relevance; some white-skinned transients, some light-skinned Parsee daughters from Bombay, wafted across the waves in pomp and splendour and acting out, all unwittingly perhaps, the undying traditions of the Raj.

On the morning of the third day I woke up early to hear unusual noises over the loudspeakers. Voices were delivering long messages, rather than announcements – I picked out words like 'port' and 'starboard' – and they were obviously meant for the crew. At the same time I was aware of the ship making unfamiliar movements, and of other strange sounds outside the cabin. I pulled on my jeans, slid down from my upper bunk, and went out to look. A few yards along, where the gangway opened into an assembly point, a steel hatch in the side of the ship had been thrown open. It was about ten feet above sea-level. A sailor wearing a life jacket and pajama pants ripped off at the knee stood at the edge holding on by one hand. A rope ladder dangled beneath him and he was peering over the side with a troubled expression.

The first passenger to come by knew all about it.

"We are having man overboard. We are going back to rescue. This sailor is volunteering to jump in the water. He is being paid higher rate to do this."

I put on a shirt and went up to the lifeboat deck to watch. It was about half-past six. The sun was well above the horizon, the sky and the sea were blue and clear, and already there was a touch of heat. The ship was into the second half of the manoeuvre to bring her back to the point where the alarm had been given. There were plenty of people on deck, all Indians, including some officers in their white ducks, and they were eager to talk.

The man had gone over at dawn, from the third-class deck.

"Did he jump?" I asked.

"Nobody knows," said an officer. "But I tell you one thing. He was an old man, but when they threw out the life belts he swam to them like a champion."

"So he's all right?"

"Oh yes. Perfectly all right. We have put down the boat. Now we are going back to pick them up."

He smiled reassuringly. I had no reason to doubt him. The sea looked calm. The water was warm. I almost envied the old man in the sea his morning bathe, and I looked forward to his rescue as a harmless but interesting demonstration of something I had never seen done before.

The lifeboat was easy to spot, but as we drew closer its behaviour seemed odd. It was floating, but going nowhere and bobbing up and down in a way that made me realize there was more of a swell than I had thought. There were three men on it that I could see. They had oars out, but the boat was so high in the water that the blades hardly touched the surface. As I watched, the crew appeared to give up rowing and pulled in their oars. Then I caught sight of the old man. He had his arms through two bright red life belts, and was floating some way away from the boat.

The officer was still standing near by, smiling equably at my questions.

"The propeller of the lifeboat has been damaged," he told me, "but we will soon get him out."

The ship drew nearer to the old man, and I saw him plainly. Only his head and naked shoulders were above water. He was a well-built, quite striking figure, with skin the colour of a hazelnut, a completely bald head and a pair of bushy white whiskers. The most extraordinary thing about him, though, was his absolute immobility. The ship came within thirty yards of him – I could have ringed him with a quoit – but he never raised his head nor let a flicker of emotion change his expression, which was one of total resignation, as he floated by, more like a waxwork effigy than a man.

I watched this with great surprise, feeling sure that in his position I would have had to laugh or shout or, at least, acknowledge the hundreds of spectators gazing down at me.

Then we were past and leaving him behind.

"Why aren't they going for him?"' I asked indignantly, thinking of the volunteer sailors waiting to swim for their money. "Why don't they get a line out?" Every new episode in this affair astonished me.

A passenger leaning over the rail shouted excitedly in his own language, pointing down. Whether he had heard my question or not, he provided the answer. Below us, beautifully visible in every detail and circling lazily beside the ship's hull was a shark. It was eight feet long or more, dark brown in colour shading to white at the tips of its fins, an elegant and menacing fish. People all around were calling out now.

"Look, look, shark! Oh dear! White finned shark. Most dangerous . . ." and so on.

A juddering vibration ran through the ship as the propellers went into reverse. The loudspeakers began to bark.

". . . Number three lifeboat," I heard.

The derricks rattled and another boat, with several men inside, swung out over the side on the two cables and slowly descended. What then followed was a scene of danger and violence I would never forget. Perhaps because the ship had lost way and was almost at a standstill, she began to roll a little more with the swell of the sea. Though it was not a movement that was even vaguely uncomfortable, it was enough to start the lifeboat swinging on its cables, and before it was even halfway to the sea it had begun to smash against the side of the ship.

The first collision was mild, the second much harder. The third was an almighty crash, the men in the boat were flung down and the side of the boat was buckled. Its descent into the sea seemed painfully slow, and it received several more tremendous blows before its keel was in the water. I could see now what had disabled the first boat, and it was a wonder to me that this one had survived. In all the times that I had heard or read about 'lowering the boats' from stricken liners or torpedoed warships I had never imagined anything like this.

Now the boat was in the sea but still attached at the bow and stern to the cables. These ran through huge steel blocks, or pulleys, with shackles attached The blocks could not have weighed less than a hundred pounds. One of the crew was trying to unfasten one of the shackles. It was clearly hard to do and took him several minutes. Then his end of the boat was free and floating with its full weight on the water, while the block swung loose on its cable. The other end of the boat, however, was still attached, and the result was practically lethal. The free end bobbed up and down on the waves and threw the boat into wild motion, making it almost impossible to unfasten the other shackle. Meanwhile the free block began to swing across the boat with irresistible and deadly momentum, knocking the sailors down and narrowly missing several skulls.

Their efforts to release the second shackle were frantic, but finally succeeded, and the boat at last got away. Miraculously, its engine and propeller were intact, and it made off to find the old man whom I was expecting, at any moment, to see pulled down beneath the surface by a devouring shark. It took the crew a long time to haul him in. By now he had been in the water for more than an hour. Then the boat went on to collect the life belts that had been thrown after him, before coming back to the ship, on the port side. But the swell prevented the crew from making fast, and they were sent off again to find the first, damaged lifeboat and tow it back to the ship.

The boats moved very slowly. It was almost an hour later that everything was assembled at the ship's side, but there was still another minor surprise waiting. Instead of taking the old man up in the boat with the crew, they decided to haul him in through a hatch. To do this, he was wrapped in a canvas shroud, like an Egyptian mummy, and drawn up by a cable on pulleys, a bo'sun's bed, as it were. Why this was done I never knew. I would swear that he was alive when we first floated past him, and I saw his face again framed by the canvas as they dragged him in, as much a graven image as ever. It did not occur to me until much later that he might have died.

The excruciating business of lowering the boats was then repeated, twice, in reverse. Exactly the same dreadful pendulum swinging inexorably over the crew as they ducked in terror, and the same fearful crunches against the side of the ship. The men stood hanging to the cables for dear life. An officer on deck shouted at them, again and again: "Sit down. SIT DOWN," but they were beyond even hearing him. Then the boats came inboard and it was all over.

The same officer I had spoken to earlier was back again, looking as pleased with life as ever. I asked him why there had been so many problems.

Ah, it was the heavy swell you see," he said. "It is a simple matter. Every two weeks we practice putting the boats in the water. Just some weeks back our radio-op jumped overboard. We had him out again in eleven minutes."

Eleven was a propitious number. I suggested that it might all have been a lot easier if the blocks and shackles had gone down a lot faster and farther than they did.

"Yes," he said, as though agreeing with me. "They go down quickly under their own weight."

It was so obvious that they did not, that I stood nonplussed.

"Was anyone hurt?" I asked, feeling sure there must have been some bones broken.

"No," he replied, happily.

Two minutes later someone came by to comment that there were several men in the ship's hospital with serious injuries.

"Yes," agreed the officer, just as happily. "You see, if the boat had been full of passengers it would have been quite different. Because of the extra weight. And also the passengers are asked to cooperate by moving to this side and that."

"But if you can't get your own men to take orders, why should hysterical passengers listen to you?" I asked.

"Yes," he said, "The passengers will certainly do as they are told. They will know it is best for them."

He rocked his head from side to side in that delightful, liquid movement which signifies not mere assent and agreement, but complete acceptance of the ineffable goodness of things as they are. The excitement subsided and life returned to normal as the ship resumed its course. Stimulated by the long drama, I became sharply aware of how strong and optimistic I felt. Every aspect of life was full of meaning. The depression which had ground me down in Penang was gone. Not a trace of it remained.

How long had it lasted? Almost six weeks. I had never known anything quite so bad, so much like death. To be alive and unable to care would be worse than death. Yet now I could scarcely believe it had happened. What had caused it? How had I escaped? I knew obscurely that my collapse had begun long before in a fateful contradiction: in the compulsion to share something I could only do alone. Well, now I was alone again, and free. I had no reason then to wonder what might become of me if, one day, I was no longer free to escape.

I looked down over the ship's side. The shark had gone. The sea looked as peaceful and lovely as ever. The big white ship gathered speed and sailed on over the beautiful blue water to Madras. Soon it became hard to believe that there had been any kind of unpleasantness at all.

At a market in the South of India

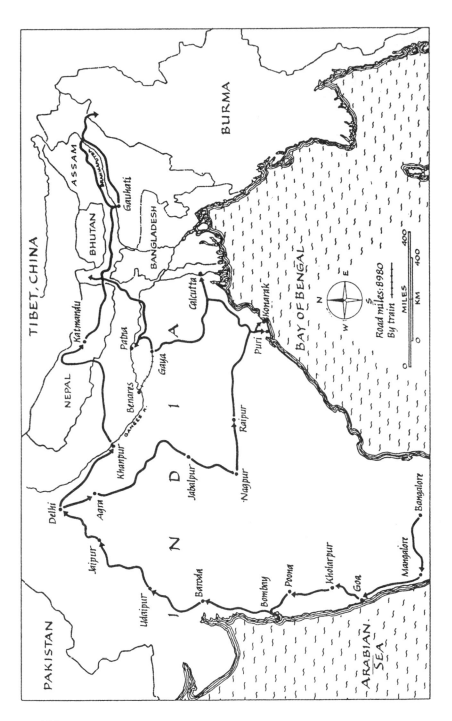

PAKISTAN

TIBET, CHINA

ASSAM

BURMA

BHUTAN

BANGLADESH

NEPAL

Katmandu

Patna

Benares

GANGES R.

Gaya

Calcutta

Khanpur

Delhi

Agra

Jaipur

Udaipur

Baroda

Jabalpur

Nagpur

Raipur

Puri

Konarak

BAY OF BENGAL

Gauhati

BRAHMAPUTRA

I N D I A

Bombay

Poona

Kholarpur

Goa

Mangalore

Bangalore

ARABIAN
SEA

N
W  E
S

MILES
0        400
KM
0    400

Road miles: 8980
By train

Soon after my meeting with the holy man, Sai Baba, I ran out of money. I didn't give him any, so I'm not saying there was any direct connection. Maybe it was just time for me to learn humility. I was in Bangalore, the biggest city in South India after Madras. One of my sponsors, the Lucas company, had offices and a showroom in Bangalore so naturally I went to see them. They had always been very helpful, with repair facilities and general hospitality, but their sponsorship did not include giving me money and I didn't ask them for it. All the same I could not conceal my predicament, and they helped me immediately by finding me a place to stay, and inviting me to dine at the club, a splendid relic of the days of empire.

There, at the bar, I met two young Indian businessmen who astonished me by saying they had planted a vineyard in Bangalore and were well on the way to announcing their first vintage. Officially alcohol is frowned upon in Hindu societies, just as it is by Moslems, and the climate of southern India seemed so entirely unsuitable to their enterprise that I thought they were mad, but they assured me it would be no problem.

"India is a garden," they said. "You can grow anything here." And they offered me a sample of their product. It tasted like a tonic wine, like grape juice fortified with alcohol. I made some polite comments which seemed to satisfy them.

Then I was introduced to Gopinath who, though I didn't know it, was destined to be my new patron. He was short, and tubby, with protruding eyes and a loud voice, but his intelligence and his sense of humour were immediately evident. He ran a car dealership and sold Enfield Bullet motorcycles. I went to visit him there next day, and we got on so well that he invited me to go on a trip with him to visit a friend's coffee estate in Chickmagalur, a hundred miles away.

Chickmagalur happened to be Indira Ghandi's home district, where she had been elected to parliament. At that time Mrs Ghandi was at the height of her power, but she had introduced the notorious Emergency Rules, suspending all kinds of democratic processes. She said it was necessary to defeat the black market and other illegal practices which were destroying the Indian economy. There was tremendous controversy about it. There were dark stories circulating, rumours of abuse of power, of people languishing in jail without due process, of unjustifiable censorship. There were other rumours too, that she was using her police powers to intimidate ignorant farmers into accepting involuntary vasectomies. The media, the bureaucracies, and the middle class hated the Emergency, and had come to hate her too. Years later it all culminated in her assassination.

Her slogans were posted everywhere. To a European they had a faintly comic sound.

WORK MORE; TALK LESS
THE ONLY MAGIC – IRON WILL, STRICTEST DISCIPLINE
DO YOUR DUTY; AVOID LOOSE RUMOURS
And so on.

Her programme was having an effect. Declared exports had increased, smuggling into India was diminished, and for the first time India could show a surplus of foreign exchange. Better still, the foodstuffs that had been smuggled out were now in storage, and there was said to be enough to feed the population for a year. In fact, I had often seen mountains of grain sacks under plastic which, due to lack of storage space, dotted the landscape. In India it was definitely the year of the rat.

Another of her crusades was to get government officials to do some work. There was no doubt that if she succeeded it would change the face of India. In no other country I had visited was the presence of government so blatant. Every large village in India was surrounded by a belt of bureaucracy. Each bureaucrat had two bungalows, his office and his residence, and each bungalow displayed big signboards blazoning forth the occupant's name, title and function. There were bungalows for Public Works, Irrigation, Sanitation, Soil Welfare, Family Welfare, Employment, Inland Waterways, Transport, Revenue, Police, Justice, etc, etc, etc. Between the bungalows marched armies of peons carrying chitties, like ants with cut leaves. The telephone might as well not exist.

The Government Service was conspicuous, immense, overwhelming. It was everybody's dream to belong to it. It meant cars, cheap accommodation, security, many privileges and enormous respect amounting to sycophancy. Again and again I was asked whether I was "on government service". Ordinary Indians could not conceive how I would otherwise have the leisure to travel as I did. And government officials were famous for their absence. They turned up late, left early, found a thousand pretexts for taking off – until the Emergency. Now government absenteeism was punishable, and it was said that officials were coming to the office almost on time.

I had an amusing conversation with a bank clerk, while he was examining my traveler's check for signs of forgery.

"How does the volume of business compare with a few years ago?" I asked.

"It is substantially greater", he replied cautiously.

"Do you have more staff?"

"They have refused to give us more staff." He was indignant.

"So the Emergency has had some effect," I suggested.

He showed a wry smile.

"In this way you could say there have been improvements," he admitted.

I thought it would be interesting to go to Chikmagalur. Maybe I would hear some more stories closer to home. We went in Gopinath's VW and arrived after dark. His friend Cyril greeted us on the verandah of his big house. He was an impressive, I would say startling man, wearing an elaborate silk robe over a long sarong. He was very tall for an Indian, and powerful looking, with a coal black skin, and a large, handsome head marked for tragedy. He might have played a wonderful Othello.

His wife, Joyce, and their daughter sat with us through dinner and stayed afterwards as we argued about Indira and the Emergency. Cyril was passionately opposed to her and all her works.

"She could have done everything she's doing now in the last eight years, and without any emergency," he insisted. "She's just trying to get rid of her closest associates – using her powers to get the black on them."

Both Gopi and Cyril were convinced that she was drunk with power, assuming such immodest titles as "Fountainhead of India" and "Mother of All Springs". I should not be deluded, Cyril declared loudly. Power had corrupted her, turned her head, and the new laws and credit policies were not helping the people. He himself employed a lot of families on his estate and he knew.

"I do what I can in my own domain to improve things," he said. "I had to borrow money to buy this place, but I borrowed a lot more to build new lines [the old colonial term for rows of homes or tents] and to electrify. Now there's a crèche. Soon I hope to start an adult night school. One day I want a hospital here . . . and let the politicians go to hell."

We argued on into the night, and I enjoyed the company enormously. Both the men, and Joyce too, were articulate, and spoke English unusually well, not just to the letter but in the spirit also, meaning that their nuances were more English than Indian, at least when speaking to me. It was rare to feel so well understood. Cyril drank whisky, copiously. His eyes were bloodshot, but he was always cogent. He was not a stupid man, but he saw things in simple terms. He had worked hard, and prospered. If the politicians would only leave it to men like him, the people would benefit more. He did not seem to realize that there might not be enough like him.

We went to bed at 2.30, and unfortunately Gopi, whose bed was in the same room as mine, fell asleep before I did. His snoring was outrageous, impenetrable, and impossible to ignore.

Next day they went pigeon shooting among the coffee bushes, followed by swarms of children. There were many shade trees on the estate, and the pigeons sat on the highest branches. They had lovely plumage and, sadly, were all too easy to hit, though I had to admit they were delicious to eat. Cyril raised a crop of pepper corns too, which grew on vines that clung to the shade trees, and I also saw many bee swarms on the trees. Cyril's estate manager, who spoke little English, got the idea that I had never seen honey. He called it "ghee", or tree butter. Later he sent me a bottle of it. On the label he had carefully written out "Honey: Sweet fluid gathered by bees from flowers." He must have got it from a dictionary.

We left the following day, and but for Gopi's snoring I would have been sorry. But there was plenty to do in Bangalore, working on the bike. I had had little chance to do much to it since leaving Penang, and I was already worried that the same problem that had been afflicting me throughout the journey was attacking the pistons again. Gopi said he knew people in Bombay who would be able to help if I needed it. Bombay was not a great distance – six or seven hundred miles, perhaps – but there was so much I hoped to see and do before I got there that I could have easily taken weeks, if only I had the money. Anyway I resolved to leave next day, and went to Gopi's shop to take my leave . . . and there the miracle awaited.

To my astonishment, I found that he had gone around his list of acquaintances drumming up contributions, and he presented me with an envelope full of cheerful, red twenty rupee notes, with a one hundred rupee note showing through the window. 350 rupees, $35! I felt no shame. In India, begging is an honorable practice, and I could live for a month on $35. With it came a letter of introduction to a couple of friends who, he intimated, should also be good for some practical assistance. So, well-heeled and well-armed, I set off for the coast, at Mangalore, and then north towards Goa, Poonah and Bombay.

§

It was usually not only difficult, but pointless to camp out in India. Difficult because every bit of ground was important to someone, and the crowds that gathered round were overwhelming; pointless because there was almost always a room to be had for fifty cents or less. As for food, every major highway was served by a string of truck-stop restaurants, generally operated by Sikhs. They were no more than tumbledown shacks, but the curries that emerged from them were delicious. I never had qualms about eating them, and the prices were derisory. Only occasionally I would look for something more stylish, just for the contrast.

At Kholapur, north of Goa, I was attracted to the Pearl Hotel for a meal and was kidnapped – in the nicest possible way – by three Indian businessmen and their wives. They became determined to show me every facet of their lives and environment, and I was only too happy to string along without questioning their motives. One of them, a slim, shy man, was an architect. The other two were tougher and more thrusting. One was a building contractor and the other an ironmonger, with a big hardware business. Next day, they said, they all had to make a business trip to one of those government bungalows where they hoped to secure a permit from a visiting big-wig from Bombay. I should go with them, and they would extend it into a sightseeing excursion. It became a remarkable journey.

I stayed that night in the architect's house, an echoing cavern of painted cement walls which I personally thought was in execrable taste, but they made me very comfortable. In the m,orning we left early so that we could first climb a small mountain and visit a famous Sadu, or holy man, in his cave. It was a strange sight. He had taken up residence in the cave many years before – I forget how many – with nothing but the shirt on his back. He had never left it since, depending entirely on others to bring him food, drink and whatever else he needed. He sat, or lay, on an upholstered bed hung with garlands of flowers, wearing a saffron gown and long black hair shot with gray. His legs were folded under a cushion but he moved them about in way which defied all normal anatomical constraints. He had very bright eyes, and a wide grin with one tooth missing in front. A small dog with a vicious temperament guarded him.

Two women were kneeling on a mat, telling the Sadu their problems. Shetti, the ironmonger, approached him, and mentioned that he had a foreign visitor, and the Sadu said that two Californians had recently stayed with him for two days.

"We can learn from foreigners about going from one job to another quickly," he said. I pondered this oracular remark for a while, but its wisdom escaped me. Meanwhile the dog attacked Shetti's little boy, who burst into tears, so we left.

There was much sugar cane grown in this area, and we stopped for a while to watch some nomadic tribal people working. Groups of women in identically coloured saris were cutting the cane. Others, men and women, were boiling down the juice in huge cauldrons over open fires to make cakes of crude brown sugar they called jaggery. Then we went to the Inspection Bungalow for our appointment with the State Engineer. We arrived on time, and the big man was there all right, but he could not be seen. His retinue informed us that he was resting, and we would be called if and when he was ready.

A stifling air of pomp and reverence surrounded this functionary. We cooled our heels outside in the yard for two hours, and I was fuming over this humiliation of my friends, but they seemed to find it perfectly appropriate, as though they were seeking audience with some supreme being. I was particularly surprised by their submission because both Shetti and the contractor, Arun, had that aggressive assurance, a driving won't-take-no-for-an-answer ego, that seemed to characterize many Indian businessmen. But eventually the call came from on high, and apparently they got what they wanted. So Shetti drove us on to our next stop.

This was when I learned that they were all Jains, one of the four great Indian religious bodies (the others being, of course, Hindus, Buddhists and Sikhs). They were not as strict in their observances as some who, in their reverence for all forms of life, wear a muslin veil over their mouths in case they should accidentally swallow an insect. But they were proud of their religion nonetheless, and wanted me to know all about it. We arrived at a place called B'haubali where they had their temple, and I was amazed by what I saw.

An entire hillside was covered by man-sized white marble models of mountains with temples on top of them, and at the foot of this cascade of sacred kitsch were more models depicting crucial episodes in the history of the religion. My friends were very proud of this Disneyesque display, and it was certainly an immense labour of love. They explained that the models depicted sacred sites in the Himalayas, and I wished that I could have found a jot of artistic merit in any of it, but all I could do was goggle at it and try to conceal my mirth. But that was nothing to what they showed me next.

The work that gave them the greatest satisfaction, to which all

Jains in that part of the world contributed, was the school at B'haubali. We walked some distance from the shrines and temples to a big block of a building made from brick and stone. By now the light was fading, and they explained that the boys would be getting their dinner, so we walked together up a flight of stone steps to the dining hall. This time I was stupefied. I had never expected to see anything like it in my lifetime. It belonged, I thought, to the early days of the industrial revolution.

At first I couldn't grasp it at all. It was a cavernous space, long and high, but the darkness made it hard tell how huge it really was. Three great charcoal fires burned at the other end of it, emphasizing the shadows and the dark smoke that curled up to the rafters. It was I suppose a bit like the central nave of a cathedral, but with a distinctly infernal cast to it. There was no furniture at all, just a stone floor, and seated on the floor, cross-legged, in four long rows were hundreds of small boys. Their heads were shaved, their feet were bare, and they wore identical smocks and shorts. Each boy had a plate and a metal jug in his lap. The rows faced each other in pairs, and down the middle of each aisle came a trolley with a cauldron of food, which was ladled out into the plates as it went by. Where the fires glowed and sparked on a raised platform, chapatis were being cooked and distributed, but the dark figures working there could just as well have been engaged in some diabolical ceremony.

I was overcome by the imagery and all its Victorian associations. Obviously I was seeing something entirely different to what my companions saw. I wanted to know whether the boys were free to leave, and had to ask several times before the question was understood. Then they laughed.

"If they want to run away we can't stop them," they said, but obviously thought that no boy would be crazy enough to give up this opportunity.

As my fevered imagination cooled down, I was introduced to one of the masters, a mild-looking man with wavy hair and spectacles, not at all the sort of strict disciplinarian this scene conjured up for me.

"I was a student here," he said, "so I am thoroughly familiar with the routine," and added that there were 600 boys altogether, from destitute homes or from no homes at all. I had to agree that in practical terms they were undoubtedly better off here than on the street.

Shetti was very proud of the school.

"Many pupils have become big men in Bombay and Calcutta," he said, and he was obviously displeased when the architect added that the government pays for 80% of the upkeep. We visited a dormitory, another great bare space, with rows of mats on the floor along each wall. And above each mat, a hook where the boy could hang his worldly possessions. It was impossible for me to express my feelings. The harshness of it was overwhelming and yet, how could one complain? What could I do that would be better? I have been haunted by the image of that school ever since.

There is one more such experience before I get to Bombay. So far the India I have seen has been almost entirely rural, but in Poonah there is industry, heavy industry. Through Gopi's letters, I am introduced to the manager of Perfect Motors, Mr Ekbote. I climb a rattty staircase, into a surprisingly modern, air-conditioned office where he gives me a great booster's spiel about India's technological advances, telling me that if I only cared to look inside the appliances I was buying in Europe I would probably find that the innards were made in India. He obviously feels that India is unjustly scorned by other nations, and he fights back.

"When I visited your country the immigration officer asked: "Do you intend to stay in the U.K?'

"I said, 'What a stupid question. Do you think I'd tell you if I did?'

"He said, 'You are insulting the Queen's uniform.'

"I said, 'I don't care. If you ask a stupid question . . . .'"

Apparently he got through anyway.

He says I should visit the Bharat Forge Company. I turn up there next afternoon, and it's another seminal experience. The plant must be a hundred years old, a huge iron girder construction full of smoke and soot. In these enormous black spaces there are staggering sights of men in floor length black protective gowns and goggles working under a steam hammer three times their height. With long tongs two men tussle with a massive lump of glowing red metal, trying to move it around before the hammer lunges down, WHAM! and withdraws, swaying, like a live thing, like a cobra waiting to strike again, and down it comes, WHAM! once more, and WHAM! again. The noise is outrageous, the smells are acrid, the lighting is wildly melodramatic, the work looks terribly hard. The men work ten hours a day, and consider themselves very fortunate because they get several days off every year.

From Poonah the road north is not bad until I get near Bombay. At Thana, where the island of Bombay begins, barges are unloading sand from river dredgers. Bombay is a major port, and the dredgers must work constantly to keep it operational. Here there is incredible activity, as mountains of sand are moved by the basketful on the heads of a vast army of women. Anyone who wonders how the ancient pyramids and temples were built need only visit Thana. The traffic congestion here also becomes deadly until I finally escape onto the expressway into the city.

The last of Gopi's letters takes me to Marine Drive, and his friend Nasir, a wealthy sportsman who likes to race cars, owns a chain of cinemas, and has a delightful Parsee wife called Katy. He has a room for me, is very hospitable, and offers to help with my motorcycle maintenance which has become urgent. The bike has now  done 48,350 miles. There is a bad oil leak out of the rear pushrod cover and, after taking the top off and noticing the scoring and pitting, we decide we might just as well do a rebore and fit the new pistons I'm carrying, as well as fitting new exhaust valves.

When I reassemble everything I make the stupid mistake of forgetting to reset the tappets. Tightening down the top I bend both the push rods. I have one spare with me, bend another one back. It works. Huge relief. It's not the only mistake I make. Three major cock-ups altogether, and I'm lucky to get away with them. Why am I making these errors? It worries me.

Bombay is a huge and fascinating city, and I spend a couple of days exploring, but big cities can't hold me on this trip, and I'm keen to get away. It's November 24, and a letter has come with wonderful news. Carol will meet me in Nepal at the beginning of December.

A hooded cobra swaying for a snake charmer – a sight of a lifetime

After all the anguish and self-doubt I went through to separate myself from her six months ago, now I can't wait to see her. And yet I'm sure the same conflicts will arise again, between my desire to be with her and my certainty that this journey, this mission, this voyage of discovery which I can never hope to repeat, has to be a solitary affair. Why do I put myself through the wringer like this? I did it with Jo. Now I'm doing it again. The same old contradictions keep surfacing – to be free, and to be committed: To wander, and to put down roots. Do I really have to choose?

On Wednesday, from Bombay to Baroda. The roads of India are really the greatest show on earth. Coming out of Bombay I passed thousands of buffalo housed in row upon row of ancient wooden sheds. A vast feed lot, presumably to supply a dairy. You had only to see it to know immediately that something like this must have been seen outside our own cities a century or two ago. A religious procession came down the road toward me, saffron robes glowing, drums beating, cymbals clashing and flashing in the sun. Then, going the other way, another procession, men women and children, a family perhaps, all carrying pieces of furniture or lacquered chests on their heads.

Then there were monster truck stops – great areas of churned up earth, pan stalls and shacks with charpoys set out around them for a quick snack and a snooze. North of Bombay the trucks really took over the highways, roaring up to Delhi, smoking and snarling, many lamed in combat, sagging or sway-backed with age but still defiant, running with the multi-coloured herd until the last, when the sun beat down on their grimy upturned bellies as they sprawled on their backs in the ditches and paddy fields.

Travelling north from Baroda what impressed me most was the number of dead trucks I saw. They were everywhere, sometimes abandoned, sometimes guarded, preserved by rigor mortis in their final dying antics. Almost all had been maintained far beyond their normal span on a life support system, until their limbs finally betrayed them and they lay helpless on their sides, or with rusted spars and rotted timbers simply powdering away, they nose-dived into the asphalt.

Coming in to the crowded city of Ahmedabad there seemed to be more carts than I had noticed elsewhere, carts of all sizes, drawn by donkeys, buffalo, oxen, and horse, but a great many drawn by people, sometimes women in tandem harnessed rather like animals. Then about fifty miles north of Ahmedabad, the character of the country and the people changed quite dramatically. I left the state of Gujarat for Rajastan, the land rose among a desolate range of stony hills and low mountains, and I saw an immediate difference. The great crowds vanished. The Rajastani men with their smooth brown faces and black, drooping moustaches, had a fiercer look. Gone were the loose, flapping white garments of the south. Here they wore woolen jackets, sweaters, richly colored head-dresses and tightly fitting pants with curly-tipped sandals. The women abandoned the sari for a voluminous skirt, usually in bright but plain colors like blue, burgundy or mustard yellow, and a cloak that billowed out behind, caught by the winds that blew frequently among these hills.

For the first time in India, some boys that I rode past made threatening gestures. The land seemed rather barren, fit only for grazing animals, and bunches of cactus lined the roadside. Yet this poor ground was jealously guarded with stone walls, and there was an ancient castle on top of every peak, frowning down upon the road – most probably, I thought, they were the lairs of robber barons who once fed on the trade that must have passed this way.

The evening was drawing in and, on impulse, I stopped at a rest house twelve miles south of Udaipur. The resident servant was out of character for the region. He wore a dhoti and a jacket, and with his gold earrings he had the seafaring look of a retired pirate. He offered me a bed, but no food, so I walked the hundred yards to the village. There was a single row of small shops, and outside one of them a Brahmin sat cross-legged behind a number of large biscuit tins containing gram, dahl, and potatoes. No vegetables, no eggs.

"Dear Sir," he said. "This is very small village, near big city. Eggs are not available."

I bought cigarettes, went back to the bungalow, cooked myself some rather unappetizing rice, made a herbal tea, and then walked back to the village, hoping for conversation, but my usual good luck deserted me. A group of men, conversing, made no welcoming sign. Farther along, another group squatted close together on the road, in a curiously conspiratorial manner. There was no electricity in the village, and only a little lamp light. Shrouded in robes, they were almost invisible in the dark. When trucks passed, they would rise up and scatter, then gather together again, rather like vultures feeding off road-kill. I could not discover what their purpose was in meeting like that.

The night was very uncomfortable. For some reason my skin itched and pricked unbearably over my entire body. It felt as though I were being attacked by insects, and I kept getting up to inspect the bed, although I knew it was just some kind of nervous reaction. My dreams, when I finally fell asleep, were strange too and, as often seems to happen, in direct contrast to my waking experiences. I found myself dreaming of a pleasant and quite explicit scene of reconciliation with the one person in my past whom I have never been able to bring myself to forgive. Again and again in the course of the journey I have had these intimations that a quite separate and parallel story of my life was being screened in my subconscious, like a soap opera, of which I only saw occasional tantalizing episodes.

In any event, for all the night's discomfort I felt bright and optimistic in the morning, ate a few biscuits, and rode on. The land was flattening out and becoming more hospitable as I came to Udaipur, a big, busy, fortified city. I stopped only for a drink and to take a photograph of a poor woman and her babies camped on the sidewalk under a piece of cloth slung over some string. Not that there was anything unusual about her circumstances, but next to her was a sign advertising luxurious accommodations with central heating, and a movie poster promising ultimate joy and fulfillment, while behind her loomed an elaborate palace. The juxtaposition was too poignant to miss.

After Udaipur I began to see camels, more and more of them, on the road, and off it. Even though I had come through Egypt and Sudan I had never seen camels in such common use for carrying and hauling. They were everywhere, and wonderful to watch, with their great padded feet swinging over the road surface, and their heads swaying from side to side so far forward from their shoulders. For the first time I began to marvel at the structural design of the camel, which seemed so unlikely and yet obviously worked so well. There was something about camel country that appealed to me. The dryness, maybe. For months I had been bathed in humid, tropical warmth, but here the hot sun struck down through cool air, and I loved it.

Some tribal Indians passed by with all their belongings loaded on three camels. On top of each load was a bed, with its legs sticking up into the air. The women leading the camels were unusually dressed, even for a country of such colourful variety. They wore saris, but only up to the midriff, where they were tied tightly under the breasts, and each breast was separately wrapped, like a package, in pink muslin.

In the fields were camels pulling ploughs, and on the road other camels pulled carts. I remembered someone telling me that camels had the pulling power of four oxen. The crazy upward angle of the shafts, which were harnessed to the camel's hump, made it seem as though the cart might become airborne at any instant.

The cows also made themselves more than usually noticeable by the extraordinary shapes of their horns which sprouted in all directions, each one, even on the same animal, seeming to follow its own whim, growing up, down, round, back, like the different characters of Hindi script that I was trying to master at the time. And then came two enormous elephants – the biggest I had ever seen – strolling down the road like juggernauts, with their riders perched on top.

After four more hours of gentle progress amongst all these wonders I came to Ajmer, an open, pleasant looking town, and liking the look of it I found a 'tourist bungalow' and stayed there with an assortment of foreigners – Germans, a Swiss couple who were buying jewellery, a girl from Brazil, another from Chile, and some Australians. The *Brasilleira* attracted me particularly, a vivacious, warm-hearted girl with striking looks and that wonderful musical language that revived all my best memories of Brazil, the beaches and the time with Lulu and her friends.

Next day they recommended a hotel in Jaipur, only an hour or two away, and I arrived at midday, to spend the afternoon visiting the stunning terra cotta center of this rose coloured city, a triumph of 17th century town planning. I thought the main street the most impressive I had ever seen, and the great palace facade too rich and beautiful for words.

New Delhi was now only a few hours away. The villages were obviously getting more prosperous, and the road conditions improved too. In fact they were good enough to be able to sustain a constant speed, so I discovered, to my chagrin, that my speedometer was mis-reading badly at higher speeds – 50 for 60, and so on. This worried me because I had been trying to nurse the engine after the rebore, and evidently I had been going faster than I meant to at times. With at least twelve thousand more miles to go, I wanted to avoid any more major surgery before I got back to Europe.

Halfway to Delhi I stopped for a biscuit and a cigarette, and sat on a stone marker looking out over the fields, with sun hot on my back. Two boys stood by the bike chattering, and I knew they would come over to question me. For once, when they did, I was aggravated by it.

"Where you dwell?" asked one.

"England," I said. "And where do you dwell?"

"Diarrhoea," he said, or something that sounded like it.

"Have you come to look at me?" I asked, smiling faintly.

To my surprise he was embarrassed, and turned away quickly. It was the first time I could recall anyone in India showing respect for my privacy. I was almost sad to let him go. I was not proud of my sensitivity. After all, I was in their country, and it was up to me adjust to their customs. Westerners often feel defenseless in India, because Indians seem blind to what the English call "reserve," the invisible walls we erect to shelter ourselves. These barriers enable us to get on with things without too much interruption. At best they represent respect for individual freedom; at worst, indifference; but we are used to having them there. When we close the gates and hang up the "No Soliciting" sign, we are astonished to find it ignored.

I don't like all the personal questions from strangers. It makes me feel that my life has become public property. So the useful exercise would be to imagine that my life is public property, and that I am both accustomed to it and happy about it. Maybe that is how it feels to be Indian?

Are there any barriers in Indian society? Of course. They are founded on respect for seniority and status. Seniority depends on age, gender and caste. Status is advertised in a number of ways, most of them the same as ours, but with certain additions. Nothing so becomes a man in India as to advance at the head of a great family army. In England or America this could be disastrous. The children might be rude, noisy and troublesome. The wife might contradict him openly and start a row. In a public place he might win a little sympathy, but most likely he would be cursed for introducing a riotous assembly.

In India that would be inconceivable. The women will be dutiful, if not positively adoring. The children will be obedient and exhibit only a pleasing precocity. The father may puff himself up and expound to his considerable capacity, and he will receive universal respect proportional to the size of his retinue and the degree of his patronage.

He pays for this privilege through the burden of his responsibilities. The Hindu is moulded under the weight of a three-tiered hierarchy, religion, caste and the joint family system. It is in the family that the pressure is directly applied. In the state of Uttar Pradesh a young executive in a cable-making company approached me, on the assumption that were of the same age. He was bewildered to discover that I was seventeen years older than him, and we began to talk about reasons for growing old. He said he thought it was the constant worry over making enough money to support not just his own small family, but many others. A nephew's education, a widowed cousin, a brother out of work, as well as his parents and other aged relatives were all a likely charge on his income.

"I am thinking about money almost all the time," he confessed sadly. He had studied hard to graduate and get this job. He had scarcely even thought about sex until he was married, by arrangement, at the age of 28. The hopes and ambitions that I took for granted meant nothing to him. No wonder, he said, that he felt as old as me.

I wondered how the pressure was applied. Suppose a successful young man just chose to ignore these obligations and go his own way? A lawyer in Tezpur explained it to me.

"His mother will refuse to visit him. Or she will come for five minutes, and then ostentatiously spend the night with a poorer relative.

Next day all the women will go to the bazaar and tell each other. It will be all over town in no time. He will be disgraced."

In return for fulfilling his duties the man would get all the emotional support an extended family could offer, and a ready outlet for his anxieties. There seemed to be less mental illness in India, but the western idea of Indian life flowing as a calm river is clearly a superstition. A factory manager in Baroda told me that his brother-in-law had managed to get a job with Monsanto in the USA. What did he write home in his letters?

"At last I am free to live a rich and fulfilling life."

Indian life is so different in its qualities to life in the West, and we who visit should make some effort to understand it. Anyone wanting to sense the most immediate, practical differences could do so now, in his or her own home. Just eat your meals – mashed potatoes, gravy and all – with your fingers for a few days, until you become good at it, and then ask yourself why it felt so uncomfortable at first. Those who feel capable of going on to college level in this subject could continue their experiments in the bathroom with a jug of water. Paper manufacturers would shudder, and a few forests might be saved in the process.

Knowing that I would have to come back through there later, I stayed only two nights in Delhi. They were spent in a dusty, deserted ballroom above the Lucas offices, because I had arrived completely broke, but fortunately there was money waiting at the bank, all of $714. There was also a letter saying that the Sunday Times was getting tired of supporting me. I could hardly blame them, after three years. On the other hand, they had had plenty of good copy from me, and I really hadn't spent that much of their money. I wished I could let them know that I had taken up begging, but in those days telephone calls were expensive, and took 48 hours to arrange. I swallowed the bitter medicine and set off for Nepal.

The first day's ride from Delhi to Khanpur was unusually hard. For the first time I encountered truck drivers who were aggressively determined to drive me off the road, and a few succeeded. In my fury I gathered a pocketful of stones, but could never get the bike out of the way in time to carry out my insane plan of launching a rock into the enemy's oncoming windshield.

After Khanpur, but long before even the foothills of the Himalayas came into sight, the air felt fresher, the sunlight seemed to bounce merrily off the stone surfaces instead of pressing down on me, and my spirits rose in anticipation. The route I had planned went through Lucknow, Faizabad and Gorakhpur to Motihari, before turning north into the mountains and to Kathmandu. In Gorakhpur, having slummed the night before, I treated myself to the best hotel. The dinner was excellent, but the first chair I sat in collapsed under me and threw me on my back. Naturally this brought me to the notice of the other diners, and a middle-aged drug salesman introduced himself and earnestly recommended, if I was going to Nepal, that I take vitamins A and D. He also explained that there was a more direct route into Nepal, that went to Pokhara. I took his advice on both counts, and left for Pokhara next day.

All in all it was a wonderful ride in spectacular weather. The road surface was broken up in places, but caused me no problems. After a flat stretch it rose up steeply, and the character of the villages changed. The houses, made of adobe, seemed more substantial, the upper half white, the lower half terra cotta, and often with designs painted on the walls. Some had thatched roofs, with painted eaves, and intricately fretted wooden shutters that reminded me of Ecuador and Colombia.

There was some frustration at the border. I didn't have a visa, and though I could get one at the police station, I didn't have Nepali currency to pay for it. The bank, of course, was somewhere else, but it was a minor annoyance, and I arrived in Pokhara by midday. A local inhabitant directed me to a lake where a colony of small restaurants was spread out along the shore, all with little rooms attached for five rupees, or fifty cents, a night. The food was mostly a Tibetan variation on Chinese, made with buffalo meat, and liberally flavored with cilantro. The population consisted mainly of blissed out Westerners and sharp, dedicated Nepali boys who seemed to run the show. The boys were gifted arithmeticians, and shrewd, impressively multi-lingual conversationalists, but their most remarkable quality was that they never hustled too hard, and after India that came as a relief.

The next day I made the really glorious ride, alongside a river and through the mountains, to Kathmandu.

It's funny to think about it now, but all Carol wrote was, "I'll meet you in Kathmandu." Not anywhere in particular, just Kathmandu. I don't know how she knew that it's easier to find a friend in Kathmandu than in Grand Central station. I don't know why I wasn't worried about missing her. Neither of us had ever been there. All I do know is that I arrived in the afternoon, signed in at the small hotel I'd been told about, and walked around hoping to see her. I went to the truly amazing square where the temple is, and down the road that the hippies called Freak Street. I met an interesting Englishman called Gavin, and we arranged to have dinner at the Swiss restaurant where he said climbers went. We had just finished eating when Carol, passing by, noticed me through the window and came in.

I saw her immediately at the door. Her face was framed in black fur, and she looked absolutely gorgeous, like a Russian princess. Soon after she had sat down, Gavin faded away. We were completely absorbed in each other, and I was as happy as I have ever been with another person. We went to her hotel first. Then she came to mine. Next day we moved to another, better one, the Lalibala, further from the noisy center of town. The following week we prepared to go for a trek on the Jomsum trail, and visited offices for permits and visas. Already we were planning what we would do when we came down from the mountains. I wanted to visit Assam, and Carol had heard of two wild life reserves there called Manas and Kazirenga, where we might see a tiger. I agreed that we could go together, on the bike. I loved her and tried not to think of where and how this episode would end.

Everything we wanted to do required permits, and money, and in Nepal officials were even more autocratic than bureaucratic. The Immigration Office, where we went to extend our visas, sported a sign that read:

> Every guest who is in immigration for their problamcs should be polite and noble behaved. Any misbehaved activities and discussion by the guest shall be proved as a crime.

Then we went to the Indian consulate for permission , to go to Darjeeling, to enter Assam and to visit the reserves. We were received by the First Secretary, who was rude and arrogant without reason. When we got our passports back there was nothing in them about Manas, only Kazirenga.

"It is good for Manas also," he said abruptly. "What are you worried about. You can go!" And he turned away.

Kathmandu was an exciting place in those days, full of bizarre people, and we enjoyed it to the full. We visited the Swayambu temple, where monkeys slide down hand rails. We had gin and tonic at the British embassy, and spent an evening with a Nepalese violinist. One afternoon we went to see the burning ghats, where corpses are laid inside tall stacks of lumber and incinerated. It just happened that a pyre was about to be lit. The corpse was apparently that of a child, because one small hand, palm upwards and slightly curled, had escaped from the lumber and was beckoning pitifully. Of course we were deeply touched by it. Just then a tour bus drew up and several dozen Japanese leaped out, all in black suits with cameras raised. As the flames rose and enveloped the pyre they snapped away furiously and then rushed back into the bus and drove away.

There was never a better example of tourism in action. Perhaps when they got home they saw something in their pictures. I don't have a picture, but I saw the hand.

Above, a house on the trail in Nepal. Below, the cook and the manager of a typical Indian circuit house or Inspection Bungalow.

W o walked and climbed for two weeks in the Himalayas, and while the natural splendors are unparalleled, what fascinated me the most was to see how people lived without power, roads or machinery, and how they adapted to the rigorous demands of their unusual environment. It was a unique window into a medieval world, and it affected us both profoundly.

The bike was waiting for us at the Lalibala, and we had difficulty packing on to it everything that we now owned. It struggled heroically on the climb out of Kathmandu, which took me by surprise, and again when we spiralled up through the clouds to Darjeeling, alongside the famous cog-wheeled railroad. I knew that if we were going to go on together we would have to lighten the load.

That precipitated a difficult decision, and we had to face up to it. How far would we go together? I was still determined to finish the journey alone. Carol had a visa for Bangladesh. We had talked about traveling in Assam together before she took off for Bangladesh, but I knew that what Carol wanted, more than anything, was to finish the journey with me, and I did love her. Would it be just too painful to part again?

The mundane decisions about what to take and what to leave brought all this emotional turmoil to the surface. In the end, what we did made no difference to any future decision. I was bound to come back this way anyway. And Carol planned eventually to go to Delhi. So we could both leave stuff behind. Later, traveling alone, I would take her things to Delhi with me. Unless, of course . . . The unspoken alternative was always with us.

At Cherrapunji, in the Indian state of Assam, 450 inches of rain falls every year, and that, according to the Times atlas, makes it the wettest place on earth. While the rest of Assam may be slightly less wet, the total volume of water falling on a state the size of Kansas can hardly be imagined. Virtually all of this water runs into the Brahmaputra River, and the Brahmaputra, needless to say, is a colossal river, five to ten miles wide for most of its length. It dominates Assam completely, splitting it in two, for there are few places where it can be bridged. Eventually it meets the Ganges in Bangladesh and helps to account for the fact that Bangladeshis have much more water than is good for them. I didn't know much about Assam when we rode in there from Darjeeling on Sunday, January 9th, but I knew we were lucky to be there when it wasn't raining

Another thing I didn't know much about was why the government was being so pernickety with its permits – or why we had to have permits at all, for that matter.

At the first check-point there was a barrier across the highway. Clearly they took these controls very seriously, but I didn't give much thought to the reasons behind them. I put it down to bureaucracy run rampant. In a roadside hut a disagreeable man in plain clothes examined our passports for a long time before stamping them and letting us go. Siliguri was the first town, and we stayed overnight at a hotel. They agreed to keep our excess luggage locked away. Then we rode to Barpeta junction, on our way to the first wild life reserve at Manas.

Assam was very different to anything else I had seen in India. There were no glaring signs of poverty, no beggars. The villages appeared prosperous, even beautiful, with houses raised high above the ground (no doubt because of the rain) but what struck me most was that they all seemed to have gardens, richly planted with flowering shrubs, slender arica palms and, presumably, vegetables. It had not properly occurred to me before that in most of India a garden or yard was a rare sign of relative wealth.

The Manas reserve is tucked in at the skirts of the Himalayas, close to the kingdom of Bhutan. A dirt road runs north off the highway at Barpeta, and it should have taken us right through to Manas. We followed it until we came to a village. What happened there is still unclear to me. The road seemed to get lost among the houses, and I wondered around for a bit before finding it again. After that it was a clear run all the way, through jungle and past marshy areas of elephant grass.

We were received by a young man who gloried in the quaint title of Beat Officer. He was a curiously evanescent character, who must have learned his English from Victorian novels. He uttered phrases like, "I will be performing my utmost to render your visit enchanting," and his answers to all our questions were an enthusiastic but uncomprehending "Yes!" When I finally got him to tell us about himself he said, "Loneliness is my companion. I am 27 years. You cannot say I have many years. Still there is the main part to come."

Although Manas had a lodge, with rooms, we wanted to save money and he showed us a site for our tent. We were the only foreign visitors at Manas, but a small group of dignitaries had come to be shown around by the resident director, and we joined the party. They seemed more eager to show off their own knowledge of tiger lore than to hear what the director had to say. One of them in particular, a Mr. Das, who was a forestry conservator, explained to me, that first evening, how tigers always move in triangles, and so on. The director, I noticed, seemed rather sullen and withdrawn, and said little.

Next morning in the lodge I was able to get the director on his own, while the others were upstairs with Carol. His manner changed completely. It was obvious that he resented having to run around after the bigwigs, and made it clear without saying so that Das didn't know what he was talking about. Sanjay Debroy was an impressive and likeable man, of medium height and military bearing. He was obviously in very good physical shape, square-jawed, with level brows, a straight mouth and honest, intelligent eyes. He was a Field Director of the Tiger Project, a campaign that Indira Ghandi had sponsored to try to save the tiger population from extinction. The numbers were very low, and dropping. The latest census showed only 54 in the Manas sanctuary, where there had been thousands before.

Debroy knew a lot about tigers, and his enthusiasm was infectious. He painted a picture of a solitary animal that joins with others only to mate, a very shy animal, moving in heavy cover through the jungle undergrowth. The tiger is not nocturnal like the leopard, but hunts very early or late in the day, eating as much of its kill as

Working elephants in India display amazing versatility, dragging logs out of the jungle , and nosing them up the ramp onto the truck bed. The sign on the truck in the picture above says Jangal Transport. Jangal is where we get our 'jungle' from. According to Rudyard Kipling, it's only a real jungle if tigers live there.

it can, and hiding the rest from vultures and other smaller cats. Then it finds water, lies up nearby to sleep, and returns when it is hungry. If there is plenty of game it won't move far, until the game has gone.

He drew some pug marks for me, one big circle and above it four small ones, like toes. You can tell the difference between male and female, because the male paw spreads wider. He had seen a female pug mark that morning, he said. There was a place along the road where he had noticed the deer had disappeared, and he had gone out early to look. I asked him if we could perhaps accompany him on such a trip if he went again. He thought about it, then said he might be going again the next morning but – and he gestured up with his thumb to where Das was loudly lecturing Carol – you never knew what might happen. But if he went, we could come.

And next morning, at dawn, he sent a man to our tent to wake us. Debroy, in a woolen hat and green army tunic, came soon afterwards with the Land Rover. His man crouched in the back, and we set off along the road we had come in on. He showed us the pug mark he had seen before, but there were no fresh prints, and he thought he must have been mistaken about the deer. If she had made a kill, she would have come back for it. Then he took us on a wonderful tour of animal spoors, explaining to us how they lived and interacted. We saw deer prints in plenty, of course, and wild elephant tracks. He knew they were wild, because they stopped short at culverts and bridges, which only tame elephants will cross. There were prints from wild buffalo, with the segmented hoof spanning eight inches, and from wild ox, or Gauer, with a closed hoof. The buffalo, he said, grew to nine feet at the shoulder, and was the sturdiest animal in the jungle. And though we had seen hardly any live animals, through Debroy's vivid accounts a feeling for their presence became very powerful for us.

Naturally the tiger's enemy was man. He described the last time he had had to shoot a tiger, a man-eater. As the village populations grew, and the villagers cut down more of the jungle, tigers had to go, but sometimes they attacked the villagers. Once they get the taste of human flesh it was necessary to hunt them down. He told a thrilling and sad story. The hunt took him several days, and he had to come very close to the tiger before shooting it. In its dying throes it had clamped its jaws around a bamboo. The trunk of the bamboo, he said, was at least eight inches thick, and with that last spasm the tiger's powerful jaws had bitten clear through it.

We had three days at Manas, and I felt I had got to know Debroy well enough to call him a friend. We might have stayed longer, but the food had run out, and we would have had to go to Barpeta anyway to buy more. So on the Thursday we ate a last egg and chapati each, then packed up and rolled out, both of us still hungry and looking forward to a meal. But the plot took a strange twist. Ahead of us a painted pole stretched across the road, barring our way. It was firmly padlocked, and next to it was a small hut. It had definitely not been there on our way in, or – and of course it struck me then – we had somehow gone around it. As we approached, a big, bull-headed man in a suit came out of the hut, obviously astonished to see us. He demanded that we bring our passports into the hut. There was no arguing with him, and we went inside. Another younger man was sitting at a desk. He looked much the more sophisticated of the two.

"How did you get into Manas?" the big man asked aggressively.

"What do you mean?" I said. "We just rode there. We went through the village"

"But there is a sign," he said

"No there isn't," I fired back.

The young man interrupted with a surprisingly suave and friendly voice, saying:

"Please sit down. Did you enjoy Manas? Let me see your papers, please."

"All right," I said. "But tell me please, who are you?"

"S.I.B." he answered. Then I knew it was serious. The Special Investigation Branch operated out of New Delhi. They were like an Indian F.B.I. and, during the Emergency particularly, they had acquired a rough reputation.

They read through our passports. Mine identified me as a builder. Carol explained that she was a history teacher. Then the younger man said:

"You do not have a permit for Manas."

I pointed at the visa. "This is the permit here, given in Kathmandu."

"But it does not mention Manas."

"The secretary told me it was valid for Manas."

"You should have a special permit."

"How were we to know? We have told everyone we were coming here. No-one mentioned that a special permit was needed. The secretary in Kathmandu was very rude, and told me this was good for Manas."

And I went on cursing that official with conviction. The men consulted together in Hindi, and made several phone calls.

"Your passports must be sent to Tezpur," said bull-head.

"How far away is that?"

"Two hundred kilometers."

"And what are we supposed to do meanwhile? Live in this hut?"

The younger man, who was obviously the more educated of the two, smiled apologetically.

"I don't suppose the First Secretary in Kathmandu will be put to the same inconvenience for misleading us," I protested.

There was a pause, and more consultation.

"We will send you to Barpeta in the bus, to save you inconvenience. Our man will accompany you with the passports."

"But the motorcycle," I said. " I can't leave the motorcycle here. Impossible."

Who was I to say what was possible. I knew I was pushing the envelope. But there was more consultation.

"All right. You will ride to Barpeta and report to the police station there. Our man will take the passports on the bus."

It was the best we could hope for.

Barpeta was not big, but it was an important junction. We went first to the Sikh truck stop, to eat paratha, rice and curry. Then we went to the Inspection Bungalow to see if we could get a room there. It was a gesture of hope. I preferred to think that we would not be spending the night in jail.

To our surprise, Debroy was there. We told him our story, and I could see that he was disturbed by it. He asked if we had receipts for our passports and I said we hadn't. He pondered over that for a while, but said that unfortunately he could do nothing to affect the issue. I could not help remembering my imprisonment in Brazil and how, slowly but inexorably, the police there had reeled me in, like a fish on a line, and how unpleasant the consequences had been.

The bungalow was very pleasant and homely, with nice beds, a clean carpet, new mosquito nets without holes, and a bulb that gave decent light. We took in our things and then walked over to the police station. It was made up of several bungalows, and a grass yard with a picket fence. The policeman on duty in the office already had our passports and asked us what it was all about. He became increasingly polite and friendly – a good looking, athletic man, in uniform and tennis shoes, who told us he had fought against Pakistan in the war over Kashmir. I was only half way through telling our story when he stopped me and apologized. His superior was at the market, he said, and would be back in an hour. Then we would surely get our passports back.

We waited a while and I looked around. Behind us was the Inspector's office. There were two barred cells on our left, labelled Male Lockup and Female Lockup. Facing us was another barred door labelled Malkhana, meaning House of Evidence, where exhibits would be stored. Apart from that there were just a few shelves holding dusty files and some empty medicine bottles. We asked if we could come back in half an hour, and returned to our bungalow.

A man was examining the map on the Triumph. He said that he could see exactly what I was doing and where I had come from. It was difficult to resist a wave of paranoia.

"And this," he said jovially, pointing, "is the Union Jack. We were saluting this flag for a long time."

Then he explained that he was a medical officer, travelling around the health centers of Assam giving small pox vaccinations.

"We have succeeded in almost eradicating small pox from India," he said, very pleased.

When we came back to the police station, the sub-Inspector was there, a rather precise, if humorless man in a khaki uniform. He asked us into his office, and we sat opposite him across his desk. He folded his arms and said:

"Now, what is your problem?"

I was too surprised to answer very coherently. How could he fail to know? I began to stumble once again through the story, but he wasn't really listening. He became indignant, however, when we told him we had been given no receipts for the passports.

"This should be penalized," he said. "I shall take action. " I wondered whether he had met Debroy at the market.

"Meanwhile, if there is anything at all I can do . . . "

I was about to say he could just give us our passports back, when a chubby man appeared at my side in a little leather hat, a green corduroy jacket and an immensely long orange scarf, wound round his neck and trailing to the floor. He too made promises of large but unspecified services, waving his arms, and adding that his jacket came from Chicago. He was quite drunk, and gazed hard into my eyes. Then, putting his head close to mine, he began to croon a song about "seven lonely days, and seven lonely nights, buh-buh-buh-buh-buh."

The Inspector buried his head in his hands in embarrassment and, in a muffled voice, said "May I introduce my colleague. He is off-duty". The tipsy inspector switched to My Darling Clementine, so for want of a better idea I joined in and we sang "Herring boxes without topses" with Carol coming in on the last line. Then the duty policeman brought a tray of Indian sweets and tea. When he opened the door the sound of drumming drifted in, and the Inspector said, "Today is Bihu. It is a great festival in Assam. Tomorrow, as soon as I get my instructions you will get your passports back. Now, if you wish you may enjoy yourself ."

But the drunken Inspector (I'll call him the D.I.) was already on his feet, dancing a little jig, and singing "Ay-yi-yippy-yippy-yay", and taking us both by the hand he drew us out of the office to a rather cramped bedroom in another bungalow where several of his cronies were already warming up on a big bottle of brandy. The duty constable was there, and a rather nice, sober Brahmin who apparently owned most of the land around Barpeta. Another man was introduced, astonishingly, as "India's foremost actor of stage and screen, Mr D. Pal." Mr Pal smiled shyly, and our tipsy host sang more songs, alternating with bizarre proverbs and sayings, like "If this drink is intoxicating then WHY is not the bottle dancing?"

And pretty soon he led us all out into the night, to the lawn in front of the station, where other constables had built a fine bonfire. I tried to forget about being locked up by the S.I.B. and join in the fun. Most of the time I succeeded, but every now and then I thought of our passports sitting in the Malkhana. At first they were all just standing around, in or out of uniform, some with bare feet, some with cloths over their heads, laughing or poking the fire. The D.I. kept up an almost continuous babble of songs and nonsense, but there were was no sign that anyone else's spirits were being raised. Occasionally he danced his strange little jig, with one leg bent and the other sandaled foot raised and jabbing at the air under his tubby body. Sometimes he took the ends of his scarf and held it out from his body in an effeminate gesture, while sweet expressions suffused his countenance.

He was just a drunk making a fool of himself, maybe, but he had promised us song and dance. A constable with a drum slung from his neck and a shawl draped over his head slouched around the fire towards us, grinning. The drum was tapered, a truncated egg shape, and was strung longitudinally over the barrel. He tapped out a rhythm on the side of the drum, while others began clapping to the rhythm – a series of double beats in four-time – and he finished each sequence with a quite subtle flourish of beats.

"This is the bull," said the D.I.

I still had no idea that anything much was going to happen.

Thinking back I'm reminded of a jazz band coming together on a gig – you know, they look like anybody off the street, standing around, joking a bit, not particularly connected until, zap!, they're into the first number, and everything comes together, and it makes your pulses race with excitement.

So here, just as suddenly, the D.I. seemed to forget his boozy bar songs and rapped out a peremptory phrase at the others, who came back with a shouted response and growling, animal noises, and he did it again, and again they shouted back, in chorus. The duty constable raised his arms and began a sinuous dance. The whole group produced a long, loud, thrilling animal howl, and launched into a hypnotic, chanting song. The drum beat and the hand clapping began and this aimless crowd around the fire became more tightly and tigerishly involved in its dancing and chanting than any tribal group I had seen since Africa. There was a special movement of the arms and elbows, and a rhythm that was quite unique. It was irresistible, and both Carol and I were swept away by it.

The Duty Constable danced with great eloquence in the firelight. Then another man joined in, with a quite different movement. The D.I. continued his strange little jig, weaving between them, coming over to us frequently to insist that they were all in heavenly ecstasy due to our presence. The Duty Constable kept telling us, "Don't mind. Don't mind." It was extraordinary, because after all here were police-men in uniform, with the trappings of their trade all around them, and we, their honored guests, had our passports locked up in their Malkhana. But the scene reached ever greater crescendos, and we were swept up in it, and joined in feeling wonderful, however absurd we may have looked.

The constables were feeding the fire with everything they could find, including parts of the picket fence. Soon Carol was wearing the D.I's scarf, knitted by his mother, and I was wearing his silly leather hat. He called us brother and sister, and we danced furiously until it was time for the feast. The food came out of buckets and was served on segments from the trunk of a banana tree. It was very good and there was far too much of it. Then quite suddenly, for no reason we could think of, we had to leave, in a hurry. The Duty Constable came over and said, "Come. It is time to go. I will walk with you," and he grabbed us and almost pushed us out into the street. But then the uniformed Inspector, who had remained sober, rushed over.

"No. Come. I will take you in the jeep." And he bundled us into the vehicle, drove us the short distance through the cold night mist, and left us with the briefest of goodbyes. Like Cinderellas after the ball, we wondered what it was all about. I was writing my notes when there was a knock on the door. It was the Duty Constable. He had walked over, and demanded to know if we were all right, as though he had expected something else. He beamed down on us, inflamed with drink and excitement.

"Anything you want you may call for me," he said and then, aston-ishingly, he advanced, seized both my biceps and kissed me firmly on each cheek. Then with an air of heroic resolution he did the same for Carol, except that there was a brief moment when his lips seemed to be aimed at hers and only by a mighty effort were they deflected to her cheek. Then he too stumbled out into the fog, nursing his Punjabi passions.

In the morning my uneasiness returned. For all the high jinks of the night before, I thought it unlikely that the S.I.B. would be so eas-ily frustrated by mere policemen. We walked over again to the scene of the festivities. The Inspector was at a table outside his office.

"Good day to you, Sir and Madam," he said. "I am sorry to say I have not yet received instructions. Will you take tiffin?"

Fortunately I knew this meant a light lunch, and accepted. Then the phone rang. He leaped to his feet, ran around the table and a flower bed, and up the steps into his office. We heard him shouting, "Yes Sir, Yes Sir, No Sir," into the phone. He did not look particularly crestfallen when he returned. He simply said that his superior felt incompetent to decided the issue, and advised that we be "produced" at the capital, Gauhati, for interrogation by the Special Branch. His man would carry the passports and we would go with him on the train. From being honored guests at a banquet we had overnight become objects to be "produced". My heart sank, and I protested again about the waste of our time. The D.I. was sitting behind us, and in a remarkably good mood considering the hangover he should have been suffering. He said that if he could get the use of the jeep, he would take us to Gauhati.

Despondently, we prepared for the journey. I was pretty sure we would not be coming back that night. Then, as were taking leave of Debroy we heard that the D.I's jeep could not be found, the passports were already on their way to Gauhati, and we were free to ride there on our own. It was no great distance, about a hundred miles, and we took our time, admiring the villages and a profusion of bird life. There was water everywhere, and particularly in huge ditches alongside the road. We found out that villagers used them as fish tanks and for growing water chestnuts. When we stopped to photograph a stork, two men who were scooping water from one tank to another to catch fish insisted on offering us a 'Bihu meal'. They were very gentle and courteous, and gave us rice cakes made with sugar and curd, and filled with tasty black seeds.

Gauhati is on the south bank of the Brahmaputra, at one of its narrowest points, but even there it was an awe-inspiring river, and the combined rail and road bridge that crosses it was an impressive piece of engineering. Gauhati, by contrast was a dull and shabby town. We found a room at a tourist lodge. Next day the ordeal began.

Twice we told our story to Special Branch agents, first to a young man called Dutta, then to a more ponderous man called Das, a name which seemed to be the Assamese equivalent of Smith. Each one affected to be convinced of our integrity but, alas, it was Saturday, and the "regularization" of our permits would have to wait until

Monday. Meanwhile we were advised to go nowhere since we had no papers. At the lodge a lugubrious plain clothes policeman with a shock of white hair pretended he was just hanging out for no reason at all, and on Sunday we got a surprise visit from Dutta. He brought a volume of poetry he had written and published, and asked me to write comments on his work. It was awful, but in the circumstances I presumed he was not looking for an objective judgement. Later he brought his wife and insisted on having a group photograph taken.

We got our "retroactive permit" for Manas on Monday, but that was just the beginning, because of course we wanted to see much more of Assam. We were shuttled around endlessly from office to office and town to town. Our visa had nearly expired, and Snow White, as we came to call our faithful watchdog, knew it. One evening, after another day of fruitless frustration, he saw me in the lobby and said, mournfully, "Mr Simon, I am sorry to see you looking so reduced."

Finally, in the nick of time, and after six days of getting the run-around we found ourselves with the Secretary of the Passport Office in Dispur, a most polished young man behind the largest desk we had seen so far. He gazed at us with the far-seeing eyes of a great administrator.

"We have to consider each case on its merits," he pontificated. "We may have reasons for refusing permission to some individuals and not to others. And of course we will not tell you what those reasons are. This is a restricted area, and the words do, after all, have some meaning. They mean that foreigners are not allowed here, with certain exceptions. "

He beamed at us.

"You are the exceptions. "

We were free to travel anywhere in Assam., except the tribal areas.

Two Germans were there too, seeking permits. With his finger tips together, and a conspiratorial smile on his face, he said to them:

"Now this, I'm afraid, may be rather difficult."

In exasperation, the woman exploded:

"I'm sorry, I really can't deal with this 'maybe', 'perhaps', 'it will be difficult'. Just tell us please whether it is possible – or impossible.

His smile became even more expansive.

"Let me put it then that, in this case, it will prove, actually, to be ... impossible."

I am ashamed to say that I felt a certain smug satisfaction.

Aside from the permit, little good came of those six days, but I did find out why the authorities had the jitters. Assam is certainly one of the most interesting and unusual places in this world and, from the Indian point of view, one of the most vulnerable. North of Assam is China. East is Burma, South is Bangladesh, and all around this long tongue of land are hilly jungle areas occupied by untamed tribes whose allegiances are as variable as the weather. But the worst of it is that because of the way India was divided at independence, India's access to Assam was reduced to the narrowest of bottlenecks, only a few miles across.

In 1962, over a border conflict, the Chinese invaded Assam from Tibet, and there seemed to be no stopping them. For ten days they advanced across the state and it was assumed that Assam was gone. While we were there in 1977 I met one of the men who had been assigned to blow up the bridges and oil wells as a last resort, and it very nearly came to that, until – and nobody knew why – China relented and left. Ever since, Assam has rivaled Kashmir as the most politically sensitive part of India. The Indian government knows that the borders are as leaky as a sieve, but it is not only worried about foreign agents. The hill tribes want more independence. The Assamese want to stop the immigration of poor Indians from other states. The possibilities for trouble are endless. So what is at stake here?

In the mid-19th century a British army captain with a few soldiers rowed up the Brahmaputra signing treaties with tribal chiefs, and found what he thought was an indigenous tea plant growing in the hills. The significance was enormous. The British, and others, were already addicted to the beverage, and the tea trade was highly profitable, but in those days it was thought that tea would only grow in China. Then came the Opium Wars, and British access to "all the tea in China" was cut off.

That little shrub set off an agricultural revolution. Assam rapidly, and painfully, became a huge tea garden. Then the British found oil. The world's second oil well was drilled in Assam. Coal was found too, and valuable hardwoods, so a railroad was built to take the tea and the lumber to the paddle steamers. Today there is still oil, coal and timber, but the prize is a million or more acres of tea estate, now owned mostly by 'rupee companies', which bring a huge amount of foreign exchange into the Indian economy.

Assam is a treasure house, and India does not want to lose it. For long periods access by foreigners has been entirely prohibited. We were lucky to be there at a time when foreigners were allowed in at all, and the government was always on the look-out for troublemakers.

So, still looking for a tiger, we went to Kazirenga. We rode an elephant, and faced off a white rhino who wanted to charge us, but the prize came next evening, in a Land Rover driving to the river. At first we saw the more predictable animals, rhino, deer, buffalo and wild boar. The sandy desolation of the river bed was strikingly beautiful, as was the life around the ponds, with fish jumping, kingfishers and gulls diving, and herons, egrets, ducks and hawks going about their business. The sunset on the grasses, reflected in the water, was altogether gorgeous and I was already well satisfied when there was a shout, the jeep slammed to a halt, and not a hundred feet away we saw a big, bright Royal Bengal tiger stalking in long grass, plainly visible and glowing in the golden sunlight. It was another of those moments when you say to yourself, for this alone it was all worthwhile. A little later a black leopard also made an appearance, and monkeys scattered into the trees. The skyline was a splendid black on red, and stars began to appear in a sky that was African in its grandeur.

We rode on up the south bank of the Brahmaputra, and by sheer chance met a helicopter pilot patrolling oil pipelines. In no time at all we were up in the air with him. And through him we made friends with an oil engineer who smuggled us into forbidden tribal territory, where we saw primitive people in loin cloths shooting fish with bows and arrows. His son was about to be married to the niece of one of India's most celebrated musicians, the sarod player, Amjad Alikhan, who came to Assam from his home in New Delhi to be at the wedding. And so we found ourselves in a room with a just a handful of people, listening to the most sublime music, with the jungle only yards away.

Near Dibrugarh, at Margherita, we arrived quite unannounced at

The beginning of the fabled Burma Road – a road I would have loved to take, but couldn't. Even to have got this far East in Assam was an achievement. Although it was illegal to cross overland into Burma, it could be done, but it meant crossing a dangerous no-man's land of war lords, drug rings, and gem smugglers – or so I was told, and for once I listened.

a tea estate, and were taken in, without question, by Jim and Jean Beven, who ran the place. For two days, as their guests, we learned the intricacies of how tea leaves are cut and fermented and turned into such a variety of different products, strange because there is actually only one tea plant from which they all come. And we visited an open cast coal mine where the coal was carried from the coal face to the railroad siding in baskets on the heads of of an endless, colorful chain of women in saris.

Every day introduced us to new wonders. The sequence of events that came our way was incredibly rich. Trying to absorb them and make sense of them my mind was racing to keep up. I was almost overcome by the exotic minutiae of so many different lives. At Dibrugarh we took a ferry across the great expanse of the Brahmaputra, and during the crossing waves of sadness engulfed me. They seemed to rise up out of the water itself, for I had no reason for sorrow or melancholy. As I contemplated the river I felt the existence of a great tide of feeling submerged beneath the everlasting, petty details of life, ebbing and flowing to its own rhythm. No doubt, I thought, at times I travel with this current, at other times against it, but with no real perception of its meaning. Yet my observations of passing "reality" must be so conditioned by it that they could only be works of imagination. How, I wondered, would it ever be possible to write a true account of this journey?

The Bevens had sent us to the manager of another tea estate on the north bank, and that visit was chiefly memorable for an extraordinary theatrical performance. It began as a mundane duty call for our host, Roy Eastment. A cultural programme was being given in the village in aid of the high school. He had to put in an appearance. It was late afternoon, but still hot. We didn't think to take extra clothing. A large tent had been set up, with a stage. We saw a few short dances and sketches, and thought it would soon be over. Already it was getting cold. Then the main event began. Apparently a group of professional players were engaged to perform a play. Everything was announced in Assamese, so of course we had no idea what we were in for. Roy thought it would be quite short.

In fact it was four hours long. In our thin shirts, we were freezing. The players had a bonfire burning behind the stage, where they tried to warm up between acts. We went back there too, to share the warmth, and it was clear that the actors were very poor. They wore threadbare clothes, and were very thin. Yet on the stage they acted their hearts out, with tremendous vigour, and even though I understood practically nothing of what was said, I was able to follow the plot.

It was an endless melodrama, like an animated strip cartoon, full of characters entwined in tales of disaster and degradation. A beautiful woman is seduced and then deserted by her lover, who leaves her with an illegitimate son. Her brother, a self-serving rascal, arranges to marry her to a rich Brahmin, but the son must be got rid of first, and never mentioned again. He sends it away for adoption. But her lover did not really desert her. He was trapped in an accident. When he returns, he is told the son has died and the mother has married. He goes off in despair. Twenty-five years pass. The abandoned son re-appears, destitute and hungry, in the company of a starving artist and his daughter. His own father, now an impoverished street musician, is also on the scene, but of course they do not know each other. The father angrily rejects his son's pleas for help.

Meanwhile his mother now has a son by the rich Brahmin. Her first son comes across them having a picnic, and begs for food. His mother, not knowing who he is, still wants to help, but his half-brother refuses to allow it. Whenever he is frustrated, the actor who plays the natural son, and who is the hero of this tale, makes a strange and striking sound – "Tettarri" – which identifies him from now on. A pock-marked villain enrolls him in a criminal gang. By now his rascally uncle, using the Brahmin's money, has become a wealthy publisher. He has designs on the artist's innocent daughter and tries to seduce her with his wealth, but she spurns him. Necessity forces her on to the street with her father, selling fake charity tickets.

The Brahmin family walks by, and the son buys a spurious ticket. Then the gang robs the artist and his daughter, but Tettari is outraged and turns the gang in by going to the police. The artist, now in desperation, commits a robbery himself. But Tettari's unscrupulous uncle finds out and uses his knowledge to force the artist's daughter, Miranda, to submit to him. (This scene is particularly long drawn out). Then Tettari's mother accidentally meets her former lover, and in dramatic tones, they tell each other what really happened to them. But the Brahmin overhears them, and finds out about the illegitimate son ...

At this point we were only half way through the story. There were scenes of arson, murder, contrition, suicide, revenge and triumph before we got to the end. Despite real physical discomfort, and not understanding the words, I was spellbound. Perhaps my enchantment was due, in part, to being reminded of the power of storytelling. I could not conceive of an audience anywhere, however sophisticated, not being drawn in by this tale. Most of all, though, it was the privilege of time travel that captured me. Just as in Nepal I had been able to think myself in the Middle Ages, so here I was present at an event that must once have been a commonplace in Europe, hundreds of years before, when strolling players like these, as poor and threadbare as these, took their homemade dramas from one fair to another, and shivered around the brazier before striding on to their rickety stages to become kings, princesses, rogues and heroes, to populate our imaginations.

Finally the convoluted epic reached its climax, and ended. Very few of the characters survived. Frozen stiff, we hurried back to Roy's estate, swallowed brandy, and warmed each other up in bed. But it was a glorious experience that has stayed vividly with me through all the years since.

We had six more days in Assam, but a good deal of the time was taken up with mandatory visits to various police stations and Special Branch offices. Although we had been free to travel, we were required, everywhere we went, to register our arrival and departure. Often the police officials were friendly and hospitable. We were several times invited to their homes, or taken out for a meal, and we made interesting connections through them, but following the rules was a major interruption to our progress.

As we approached the end of our time together I felt, more and more, the pressure to change my mind and take Carol with me the rest of the way. The pressure did not come from her. She was warm and loving to the last, and scarcely mentioned her hopes. I was at war with myself, but still I could not bring myself to abandon the journey as I had conceived it. I remembered the bitter regrets I had experienced earlier, and did not want to repeat them, but I did not know just how crucial my decision would be for both of us.

We rode on to Tezpur, to Gauhati, and then to Shillong. From Shillong to the border, at Dawki, was only a few hours, and I remember that empty road through the green hills as the most beautiful ride in all my experience. Dawki was a tiny village in a peaceful valley by a river that issued from a rocky gorge. A mass of wild flowers embellished the grassy banks, together with arica and coconut palms, and jack fruit trees with their heavy fruits hanging in bunches from the trunks. There was nobody around, and we stripped off and swam in the clear green water. Then we cooked a dinner at the Inspection Bungalow, and made love. Somehow we were both able to put away the thought of what tomorrow would bring, and we were very close.

I took Carol to the border next day, and we came first to  the Indian customs shed. I was very moved by the thought of her wandering off alone again, and thoughtlessly I brought out my camera to take a last picture of her. The customs official shouted angrily at me and threatened to confiscate the film, and our parting was a miserable hurried thing. Long, long afterwards Carol told me that it was the memory of that separation that decided her finally not to wait for me. Although we met again briefly in Delhi, and then much later in France, we were never quite as close as we were at Dawki, and in the end I lost her.

# 11. Ends & Beginnings

**B**ack in New Delhi, burned by my transit across the Deccan plain, frustrated by weeks of waiting for spare parts, I felt my spirits to be sinking. Although I was still ten thousand miles from Europe, the end of the journey already seemed imminent. What was ten thousand miles to me then? As a physical challenge it represented a mere thirty or forty days of riding. The perils of free-shooting tribesmen on the Khyber Pass, of stone-throwing Kurds, of the Shah's ruthless police, of the frozen passes into Turkey, prompted scarcely a flicker of concern. And the prospect of seeing so much that was rich and rare and beautiful left me sadly indifferent.

In Delhi I drank beer, haunted offices and plunged into the acquisition of souvenirs which before I had largely scorned. In Kabul I wallowed in Western food and wine, and bargained for a samovar. In Rasht I sank gratefully into a sea of gin and tonic, and in Meshed I dabbled in rugs. Along the way my heart could not but rise frequently to meet the glories of the Himalayas. I responded as best I could to the fascination of Afghanistan, Iran and Turkey, and to the many unavoidable incidents of such a journey, but the steady inspiration was gone and I hunted for it in vain. I was going back, it was all over; I was longing for the end, dreading it, completely unprepared for it, unable to take my mind off it.

Because the old building was still there, still mine, it mesmerized me. I could think of nowhere else to go. All my self-knowledge and my airy detachment deserted me, and I wanted only to be back in

Some things should never just be seen in passing. This one corner of one small part of the temple at Khajarao could occupy a visitor for hours with its extraordinary portrayal of human life. It was here that I saw some young women in conversation with one of their Gods, Shiva. They were dressing him with flowers, and talking to him as though he were a friend of the family.

that familiar refuge, to gather my wits, to write my book and, with that, I hoped, to recover my strength and my wisdom. Yet already I had an inkling that such wisdom as I had gained could not be stored, to be brought out and dusted off in moments of need, but had to be regenerated through the spiritual energy of the moment, and I wondered quite seriously whether I had burned myself out, whether the source of that energy was dead for ever. Every day I felt the fear of overexposure more sharply, and finally, from Istanbul, I ran for sanctuary as if for my very life.

I installed myself in the old house alone. My former partner had made another home for herself elsewhere, though not so far away as to be forgotten. She had a claim on the building too, but she was patient at first and did not press it too hard.

The book was all that mattered to me then. The journey was still bright in my mind and my memory was full to bursting with marvellous detail, but it was a fragile cargo and I needed desperately to get it down on paper before it became faded and lost for ever.

The laws of the physical universe govern us too. Nothing can be accumulated in this world without a corresponding debt; not experience, not beauty, not wealth, not even love, and the price can never be estimated in advance by the one who has to pay it.

The book took eighteen months to write, with little respite. It was too long for those around me. I had learned to make intimate contact with strangers almost instantaneously, but I had lost the habit of nurturing relationships over a long period. I had become literally unsuited for a settled life.

The old man was still alive, now older and more cantankerous than ever. He received me happily at first, as was his style, but soon little matters began to irritate him. There was a stone path which we shared. He wanted to cement it over. In fact he would have cemented over the entire village given a chance. I refused, as always, but now I could not spare the effort to be diplomatic. With no woman around to mollify him, he became surly and secretive. He claimed that his cellar was leaking again, and that the magneto of his archaic tractor had been ruined by moisture. This was a disaster, not because he could not work his vines, since he had none left, but because he couldn't take his family to market.

None of his family had ever been able to pass a driving test because, the old man explained, the inspectors were all corrupt and gave licenses only to those who paid bribes which he certainly would not. The horse also having been sold, the only vehicle he could legally take on the road was a tractor. The family sat on a flat trailer, usually with a sheet of plastic over their heads. Now, he said, I had rusted his magneto.

He shouted the accusation at me one day, and I was too sensitive to remember that he always shouted. We became even further estranged, and his daughter had to act as intermediary. Then a situation began to develop that must have been hilarious to onlookers but was deeply depressing to me.

Having no more vines and no horse, he had no income other than his pension and, of course, no further need for the cellars under my house. His next move was obvious. He would sell the cellars. It could not have happened at a worse time for me, in every respect. I had no spare money at all. I could not afford to be embroiled in negotiations with an irascible and irrational old man. Worse still, he let it be known that he was looking for an exaggerated sum.

This upset me deeply, because we had agreed, but verbally, that when the time came for him to sell me his cellars the price would be reasonable. It was too much for me. There I sat trying to write a book about grand aspirations, great open spaces, visions of freedom, the generosity of the human spirit and so forth, while beneath and around me scuttled a crablike peasant, hinting, scowling and plotting betrayal.

I wrote him a pompous letter reminding him of our agreement and offering him the sum, corrected for inflation, which seemed appropriate. The next morning I found the letter sprinkled in tiny fragments on my doorstep.

Unfortunately, one of the cellars was an integral part of the house. It was not really a cellar at all, but a ground-floor space immediately below the room in which I worked and with a wooden ceiling. While it was used only for storage I was unaffected, but if it should ever be occupied by people the noise of their activities would resound through the floor and drive me out.

At first, the prospect of anybody else wanting to buy the space seemed remote. I had only to wait, plug my ears to the old man's mutterings and hope that in time the book might earn me a few pennies. This was easier said than done. The family surrounded me, for they lived on one side of my house and had their vegetable garden on the other. We had to pass each other. Each time we did, our mutual silence and hostility was painful and clouded my thoughts. From my kitchen I saw them every evening in their garden, bent double over their crops, with their ample posteriors pointedly aimed at my window. And when the bread van came and parked outside my door, we played games of hide-and-seek to avoid each other.

The old building which had once guarded the village from attack became a fortress again. Then one new ingredient was added to bring the farce to its climax. The old man found another buyer. He was a Parisian who some years before had bought a small holiday house some doors away from my own. He was a seemingly inoffensive accountant with a toothbrush moustache, a warbling wife and a weedy son, who came for a month every summer, supposedly to relax.

Riding high among my splendid dreams, I sadly underestimated the acquisitive instincts of this *petit bonhomme*. With the greedy tenacity of a gopher, he gnawed away in obscurity, burrowing through the neighbouring property to expand his empire. Thanks to the complicated way in which the houses were joined to each other, he found himself that summer with the wall of 'my' cellar at the end of his tunnel. He could not help his nature. At all costs, he had to gnaw on.

Rather than risk my working conditions, I decided to eat humble pie. One afternoon I approached the old man in his garden. With sickly hypocrisy, I said I regretted our misunderstanding and hoped for a compromise.

'You see,' I said. 'While I am writing over there I find the possibility of noises from below too disturbing.'

'Ho ! ' he shouted contemptuously. 'Ho, you and your writing ! What's that to me? I shit on your writing and your derisory offer. You will never have that cellar. Never! You understand? Never!'

'You must be mad,' I said, and walked away. The peasants, I thought bitterly, are revolting. It's war.

The gossip began to spread through the village, and my allies reported back to me: 'The Parisian has made them an offer.'

I feigned indifference.

'So what?' I said. 'They have to offer it to me first.'

'He has proposed a large sum of money.'

'I'll believe it when I see it in writing,' I said.

But from my window I saw the comings and goings between my enemies. And when I saw the old man bring lettuces and tomatoes from his garden and hand them to the Parisian's wife, with ingratiating cries of 'Think nothing of it. Glad to be of service,' and so on, I knew it was serious, because once I had been the object of these attentions, and I knew they meant business.

Then I began to hear sinister sounds in the cellar below me. The old man and his grandson were clearing it out and singing as they worked. Their work may have been quite innocent, for all I knew, but by now I was gripped by a siege mentality. The sappers were undermining my foundations; the hooks and ladders were rattling against the walls, and the enemy was already singing in triumph.

I needed only another month or two to finish my work, and I was ready to do anything to win that peace. I swallowed my pride again and went to visit the Parisian.

'I hear you have an interest in the cellar,' I began, as mildly as I could manage, 'but perhaps you don't know that we have an agreement, the old man and I, that dates back ten years now. He promised to sell it to me at a reasonable price when he had no further use for it, and I have always assumed that it would become part of my house. Yet now he is talking about prices in the millions.'

His face remained blandly polite.

'Ah,' he said. 'I did not know of the existence of an agreement. I have simply said that, in the event of his wishing to sell, I would be interested. I have certainly no intention of paying millions for it.'

Being a poor businessman, I was relieved beyond measure. In fact, my naivete served me well, for once, and I was able to put the whole thing out of my mind. The holiday season ended, the Parisian returned to Paris, the old man and I ignored each other and the subject of the cellar went under ground.

Eighteen months is a long time. The writing went on without interruption, but all my energy and imagination went into reliving the past. There was nothing to spare for the present. The pressure was great and I was thrown wildly off balance. I was hungry for affection and stimulation, but could give nothing in return. My guilt made me oversensitive and awkward. To protect myself from my own anxieties I provoked hostility and exploited my friends.

The worst of it was that I knew I was living my life in contradiction to what I was proclaiming in my book. Having to defend my territory from the old man, the Parisian and others made me want to cling to it all the more. While I extolled the virtues of freedom and detachment from material things, I knew I was becoming once again bound to this great pile of ancient stones. While I wrote about the advantages of solitary travel, I knew I longed to be loved, understood, protected and cared for, whatever the cost to my freedom.

I resented these impulses, and fought to overcome them, but the pendulum had swung too far one way, and now it came rushing back with unstoppable force I dreamed of gardens and families, and drew sketches of the improvements I would make to the house.

When the book was finished (and I got to the end perhaps a little too soon) all those repressed desires welled up. The book succeeded far beyond my expectations. There was some magic in that too, as of a prophecy fulfilled. I began to believe I had the power to reconcile the inner liberty and detachment of the traveler with roots, houses and families.

My euphoria increased beyond bounds. I fell in love, and the woman who soon afterwards became my wife would have been well within her rights to wonder whether she was not so much an equal partner in a marriage as the victim of a flood disaster.

With an optimism and confidence that belonged more properly to a traveler than a husband I brought my wife back to that same old building, persuaded somehow that my happiness and good fortune would have the same magic effect on others that it had on me.

The reverse was true. The old man and the accountant revived their conspiracies more intensely than ever, and became involved in elaborate schemes to get round the law and defeat us. And there were other rumblings and disturbances which failed to die down. There were skeletons in every cupboard, and live apparitions at the door, and the more my wife came to love the building, the more hateful she found it. Finally, when it was almost too late, we fled as hastily as we had come, pursued by furies, bewildered by our bad luck and by each other.

At times like that I had to wonder whether I would ever be fit to live with another person: whether my four years of travel had changed me more than I knew - or rather, not changed me so much as revealed me, clearly and irrevocably for what I was, a solitary being incapable of finding myself in harmony with someone I loved.

My thoughts returned constantly to times of peace and clarity on the journey, feelings I had wanted to bring back as a gift to others, but which seemed to have no place or purpose in this everyday world.

# 12. By Jumbo

I can't help grinning. It's all I can do to stop myself from laughing out loud. I can't explain it, but it's as close to pure happiness as anything I know. I always get it at the beginning of a journey — even a journey like this one, which is unlike any I've made before.

I'm very lucky. Looking around me in the crowded Boeing I don't see anyone else ready to burst for joy. I could be wrong. Maybe it doesn't show on my face either. But they don't look the types, any of them. They're all too busy to be that happy. Maybe that's why they're keeping themselves busy – in case of improper happiness. A lot of people can't handle that much joy when they don't know where it's coming from. It frightens them. It makes them think they might be wasting their lives. They work so hard for their happiness, it has no right to sneak up and take them unawares. It spoils everything.

My wife, Francesca, can be a bit like that. She's there beside me now, sweet and beautiful. And pregnant as well, although it's too early for anyone but me to know it. If a wave of happiness should come her way at the wrong moment she might raise her hand like Canute and say "Wait a minute. I'm not ready to be happy. There's this and that and the other thing all wrong. I'm having a rotten time. Can't you come back another day?"

When we married I thought we'd be laughing all the time, but I was wrong about both of us. In fact I seem to have been wrong about a lot of things. Well, never mind about that now. We married for better or for worse, and now it's time for better. I love my wife. I love her tenderness, her passions, the crazy impetuous courage with which she threw herself into this marriage with a global hobo and chronic misfit like me. She cares so much. Every smallest particle of life matters. She rescues moths and people in an equal agony of concern, but there is too much pain in this world, even for a lion-heart like hers, and it leaves little room for what I call happiness.

Perhaps my sensibilities have been numbed by an overdose of experience. I have made such a habit of laughing at misfortune, maybe I am blind to the pain of others. Sometimes my laughter hurts her, as though it were meant to exclude her from my life.

There's plenty to laugh at here if you can get yourself into the right frame of mind. I try to imagine that I've never flown before. With practice this view of things comes quite easily. Then the whole idea of a Boeing 747 flying at all becomes quite hilarious. How can it? How could this immense silver eggplant ever leave the ground? Seen with an innocent eye, the Flight of the Jumbo is plainly absurd. A great lolloping bulbous thing like that, supported by thin air? Ridiculous! Yet here are hundreds of sane adults solemnly certain that in eleven hours from now this crazy contraption, this mad inventor's fantasy, will land them in San Francisco.

Anybody here know how much a jumbo weighs fully loaded? Hands up. Yes, you over there? Wrong. The answer is 350 tons. Now who seriously believes that 350 tons are just going to rise up into the stratosphere? It's nonsense. We will sit here fussing with our bags and coats, twiddling the air nozzles, and squinting slyly at our neighbour's face. Then, after an hour or so, we'll all get out and take our buses and trains home.

"Ladies and gentlemen, this is your captain speaking. I guess we didn't make it this time. A few more wrinkles to iron out. We hope to try again soon, and hope that you'll be here to join us. Meanwhile, thank you for coming along, don't forget your duty frees, and have a safe journey home."

But the jumbo will take off. I know that too. That's the problem and the virtue of a childish eye in an adult head. Everything is simultaneously evident and incredible. We're trundling over the tarmac now. Look at these long, regimented lines of grown-ups. They've not been so obedient since their school days, all children again, cowed by the miracle of flight.

"Smoking in the toilets is forbidden." I should think so! "Fasten your seat-belts. Place your seats in the upright position. Extinguish all smoking materials. Soon the headmaster will be here to address you."

Air travel isn't travel at all. We just sit here getting older and more tired. In twenty minutes' time, when we're tens of thousands of feet above the Irish sea nothing will be significantly different. Some people may experience a flutter or two before the wheels leave the ground (*'The damn thing isn't going fast enough – we'll never make it.'*) and shudder at the double CLUNK of the undercarriage retracting as the ground swoops away. Then, after a moment of mild relief, all consciousness of the outside world fades away.

True, somewhere in the aircraft there may be a child transfixed by the notion that beneath its feet, through that thin metal skin, is a heartstopping plunge past clouds and whirling flocks of birds to an ocean of whales and fishermen and people feeling ill on the ferry to Fishguard. For the rest of us, we may as well be sitting in a waiting room.

A long time ago, at Christmas, I was taken to a big London department store where there was a model submarine for children to sit in. I went inside, the lights turned green, there were bubbly sounds and plangent music, and through the porthole I saw an aquarium complete with treasure chest, octopus and diver's helmet. Afterwards Santa Claus gave me a present. That was much more like real travel.

And still my excitement is real enough. The champagne effervescence of it is clamouring for an outlet. My mind is fizzing with memories of encounters on boats, trains, buses and the long, long road. I look around me ready to delight in the variety and complexity of my fellow passengers. I know better than to expect a Nubian camel driver, or a Guaraní Indian woman taking chickens to market, but I'm ready to find fascination in anyone. I scan face after face, registering the differences between fat and thin, light and dark, old and young, hirsute and balding, but in some indefinable way everybody looks the same, flattened and reduced by the mechanical regularity of our situation.

My eye is held at last by the rhythmic jaw movements of an elderly couple sitting side by side in one of the central rows. They are both staring straight ahead, glassy-eyed. What makes them extraordinary is that they are chewing in unison. It can't be chance. Must be the unconscious expression of a need, the same one that makes certain orderly persons always walk in step. Alone, neither one would attract a second glance. Together, as their prominent jaws rise and fall with military precision, they look grotesque.

Their obliviousness is remarkable. They seem to be aware of nothing except the salivated material slipping past their palates. There have been philosophers – Bishop Berkeley among them – who proposed that the world only exists in our recognition of it. I would like to see the world as this masticating twosome recognizes it. Almost everything around them would disappear. The other passengers, the aircraft itself, would cease to exist. They would be left, with perhaps a few shreds of seat attached to their backsides, sailing alone in space. They would chew their way over the North Pole at 33,000 feet, port and starboard jaws champing together at an even eighty revolutions per minute, fuelled from the same large packet of onion-flavoured potato snacks. But then, according to the same hypothesis, while the rest of us have vanished, their thoughts would manifest themselves as reality. I would see them in a vapour trail of unpruned rose bushes, revised wills and testaments, inconsiderate children, leaking taps, ancient sexual encounters, collapsed soufflés, humbled bank managers and all the paraphernalia of retired life in the suburbs.

Happy to find something, however silly, to fasten my pleasure on, I lean back and watch London slip away past the window. It's amazing to think that I might never live in Europe again. More than amazing – impossible. I have to suspend my disbelief. The capacity of human beings to suspend their disbelief seems to be infinite. Without it, all the benefits of rational thought would be lost – and all its horrors avoided. How else would we fly in airplanes, operate gas chambers, submit to surgery, immunize children with toxic vaccines, or emigrate to foreign lands.

Only two weeks ago we were still enmeshed in our life in France, dominated by resentments, misery and cruel disillusion. And finally, it was such a simple thing to do to take the decision, close up the house, pack our bags, travel to London, and fly. The very speed of it was cauterizing. In the rush of events I could put those old, harrowing emotions aside. Now, for a moment, they threaten to engulf me, but mercifully the cabin staff have come to my rescue with a distraction.

They are about to instruct us on what to do when the aircraft plummets to the ocean. Airlines loathe and detest any reference to disaster. Their fear of it amounts to obsession. People who run other forms of transport, which kill countless thousands annually, never give it a thought, but airline operators will do anything to convince us that an aircraft is sustained in flight by arrangement with God. To doubt is to sin, and only sin could make us fall. But they are forced by regulations to prepare us for this unthinkable catastrophe, and they have spent years and fortunes figuring out how to do it without causing a moment's loss of faith.

The result is a profoundly funny ritual, and it is about to begin. Two flight attendants take their places on either side of the movie screen to present the British Airways' production of The Ditching and Breathing Ceremony. They have already prepared their facial expressions, ready to make light of such sordid and shocking matters with the jolly propriety of a vicar's wife talking down a rapist. A voice chatters happily over the speakers about vague emergencies, and the girls begin their silent dance. It is richly oriental in its symbolism. Smiling benevolently, they reach up for The Dropping of the Mask. This refers discreetly to the unmentionable prospect of a hole suddenly appearing in the side of the airplane. Then comes The Donning of the Jacket, a traditional orange costume, and the nimble Tying of Bows, followed by Tugging the Cord and Blowing the Whistle. Finally there is The Pointing Out of Exits, four gestures which might seem uncomfortably rude if they were not accomplished with such style.

The ballet passes along so merrily that I have sometimes caught myself wishing we could have an 'emergency', so that I could play with all these pretty toys. It takes an effort of the imagination to conjure up the horror and confusion of a Boeing falling into the Arctic Ocean with four hundred people, but since my experience on the *Chidambaram* I am more willing to make the effort. I used to think about lifeboats the way the airline would have me think about life jackets and rafts. Now I am less convinced that I might somehow escape from disaster by tugging my cord and blowing my whistle. Of course, I admit there would be no harm in trying, but my memories of the boats smashing into the side of the ship are still vivid. They have made me quite suspicious of all the soothing procedures and provisions that the authorities say they have in hand to save me from one crisis or another.

It is almost four years since I sailed on the *Chidambaram* ChiDUMbrrRUM. I have never told Francesca about it and the man who fell, or jumped, overboard. I would like to tell her now. It seems a perfectly natural thing to do to pass the time, but I have become circumspect about memories. My traveler's tales are not her favourite form of entertainment. They remind her of my past, of the many years of my life before we met, of people I knew, of women I loved.

'And this house,' she used to say, in a crescendo of fury. 'Even this house is mixed up with another damned love of your life . . . How could you bring me here? How could you be so heartless?'

And I was outraged against my better sense and nature, and said I could hardly help having a past any more than she could, and anyway she loved the house or we wouldn't have stayed in it . . .

'Love it,' she shouted. 'I hate it. It's a bloody medieval slum. . .' and the fight would go on with each one of us thinking, God, what are we doing? God, what have we done?

And so, after a year of trying, we left the house.

For California. To find some land, and start again.

I have such hopes of California. The sunlight. The ocean. The feeling of liberty and space. I remember those feelings so well from my journey. That journey! Is it an obsession? Will it poison California for us too? But what can I do? I can't forget it. Four years, the most intense years of my life.

I think that journey changed me. I think that journey is part of me now for ever, and what I learned and discovered on that journey must have just as much meaning and importance as it did then.

So what got us into this awful mess?

Will this be the end of it?

**13**

My first exposure to California, in 1975, was unexpectedly shocking. The conspicuous consumption almost did me in. I came to Los Angeles across the Mojave desert, and nothing had prepared me for the experience. I am told that when starving prisoners were released from Nazi concentration camps one had to be very cautious with their diet. Steaks and ice-cream were likely to kill them. The analogy is far from perfect, because I was certainly not suffering in Latin America, but there were long periods when I felt deprived and was looking forward to a bit of luxury. I never dreamt how far California could take it, and the effect it would have on me.

I still remember, quite vividly, my first visit to a big American supermarket. I was used to stores where even the most basic needs were hard to come by. At the first Safeway I visited, I was so overcome by the sight of so much trash and trivia that I had to leave for fear of throwing up. This is almost impossible for me to imagine now, but I know it is true. I watched television with fascination and horror, and wandered around the freeways looking in vain for something to connect with. A few days later I went to Disneyland, and was inspired to write an article for the *Sunday Times* which they published a month later. Some things have changed since then. Most are the same, if not more so. The article was titled:

### RIDING THE GRINGO TRAIL

Glowing gently under the great solar grill of California, the people came rolling over the tarmac on human baggage trains, hundreds at a time, starry-eyed again, about to take those rides again, through the longest row of turnstiles this side of Florida.

First thing inside the gates is Main Street, where America grew up. Gas lamps, trolley cars, barber poles, candy counters, mutton chopped waiters with baize aprons, and girls in gingham, all clean as a whistle and neat as a nip (though not since Libya had I been in a land where alcohol was forbidden).

I watched the American families of the seventies parading past – "Wilbur, don't touch the gentleman" – in pastel pinks and greens, chiffon and jersey, bare backs and bermuda shorts, stetsons and side-burns, freckles and sneakers, and tons and tons of deodorant to keep them "dry, dryer, driest" for longer than ever before with absolutely NO ZIRCONIUM as advertised. They spill out over this kingdom of fun and thrills in their tens of thousands, but sooner or later they disappear, like bees among hives. Where are they going? How do they all fit in? The mystery is resolved underground, for Disneyland is an illusion floating on an illusion, and the heart of all this labored hilarity is a subterranean labyrinth. Here the technology of trivia comes to its climax. You float on a barge through a seemingly vast grotto, where humanoid pirates enact scenes of battle, arson, pillage, rape and various other rum doings under a moonlit Carribean sky. I stumbled out to contemplate the immense resources that had been marshalled to distract me for a few moments.

It wrenched my mind, standing there, to recall that I was the same person who, only a few months ago, was riding alone across the Bolivian Altiplano, more than two miles above sea level through a curtain of freezing drizzle. The day before I had fallen in a river and lost the last of the plastic bags I used to protect my gloves from rain. My hands were frozen tight, and the cold was reaching up my arms. My usual defence against cold was to sing, uproariously and defiantly, into the flying air—sea shanties and folk songs dimly remembered from the *News Chronicle Song Book* of 1937. For once the antidote failed. It became intolerable to continue, intolerable to stop. Rummaging in my mental attic for other remedies I came across a story told to me about an Italian climber who survived a four-day blizzard on a vertiginous alpine shelf while his companions perished. His method was rhythmically to clench and unclench his fingers – the only movement he could perform without falling.

I began to do the same on my handlebar grips. At first it was simply agonizing. Then a biological miracle occurred in my arms. Warmth flooded down to meet the cold. It was such a precise reaction that I could tell where the interface was at any time, felt it moving down past my wrist to the knuckles, then the finger tips. Soon my whole body was tingling with life, and I traveled on to La Paz in an invisible bubble of warmth and comfort. There have been few other moments on this journey when I have known a greater sense of triumph.

On the bleak and frigid plain around me small herds of llama sat among the stony scrub, their long necks sticking up through the gray haze like periscopes in the North Sea. By the roadside, also squatting, were occasional Indian herdsmen wrapped in woollen mantles. The rain ran off their hats and trickled down over the sodden material. I pitied those gray pyramids of humanity, and was as astonished by their stillness and acquiescence as they must have been by my frantic motion. I think now that they were probably quite as comfortable as I was. Perhaps we each wondered how the other could stand it.

It is customary to explain all feats of Indian endurance by their use of the coca leaf, but the information I gathered about that, in Potosí and other places, doesn't support this view. Coca is an aid and a strong habit, but Indians (like all of us) have other, more personal ways of generating defences against hunger and the elements.

Here in Los Angeles I think about those Indians and for the first time it occurs to me to wonder how much they were worth, in dollars. How much money, I mean, is represented by their possessions and the services provided to maintain them in their way of life? I don't suppose it comes to $100 a head, if that.

The question is unavoidable. Here everything speaks to me of money. First the vast freeway constructions, a mesh of concrete carpet, four to eight lanes wide, laid out over thousands of square miles, with spiralling flyovers at every intersection. And the machinery that pounds over them day and night; it's thirty miles there and thirty back just to see a movie, visit a friend, eat a hamburger on the beach, do a job of work. Then the supermarkets and shopping malls, temples of a thousand options where you must look hard to find anything that a person really needs. Or the Marina del Rey, a nautical metropolis where unimaginable numbers of pleasure boats sprout from the quaysides like figs on a stick, most of them never having gone beyond the harbor wall.

What then would be the capital investment to maintain a citizen in his Los Angeles lifestyle? Divide the population into the value of rateable property, throw in the roads and freeways, the utilities and services which protect and succour him, and the figure cannot be less than $100,000 a head. It may be twice that. Whatever the amount, it strikes me as absolutely preposterous.

Is life a thousand times more rewarding, more healthy, more secure in LA than on the Altiplano? If I want access to education and medicine, to libraries and blood banks, must I first defend myself against crime, smog, noise and ugliness on every side? It is easy to understand that the Indian has little choice, and even less practice at exercising it. But why, in Heaven's name, does anyone choose to stay in Los Angeles.

Los Angeles is certainly at one end of my American experience, just as the Altiplano is at another, and there is a perversity that attracts certain kinds of person to extremes. I found that while most North Americans living elsewhere profess to detest LA, those I met who lived there seemed quite content. They seem to deal with it by creating an enclave for themselves in one of those rectangular lots that this megalopolis is divided into, and from there to exploit the rich resources of stores, offices, studios and factories, paying high rates for the privilege. The car is the instrument of survival. Moving along the freeway, as though on a conveyor belt, it becomes a monkish cell. At other times it enables them to escape altogether. The art of life in LA, in short, is to block out as much of it as possible all the time, and to escape quite frequently. As a strategy for living it is fairly successful and ingenious. It is also fearfully expensive. Consumption is more than conspicuous, it gallops.

Take paper products, for example. In many homes paper plates seem virtually to have replaced china. In California rest rooms, by law, there must be a dispenser of large circles of sterile paper to interpose between your squeamish self and the seat, dubbed "Nixon party hats". On TV I saw a new product advertised, a douche, which is so disposable that it is apparently gone even before you use it. "Just read the directions", says the voice, "and throw it all away."

If I had flown in from Europe all this would have seemed merely extravagant (perhaps pleasantly so). But I come from nearly two years of living in open spaces, tents and huts, where human life is simple, and the extravagance is left to nature. I find this custom of perpetual consumption physically and morally offensive. I can't stomach it, and it seems important to track that feeling to its source before it fades.

In the last 13 months I have traveled 15,000 miles in Latin America, from the north of Brazil to the south of Argentina, then from Chile through the Andes in Bolivia, Peru, Ecuador and Columbia. Then into Panama, Costa Rica, Nicaragua, Honduras, Guatemala and Mexico. Trying now with my mind's eye to encompass that experience three related impressions stand out.

First was an intrusive presence everywhere of North American products, sales methods and cultural appendages. Second was the sense that, while Africa was a colonial empire dismantled, Latin America is an economic empire still at its peak. Third, that compared with Africans, Latin Americans carry a heavy load of trouble and frustration.

Don't let me give the wrong impression. We live in a world of trouble. The essential thing is to distinguish between different kinds and degrees of trouble. I am not speaking here of revolutionary movements or clashes between nations, but of the quality of individual lives.

I want to explain why the motorcycle turns out to be such a good instrument of exploration. It exceeds my greatest hopes. Its outstanding advantage is the very quality which once worried me most: it attracts attention.

Along all the endless thousands of miles of roadside in Africa and South America, excepting only the arid wastes of Northern Kenya, and the empty Argentine Pampa and Chaco, there is human life in all its manifestations. So much of my last two years have been spent riding past people that I have learned, inevitably, to read a great deal from people's expressions. The Triumph and I are a rare, if not unique event in most of these places, and the reactions to our passing are spontaneous and revealing.

Above all there are the children, and I know by heart, as though engraved there for ten thousand years, the attitude of the small boys, naked in the sun, half crouched, arms thrust out, fists clenched, grinning and howling, half in fear, half in wonder, ready to fight, to run, to submit. Or the little girls, up on their toes, arms outstretched, palms open, arched towards me, wanting instinctively to embrace this marvel before they turn to flee leaving a trail of enticing giggles behind them.

With age, dress and social conditioning, this basic vocabulary grows and ramifies to become the subtlest language of any, but because it is my language too I have learned to read it. There is no time for dissimulation as I hurtle past. The messages I read are true, and they tell me whether these people are clear or confused, hostile or hospitable, oppressed or free, industrious or indolent, bright or dull.

Against the almost continuous input of information there are the casual meetings, at gas stations for example.

Here's one in Africa.

"Oooh, where you come from in that one, Baaas?"

He's black, short, boiler-suited, working on the pumps. His face is a pantomime of wonder and appreciation. The servility is a game. It suits him to have me on a white man's pedestal. He can enjoy me better up there. For us to meet on the same level in this white racist territory would be a long-drawn-out and painful process. I protest mildly at the Baaas bit, but then we agree to humour each other.

"From England? Oooeee! No! I couldn't believe! "

And so on. He's sly but there's no bitterness. I'd lay my life on it.

Another in Argentina:

"Where do you come from?"

The question is abrupt, even harsh, and uttered with a studied absence of interest. He's 19 or 20, wearing salmon-colored bell bottoms, a plastic crocodile belt and a polyester shirt with the names and pictures of the world's capitals printed all over it. He wears it open to the waist and the short sleeves stretch nicely over his biceps.

He's one of a group who are hanging out between the pump and the bar, punching each other occasionally on the arms. He wants to know only how fast the bike goes and how much it cost. He suggests that I came most of the way from England on a ship. When I tell him otherwise, the explanation hardly appears to register. He's so muscle-minded that he can't see through his own image of himself. He's proud, resentful, and curious in that order. It's too much work for me now to dig down to the curiosity. He saunters off disdainfully, satisfied that at least I am no threat.

These two meetings, I find, represent very well the major social difference between Africa and Latin America. In Africa things appear much more straightforward. People seem to have their motivation fairly clear and simple, and look reasonably at peace with themselves. There are glaring injustices. There is great cause for anger, confrontation and change, but in thinking how people are in themselves, I am left with a general sense of tranquillity and good humour. (The one exception, Ethiopia, seems to prove the rule almost too nicely).

Latin America leaves a different trace. The self-destructive aspects of the *mestizo* personality are eloquently described by many writers (e.g. De Madariaga's Fall of the Spanish Empire). A great part of any Latin American male's behaviour is formed by a continual pursuit of his own identity, since he seems to exist for himself largely through the eyes of others. This makes him particularly susceptible to flattery; vulnerable to any challenge to his manhood, however puerile; and reluctant to seek information if doing so might reveal his ignorance.

He is, in short, a natural victim for anyone taking a colder, more collected view of his environment. A person for whom social respect opens the way to profit cannot hope to compete well in business with one who seeks profit first and then buys respect. The scene for the sacking of Latin America by the Anglo-Saxons was set centuries ago by the Conquistadors.

My journey to the United States began, I now realize, when I stepped off the ship in Brazil. I don't know where else in the modern world one could pass over such a great land mass, among so many different races and nations all paying tribute to one distant power. At first, though, this didn't occur to me. For one thing I was locked up almost immediately by the Brazilian police, which concentrated my mind for some weeks on a much closer and more frightening power. For another, motorcycling Gringos are a rarity in the north east, and people did me the courtesy of asking me where I came from without assuming that I was a North American. I was two thousand miles farther south, in Rio, before the prejudice became unavoidable.

Then I was on foot, in a laundry, looking for some clothing they had lost.

"Are you an American?" the man asked, with his own peculiar brand of an American accent, and an expression which indicated to me that he was ready to jump either way. I said I was English

"Good," he said eagerly. "Americans are shit."

If I had said I was American he would probably have told me about some relation of his living in New York. It didn't occur to me to protest. I am no stranger to prejudice. The Libyans are contemptuous of the Egyptians. The Sudanese despise the Ethiopians. Africans have little good to say about Arabs, and none at all about Asians. Whites turn their noses up at Blacks. There is no shortage of prejudice between nations and races in South America either. It exists between Indians and Mestizos, between Chilenos and Peruanos, Argentinos and Brasilleiros. Even in Brazil itself, supposedly a melting pot of races, the rich white south is openly content to have few black skins to darken the view, and it is all too clear everywhere that the whites are on top of the pile and mean to stay there.

Yet none of this compares in generality and virulence with the prejudice against the United States, its power, its policies and its people. Whether expressed by thousands of voices chanting slogans, or by hypocritical asides from the Spanish gentry; whether directed at dollar diplomacy, the US military, the CIA or Yanquis and Gringos in general, it is heard everywhere as the one unifying idea in Latin America.

It is hard not to share the resentment. South American towns are often a parody of North American life. Shiny curtain-walled banks loom over hovels. In countless decrepit streets a brightly enamelled Coca Cola or Pepsi Cola sign juts out above every single doorway. Village shops are stocked less with what the peasantry needs than with what American technology produces. Everything has this lopsided, disjointed feeling. The two cultures do not meet, they collide, and in spite of themselves Latin Americans know they haven't the force to resist.

They never had time (nor the inclination, perhaps) to evolve their own independent systems. And yet, unlike the subjects of the British Empire in Africa, they were always nominally in charge of their own destinies. The gap between the myth and the reality was far too wide to bridge, and corruption was the only possible consequence. Nobody I have met in government or law really believes the process can be reversed. I am bound to say that I much prefer the consequences of British rule in Africa to what United States economic domination has done for the Americas.

The "Latinos" are quite imaginative enough to perceive the humiliating position they occupy *vis á vis* the Gringos. Their accumulation of rage and resentment is sad to observe, and sometimes personally unpleasant. On the west side of the continent, where the so-called Gringo Trail of tourists begins, I was spat on once from a lorry, had mud thrown at me twice, and heard the mocking cry of "Gringo" most of the way from Bolivia to Panama, and beyond. How I wished I had remembered to bring my Union Jack with me.

The British, in fact, are now perfectly placed in South America to enjoy maximum respect and affection. A once great nation reduced to "harmless uncle" status, we suit the psychological needs of Latin America very well. It is half a century since the pound gave way to the dollar as the major source of foreign investment. There are nostalgic references to the railways we built, the polo tournaments we played, the shops and clubs we opened, and much flattery of London as the best city to live in.

I happened to follow the Royal Yacht's progress along the coast of Central America (at a respectful distance, of course) and saw how well the old royal magic still works. By popular consensus we are now all that North Americans are not. We are civilized, sensitive to the feelings of others, clear of speech and clean of habit, and of course imbued for ever with the spirit of fair play. We are also comfortably old-fashioned.

For a traveler in search of space and beauty, South America is a heart-stopping experience. Everywhere I saw spaces where I felt I could cheerfully spend the rest of my days. Like the Atlantic beaches between Bahia and Rio, the luscious farmlands above the Páraná river, or the lower slopes on either side of the southern Andes. I revelled in the spectacular fertility of the Colombian valleys and mountains, and countless other times felt myself to be in harmony with my surroundings.

For nearly two years now I have been self-sufficient with what I carry on the motorcycle. I am delighted to discover how little a person needs, or even wants, as long as the mind and senses are kept open to the excitement that life itself has to offer. It is this knowledge, finally, that made my ride into Los Angeles such a bruising shock. I see the American consumer as an addict in the grip of a habit at least as demanding as, and vastly more expensive than the Indian's coca leaf. It is a habit that the planet cannot support for ever, certainly not for all its inhabitants.

Worst of all, it seem such a pity – that all those resources, all that effort and ingenuity and promise of freedom, which people in Africa and Latin America envy so much, should lead to a sea of waste paper and a desperate attempt to get people to recycle their aluminum beer cans.

**14**

They showed a Clint Eastwood film I hadn't seen before. I put on the headphones, tuned in to the soundtrack, and watched with curiosity, then astonishment. Eastwood was not my idea of *avant garde*, yet here he was in a piece of daring, experimental cinema. It was the more amazing because the screen images were entirely conventional. Within minutes of the title, the hero was involved in fist fights and the wrecking of cars. But instead of Eastwood's predictable clipped repartee I heard his thoughts, crazy fragments of association surfacing from a schizoid mind. There was a maniacal ape in the movie too, and a stream of spoken symbolism flowed over the action shots of flying fenders and crunched bodywork. While the muscled hero on the screen squared up to his neanderthal opponent, a whispering voice breathed words of love and nostalgic regret for the taste of apple pie. Totally gripped, I watched the American fighting male disintegrate and collapse in front of my eyes as his mind, disgusted by the senseless violence, deserted his body and wandered off into cloud cuckoo land. Then, just as Eastwood's craggy fist landed on a fleshy nose opposite him, a giggling female voice burst through with: "Hey guys, what say to a chocolate sundae?" and I realized that I was plugged into the soundtrack of another film.

A sense of the surreal stayed with me throughout the flight. Somewhere near the end I woke up to see, far below the airplane, a vast area of bare ground all on fire. Surrounding this smoking waste was nothing but an expanse of snow and ice. It was quite beyond me to account for it. It was the sort of thing I would have imagined on

Jupiter or Mars. I stared until my eyes hurt, and then went back to sleep.

We came to earth on an April afternoon, twenty miles south of San Francisco. Because we were flying toward the sun, all those eleven long hours of expectation, weariness, hope and doubt, were telescoped into three. My fantasies, my mind-boggling visions through the window, were shrouded not only in sleep but in a time warp which took them, in a sense, out of my earthly history. All this was part of the magic of coming to California by air, a feeling of having, somewhere along the way, escaped from the earth altogether and then returned to a world that was, subtly but completely, different.

San Francisco then still had a Third World airport, overcrowded and underventilated. We followed the rat run of corridors and tunnels until it brought us, like prisoners on remand, to our judges at the immigration desks.

Francesca did not seem to share my own impression of having arrived by way of another planet. She walked alongside me, quiet, set, reluctant to give way, a small dignified European person in a pink print dress carrying a baby in her womb.

I studied the officials as we waited with the crowd, contemplating the remarkable power they exercised over our fate. They had their own brand of taciturnity but I felt they had to contain their spirits to achieve it, unlike their British cousins who so often looked as though they had to raise themselves from the dead each day to perform their churlish functions. Everything here now confirmed my feeling of heightened vitality, of a wider life.

Then we were called, the aberrant noose failed to close, and we were through into the light and became part of it. From the customs area we spilled out through the stiff wooden door on to the sidewalk, like bemused revellers at the end of some mad funfair ride. I was phenomenally glad to be there. The sun hit us for the first time and I felt like an irradiated crystal, glowing and vibrating fit to split. I wanted to touch people, shake their hands, joke with the porters and get wise with the cops.

Tee was there to meet us, splendid Tee from the old days. She stepped, unhurried, from an old maroon Saab and came towards us with her deliberate, almost formal smile.

"Hello," she said.

Then she turned to hold out her hand to Francesca.

"Francesca," I said, "this is Tee," and they shook hands.

I blessed and double-blessed Tee's Southern manner, her English ways, her instinct which told her that the one thing Francesca dreaded was to be swept into a heated embrace by a Californian goddess with flashing teeth and unknown antecedents. Tee was always one of those precious few who express their friendship in deeds rather than words. Francesca's pleasure was undeniable now. We could not have fallen into better hands.

"You can stay at my place, if you like."

"Oh, are you quite sure you've got room?" Francesca asked.

Her perfectly reasonable politeness still surprised me. I forgot I was no longer a phenomenon in people's lives. If we hadn't had a penny between us, if the nearest hotel had been in Alaska, she would have said the same thing. It was something about her I had been slow to appreciate. On the road I never questioned an offer. I even believed it did people good to have me stay with them.

"No, it's fine," said Tee. "There's room."

She didn't say there was plenty of room, or that she could squeeze us in, or that she wouldn't dream of letting us go to a hotel, or any of those phrases people use when they want to sound generous.

"Well, you're very kind," said Francesca. "Just for a few days."

"How are you doing, Tee?" I asked.

"I'm good," she said. "How're you?"

"It's just fantastic to be back."

It was too. I felt Francesca melting with the relief of meeting someone she could understand, someone who might be even more reserved and private in her nature than she was herself, giving her a chance to release some of the warmth and generosity of spirit that she had in abundance when she felt safe. It would have been foolish, of course, to suppose that this one fortunate encounter guaranteed our happiness, but I could not resist the soaring optimism that simply being in California inspired in me. It was easy to forget that those ebullient feelings had been born out of the circumstances of my first arrival there, on a motorcycle, five years earlier, in a state of freedom and detachment which would be impossible to repeat. Indeed, that previous visit might, from Francesca's point of view,

prove to be a serious handicap in her own search for an equal freedom. But then there was virtually no place left for us to go which did
not suffer from a similar drawback, or so I told myself.

So far at least the omens were good. I lay back in the Saab among
our bags and bundles, and gave myself over to the enjoyment of it.
We rolled up the highway to the city, over the brow of the hill
crowned by the notorious rows of houses that are 'all made of ticky-
tacky and all look the same', and came down through 19th Avenue on
our way to the Golden Gate. Tee was giving us a methodical account
of the state of things in her house and work. She was good with information anyway, being a computer programmer at quite a high level,
but was perhaps taking extra care because I had once accused
Californians of never finishing their sentences.

She shared a house in Mill Valley with a girl friend from New York
called Anna. Anna was in love with Seamus. Seamus had a small boy
called Sue.

"Sue?"

"No, Sioux – like the tribe."

"Does Sioux have a mother?"

"Uh-huh, but she split."

"Does Seamus love Anna?"

"Kind of, I guess. He hangs out a lot at the house. Sometimes she
hangs out with him. Sometimes he splits for a week or two. Anna
wants to move in with him, but I think he's afraid of the commitment. They're away right now, so you can have Anna's room."

"What does he do?" I asked. A British question, I thought.

"Mostly he runs dope. He's on a dope run now, to the border."

"What border? What dope?"

Tee's patience had a surface like obsidian, tough and opaque,
which concealed a serious aversion to any show of temperament. You
could ask any damn fool question you liked and she would answer it.
Her face might tell you what she thought of you, but her voice would
never waver.

"He runs marijuana to the Canadian border. They rented a
Winnebago. Do you know what that is? A mobile home? He's got several bales this time. He takes it up to Washington, then someone else
runs it through the border. That's the dangerous bit. Anna's going

with them this time. They're going to have a vacation on the way."

"And the kid?"

"He always goes. Seamus would never leave him behind. They're inseparable."

"What's he like?"

"He's a real sweet kid. But he's just wild."

"I meant Seamus."

"He's real nice. He sits in front of the TV all day drinking beer. It's really amazing how much beer he drinks. It doesn't seem to affect him. The kid runs wild in the house, and Seamus just lies on the couch. Sometimes I can't get into the kitchen because of all the empty beer cans, but he has a real kind nature. Only once I remember we were in a bar and he frightened me. I saw the violence in him. There were some men doing something – I don't know – something he didn't like, and he showed it. Suddenly I saw how big he was – he's a big man – and there was this real feeling of violence in him. Do you know what I mean? He didn't have to do anything. It was just there. It scared me, but at the same time I felt really protected. You know?"

I couldn't make out how Francesca was taking all this. Drugs had never figured in our life together. I was only a little bit nervous myself, that same old fear of being caught doing something illegal when the consequences were out of all proportion to the benefit. It was only the mildest frisson though. I knew Tee well enough to believe she was safe, and I knew also that marijuana was currently the biggest dollar-earning cash crop in California.

"Anna sounds as though she might be in a bit of a mess," I said.

"Yes. She's screwing up her life. She's clever too. She used to work on a magazine in New York, but she can't do any regular work now. She wouldn't see Seamus. It's all getting a bit heavy, and I hate coming back to a house full of garbage. I find it really hard to talk to her, but I guess I'll have to. I have to keep asking her for the rent. You'll like the house. It's pretty, and there's a good view from the deck."

All around us the Bay was blossoming out.

"Look, here's the Golden Gate Bridge coming now," I said.

The big red-leaded towers rose up ahead, tied by their swooping cables.

"How funny," said Francesca. "I always thought it was golden. What a beautiful view."

It was really getting to her now. I pointed out to the right.

"There's the city, down there."

The skyscrapers of San Francisco were clustered at the water's edge below the hill, like a flock of tall birds. The sun burst in from the Pacific, skipping over the Bay and shimmering in the windows of Berkeley far away on the ridge. I could look down on Pier 35 where five years before I had sailed away on an ocean liner in such a confusion of happiness and heartbreak. I saw the excitement on Francesca's face and felt a choking pleasure and pride in having brought her to this lovely place. Surely, my heart sang, this is going to be all right?

Then we climbed up to the rainbow tunnel and came out over Sausalito and down to Mill Valley.

The first thing I saw when we turned into Tee's street was a huge mobile home with Winnebago written all over it.

"They can't be back already," said Tee.

It was a pretty house all right. There was a hedge with a gate, then a bit of grass, then a glass door and a little hall, then the living room. There were windows in the far wall and, because the house was perched on a hill, you could see a long way. Beneath the view, stretched out on the sofa watching TV, was Seamus. He was long and blond, with a lot of whiskers, long straight hair tied behind his head, and not a drop of Irish in him anywhere that I could see.

He had a can of Budweiser in his hand, but I was not prepared for the exceptionally warm and friendly smile he gave us as we came in. Tee introduced us and, without getting up, Seamus stretched out an arm to each of us and said "Hi, man." Then he shouted:

"Sioux ! C'mere. Get your ass in here and meet some folks."

A cheerful little voice chirped back from the wooden balcony that Tee called a deck.

"No. I'm busy."

Seamus got up, then, towering above me, uncomfortably tall in those low-ceilinged rooms. As Tee had said, he was spare and lean despite all the beer, but without a hint of menace. In fact his voice was all chuckles, and his expression remained affable almost to the point of seeming foolish.

"You jest come here now, and no messin'," he said, and I heard the reluctant sounds of Sioux dragging himself to the room.

He also exceeded Tee's description. His face was truly angelic and his round blue eyes appeared utterly fearless. He was four years old, and his quality was such that you could not help trying to imagine the rest of his life and what he would make of all the confusion.

"This is Francesca, and this is Ted."

He slapped my back and I tottered forward involuntarily.

"He's been round the world on a motorsickle."

I got it then, just a touch of what Tee called 'violence'. It was not in the slap itself, of course, but in the way he referred to my journey accompanied by a physical gesture. The message I received read: "You've done something I respect. Maybe you're tougher than you look. So be careful. Don't underestimate me. I want your respect too."

I would not have called it aggressive. It had nothing in common with the spite of football hooligans or the hate of bigoted fanatics who need great jolts of adrenalin to overcome their inhibitions before plunging in the knife. He was a peaceful and, I judged, a naturally contented man, who simply took the law into his own hands when he thought it necessary. It was something you were expected to understand, just as there would be many things you would need to understand if you wished to associate freely with bears. Whether she knew it or not, Seamus was my wife's first introduction to the Wild West.

Seamus subsided on the sofa once more. Sioux scuttled back to the deck where he was taking one of Tee's chairs to pieces. He had already removed some cross struts and was now hoping to detach one of the legs.

"Would you stop that, Sioux," Tee said, then "Where's Anna?"

"She's out getting hamburger or something. You hungry?"

"Oh no," said Francesca, and described all the meals we had succumbed to on the plane. Her account was very animated and funny, and she made them sound even more awful than they were.

"Weren't you supposed to be up in Washington State by about now?" Tee asked Seamus at last.

"Man, did that one screw up." Seamus began to leak laughter like steam from a burst radiator. "That was a bummer, I tell ya. We got let down. Cops everywhere. We had to dump it all in Crescent City. But we're goin' again tonight. It's all fixed. Soon's Anna's back with the meat. Boy, I tell ya, farmin's a great life."

He sank back on the cushions, drained another Bud, and closed his eyes. The TV was twittering away irrelevantly in the corner. With every voice and image competing with every other it was like canned bedlam. I wondered why Seamus watched it. It couldn't have been for the excitement.

The haziness of imminent jet lag was stealing over the two of us, but we were determined to stay up at least until ten. Francesca disappeared into the bathroom to take a shower, and I wandered out on the deck. Sioux was rattling his chair-leg against the railing, and I took it from him and stuck it back into the chair and collected up the other bits and pieces and put the chair back inside. His protests were half-hearted and brief. It was clearly something he was used to, and he set about dismantling a desk instead. Below the deck was a small garden. A lemon tree and an orange tree both bore fruit, and I felt an absurd ecstasy at the sight of them. I suppose they made me feel that I was out in the wide world again and free.

The valley stretched ahead into the Bay. This was not Mill Valley's most picturesque aspect. The valley floor was marshy and dotted with industrial buildings, and the big freeway viaduct crossing it was squat and uninspired, but the hills around were interesting and the distant view was fine. I lapped up all the small differences from Europe with an insatiable appetite, the wooden houses, the shingle roofs, the stop signs and letterboxes on stilts, the big firs and redwoods standing high above the low single-storey buildings. Even the whooping of the police cars, such a hideous sound in itself, had its charm that evening.

Then I switched places with Francesca, following her into the bathroom and telling her about the oranges and lemons. The bathroom too had satisfying differences in its chunky enamelware basins with chamfered corners, the push-me-pull-you taps, the solid tiles curving up where the floor met the walls, the characteristic musky scent of American toiletry and the profligate cascade of water from the shower head.

What surprised me, what had always surprised me on other visits to the USA, was how immediately at home I felt with the domestic detail of America, the plumbing, the layout of the homes, the shops and gas stations, bars and restaurants. It was the familiarity of *deja vu*. Soaked up doubtless from a lifetime's exposure to mediocre and unremembered movies, it made me comfortable and gave me pleasure.

I wondered whether Francesca shared those feelings, and, if not, how long it would take her. Of course we didn't have to stay. It was all an experiment. But if we didn't stay, what *would* we do? My old passion for the landscape of Northern California flooded back, my old longing to find a few acres somewhere among those mountains and forests, to build a house, plant food, live a wholesome life. How I wanted it to work. But all that was a long way off. Meanwhile, we would stay down here and see how it went. And if we liked it we could stay long enough to have the baby here. And then, maybe, we could find that place in the hills . . .

The baby. It hardly seemed real to me yet, but it already had a name. ISWAS. On the drive through France we called out names to each other, all the boys' names first.

"Adolph, Adam, Alan, Anthony . . . what about Anthony?"

"No, hate it. Arthur, Andrew . . . don't mind Andrew."

"Ugh. Not for me. What about the B's. They're all nicknames. Bert. Imagine being called Bertie. Bob. Billy. Bernie . . . Hey, we forgot Alexander. I like that."

"Not bad. Let's go on . . ."

We finished up with William Alexander and went through all the girls' names we could think of, but only Isabel came up to scratch. Isabel Simon or William Alexander Simon. We called it ISWAS. Is Was Will Be. A strange thing coming into our lives, a welcome but unsettling dot on the horizon whose arrival was as predictable as a collision with a comet, and whose consequences were just as unimaginable.

Anna came back with pounds of hamburger meat and another twelve pack of Budweiser. She was a dark, lively girl, thin and a bit distracted. She smoked incessantly in nervous puffs. With her elbow resting on the arm of the chair her forearm traveled constantly to carry the cigarette between the ashtray and her lips like a robot on an assembly line.

We were hungry enough to eat by then. Anna confirmed that we were welcome to her bedroom, saying she would be back in a couple of weeks. Soon they were all leaving. Sioux had fallen asleep under the desk and Anna carried him out, promising to clean up when she got back. We filled several more grocery bags with empty cans and cigarette ends and went to bed among mountains of embroidered, piped and beaded cushions, dimly illumined by a glowing electric goose.

The next day was idyllic. Tee rode off to work on her bicycle and we were left in tranquil possession of her house and car. The sun streamed into the kitchen from across the Bay. We fixed our breakfast, enjoying the endless small novelties of American life: the vast containers of milk, the tiny sticks of butter, the cavernous refrigerator full of bits and leftovers going bad, the clever rubber nozzle on the kitchen tap, the flimsy little rashers of bacon. The *San Francisco Chronicle* was lying outside the front door and we took it to the breakfast table and shuffled the sections between us, laughing at its parish pump inanities. We seemed to be at peace with each other as never before, and we were in no hurry to do anything that might rob us of this unfamiliar feeling.

The flight to California was an inspired whim. We hoped it would satisfy our desire for a rural life, a good climate and reasonable access to intelligent society. There were problems, too, but none of them seemed insuperable. Most of all California had that pervading sense of freshness and freedom which now seemed to be infecting us both.

We were very fortunate to find ourselves in Mill Valley. I had never been there before, and it was the first time we had discovered something together. It obviously did a good deal for Francesca's morale to know that she was not once again following in the tired trail of some earlier adventure. When we couldn't make our breakfast last any longer, we took Tee's car down the hill and followed the main road round to the town center.

We passed the High School, and entered the rather ill-defined mouth of Miller Avenue. There were stores, bars, gas stations, surgeries, undertakers, realtors and take-away franchises on both sides of this main dual carriageway. To my European eye they looked like counters on a board game, moulded in one piece, forecourt, picket fence, ornamental shrubs and all, that you might move around at will.

Farther along the avenue, where the hills close in and the two carriageways merge into one, things became more sedate and controlled. We drove past a number of formal and elegant private houses with carefully tended gardens, and there were no more patches of rough ground between buildings. Above us on all sides we saw glimpses of other houses hiding behind big redwood and eucalyptus trees, and although the general sense was always of being surrounded by forested hills I began to realize that the forests concealed thousands of homes, as well as the streets to serve them.

The houses surprised me. Until we came to Mill Valley I found modern American domestic architecture depressing. The plumbing might be fine, but the homes themselves struck me as dreary, mass-produced shanties, crude pieces of carpentry held together with staples and glue, worth less than the shiny new Chevy outside. It was a prejudiced view, perhaps. Most small English towns have been ruined by millions of new houses as shoddy and monotonous as any, but they are built of brick and rooted in the ground to give an impression at the very least of solidity and permanence. Whereas the average American tract house seemed ready to fall over at the flap of a fly screen. Nobody could have persuaded me that a real house should be built of anything but brick or stone, until I came to California. Then my mind was changed instantly.

The houses I saw clinging to the hillsides and peeping out through the foliage were as adventurous as they were discreet. Every one seemed different, and most had the unmistakable stamp of somebody's dream come true. The ease with which they sprouted terraces, balconies, dormers, turrets and annexes of all kinds was a wonderful promise of the versatility of wood framing. The miracle was that it did not lead to aesthetic disaster, but was saved from confusion by the unifying effect of raw wood exteriors. From those first days in Mill Valley I began to develop a feeling for building in wood which did a lot to release me from the medieval world of stone and tile we had left behind in France.

The avenue split into two again around an island which accommodated the Mill Valley Lumber Yard and one or two old lap-boarded buildings, including the defunct mill that gave the valley its name. Once past this we were plunged almost immediately into the center of the town, a large square with shops on three sides and parking spaces and a bus depot in the middle. Beyond the square the land rose steeply to form the inland face of a ridge of hills and low mountains, part of the range that runs up the Pacific coast. Several thousand feet above Mill Valley and clearly visible was the peak of Mount Tamalpais.

Our first walk around the center of this small town was as exciting as any movie, as revealing as the best social documentary. More than any other place I knew, Mill Valley wore its heart on its sleeve, the heart of Marin in the seventies, the scene of Cyra McFadden's hilarious satire *The Serial*. Here every fad, fancy and fetish of the Californian lifestyle was brought to seamless perfection as yuppie couples went in pursuit of eternal youth and the latest wisdom. Here you could put your body and your senses through any combination of all the most bewildering processes and positions known to the human potential movement, and more. You could be focused and dispersed, centered and centrifuged, oxygenated, dehydrated, iced, steamed and boiled, you could hang like a bat in gravity boots, twirl like a dervish for Gurdjieff and learn to swallow your tongue. You could be pummelled, tickled, stroked and walked upon. You could be dragged back screaming to the womb, projected to the asteroids, taken through all the stages of human evolution from worm to ape and reduced to a macrobiotic dot. You could swing like ginseng in a macrame pot-holder and live on an exclusive diet of banana bread and bean curd without causing an eyebrow to twitch. And, most extraordinary of all, you could eat, drink, smoke, dress and talk like any ordinary unenlightened jerk from the rest of the universe, and that was okay too.

We sauntered around, looking into shop windows and doorways, delighting each other with readings from breathless notices for transcendental meditation, aerobic dancing, sufic perception, beansprout germinators, yoghurt incubators and sitar recitals. But it was very clear that amongst all this exotica the normal necessities of life were well provided for. There were banks, supermarkets and stores just like anywhere else. If they were a shade more expensive, it was a small price to pay for the privilege of living cheek by jowl with such affluent members of the counter-culture, the rich refugees from Haight Ashbury, who now supported their alternative habits on executive wages earned from nine to five in downtown San Francisco.

We talked to people in the street. It was easy. Most of them were already smiling, just as we were. It was the sun that did it. I had never known a more benign sun than the one which shone on Mill Valley. It was like a constant companion, a positive presence that amplified and enriched my mood; bright and cheerful in the morning, warmly encouraging through the day, gentle and golden in the late afternoon and always inspiring at sunset when it set the heavens on fire. It was reliable and irresistible, and it had a profound effect on the quality of life – not by making people better than they were, for only they could do that, but by urging them to be at least as good as they were able. Sometimes people seemed to become almost comically determined in their efforts to show goodwill. The greeting "HI" and the parting "HAVE A NICE DAY, NOW" always carried more emphasis than anything in between. All of life was qualified by those gilded brackets. Even if the message was bankruptcy or bereavement you could not, under such a sun, quite abandon hopes for a nicer day.

At any rate, what with that sun, the prospect of a small house on a hillside hidden among the trees, and the pleasantly eccentric village atmosphere of Mill Valley, we were quite taken with it, and before long we agreed that it would be a good place for Iswas to first see the light of day.

Our mysterious and distant child became suddenly and wonderfully real to me a few days later. I had other friends in the Bay area, and one was a doctor called Joe, an intensely loyal and generous friend who always made visits doubly pleasurable because of his passion for French champagne. He and his wife Pamela lived high on the ridge above Berkeley, and his windows were among those which had twinkled at us when we first crossed the Golden Gate. Now, on his deck and gazing down on the whole Bay, we toasted ourselves, and everyone else, in Mumm's before explaining our problem. Francesca was in her fifth month of pregnancy, and had not had a check-up for almost a month. We had not decided yet where to have the baby and who to sign on with.

Joe did acupuncture and his surgery was not equipped for antenatal care.

"Magde," he cried. "Magde Girgas. I'll fix it. You go and see Magde. You'll like him. We were at medical school together."

Magde Girgas was an Egyptian obstetrician (try saying that in a hurry) with a practice in downtown Oakland, where he had a few rooms in a cramped warren of doctors' offices. Oakland being what it is, his patients were a mixture of races and most of them seemed to be there when we arrived, so that I felt an immediate warm nostalgia for the crowds of Cairo and wished I were back on Talaat Harb chewing a spiced bean roll and with my whole journey ahead of me. These fantasies of lost freedom were still quite frequent and painful, and might hit me at any time like a migraine attack. Then, involuntarily and swift as thought, my mind would follow the events and decisions after my return and taste gall, because in that moment it would seem that I had tossed away the whole world and gained nothing but misery.

This time the moment was short-lived. Girgas called us in to see him, a strong, energetic man trying to work through an overload of patients before he left on vacation. He was merry and warm, and it was clear that Francesca found him sympathetic. He listened, prodded, and declared everything and everyone to be exactly as they should be. Then he asked me:

"Have you heard your baby yet?"

"No," I said, surprised. "I haven't. I thought that. . . well, isn't it much too early?"

We were both still quite ignorant of the boons and complications that medical science had brought to childbirth. Girgas smiled sweetly. He brought out a small piece of apparatus with a long cord attached to an earphone, and placed it carefully over Francesca's nicely rounded belly. Then he passed the earphone to each of us in turn.

I was unprepared for what followed. I had had no time to anticipate what I would hear, let alone what it would do to me. Suddenly I was listening to a heart beating very fast. It was disturbingly loud, pumping away vigorously and inexorably. What I heard was not the frail, scarcely viable embryo of my comfortable imagination. It was the drumbeat of a conquering army, an unstoppable force, overbearing and threatening. I was overcome with wonder and not a little fear. It was like traveling in time, more eerie than a voice from the dead. The dead, even if they speak, cannot return, but this was a voice from the future, and the future cannot be avoided.

There it was, saying 'I'm coming, I'm coming, I'm coming', and it hit me, like a punch in the solar plexus, that the life I had known for forty-eight years would be ended irrevocably by the arrival of this being. Once this child was born, I thought, I would be bound to it for as long as we both lived. I welcomed it, I marvelled at it, but I dreaded it too.

When Francesca heard the sound I saw the colour rise to her cheeks. She seemed electrified, bristling with awareness like an animal in the wild. She felt a different kind of awe and ecstasy which she beamed across at me. My own transparent emotion also impressed her deeply, as she saw me register the reality of the gift she was preparing for me. So, in that small, faintly oriental cell in Oakland, Iswas brought us together on a level of raw feeling that we had probably never reached before.

That incident was the beginning of my career as a father-to be. From that moment every decision I took, every plan I made, every ambition I formed was qualified by Francesca's pregnancy and the overwhelming prospect of the 'due date'. It was a strange new experience because the outcome was virtually inevitable. Regardless of how we prepared for it, on or around the first week in September Iswas would appear. We could try to make it more or less pleasant for ourselves and more or less healthy for the baby, but the event would occur whether we liked it or not.

For a while, though the biological clock went on ticking away relentlessly, life was little affected in its detail by 'our' pregnancy. We stayed with Tee for a month, still testing our resolve to stay in California. Usually we had the use of Anna's bed, but when the tribe returned from the north for brief periods we made do with a mattress on the floor of another room. During that time we hired a car and for five days explored the mountains, the valleys and the wild rivers of Mendocino, Humboldt and Trinity counties to get the feel of the country.

I was deeply concerned to know how Francesca would find it. Big wilderness areas were a part of my life now. I took to them as easily as a duck to water. I had only to wander on to a wooded mountainside with a stream below to see my cabin already built, my garden planted and my chickens clucking busily around the porch. Mill Valley might be a fine civilized place to rest, enjoy life and have a baby, but it satisfied no deep yearnings for me. We had often talked and agreed about the sort of country life I had in mind, but now we were beginning to face its physical realities, and they could be awe-inspiring and intimidating too.

There was no question that she was impressed. The great redwood groves north of Garberville lifted her heart as high as any of her beloved European cathedrals. The rivers swollen tumbling along their rocky beds made her heart race too. We came back over the saddles and peaks of the back country, majestic firs crowding over us cloaked in dark green with snowy mitts, sheltering a silent, mysterious world of life unseen.

I questioned her as often as I dared.

"Yes," she said. "I love it. It is beautiful. I'm so glad we're seeing it. Isn't it spectacular." But behind the praise and the enthusiastic acknowledgement I sensed a lonely figure, nervously hugging herself. And she did not say: "This is where I want to live."

I comforted myself with the thought that it was early days yet, that with the winter only just lifting off the mountains the splendour was perhaps also rather bleak, that a woman expecting her first child would hardly be in a mood to embrace the challenges and hardships of a pioneering life. Time and familiarity might change that.

"I don't know whether I could live without people," she said.

"Well, we wouldn't exactly be without them, would we? I mean, the only kind of land we could buy would have to be in areas where people were already settled. Anyway, there will always be some small town near by."

I had a sinking feeling as I said it. The towns were the biggest disappointment of the trip. After three years in Europe I had forgotten how primitive, how crude and unappetizing the small towns of North America could look. We had passed through many on the way but I saw no buildings to admire, no restaurants worth stopping at, no signs of a community with any interests outside commerce, domesticity, and perhaps the church. What could we find in common with the people who lived there? It required an act of faith to believe that wherever people lived there was always good company to be found. I was willing to make that gesture for myself, but I could hardly insist on it for both of us. And I had to remind myself that it was easy for me. After all, I had proved that I could do without people altogether.

My beautiful dream began to seem heavily compromised as I stumbled over the forgotten fact that there were two of us to please, and that it was not just a question of persuasion. It really had to work for both. Oh God, I thought, we'll never be able to get a clear run at anything. To hell with marriage!

"Anyway," she said. "What about schools?"

We almost had a row then, and drove on in tight-lipped silence through all the beautiful scenery until she said: "Look. I'm sorry. It's just that . . ."

And I said: "I'm sorry. I know we've got to have people and schools and all the rest, but can't we wait until . . ."

"It's no good you thinking you can stick me out in the wilderness somewhere," she said. "I won't do it. You've always got these grandiose schemes, and you just sweep everybody along, and look where they landed us. And now you're doing it again. Well, let me tell you that if we're going to live here I want electricity and hot water and people to talk to I can trust . . . "

And I said: "Of course you can have hot water, and we can always generate electricity and . . ."

Then she said, suddenly soft: "Oh Ted, it isn't that really. It's not your fault. You're a good man and I love you. I'm sorry to make you a battering ram."

She meant scapegoat. She had a genius for recycling jaded metaphors.

"Ted, it's just that I feel such a stranger here. I think I'll always feel like a European. I can't believe I'll ever want to share my thoughts and feelings with people who go around saying 'Hi! Have a nice day' all the time. Do you know what I dread. I think one day a scrumble of loud, well-meaning athletic women are going to break into our house and shout 'Hi! This is your baby shower!' and I shall run screaming all the way to the airport. I'm sure they're wonderful people. I'm sure baby showers are a really good idea. But it's not for me, and I wish to God you hadn't brought me here. I wish you would just stop meddling with my life."

So I got furious and stopped the car, and got out and rushed around under the trees kicking things, because I knew that the worst place, the deadliest place of all to have a row was in a closed car. Then she got out too and with her lips pursed she said:

"Why don't you say you're sorry? Why can't you help me? You hurt me so much . . ."

"I HURT YOU?" I screamed. "What about the way you hurt me?"

And so it went on for a while until we came to our senses again, and I said we really didn't have to decide anything yet, and she said maybe it would all seem different after a while, and we both said how sorry we were. Sometimes it seemed to me that marriage meant always having to say you're sorry. That's when I hated it most.

But as always we became very close and loving again, and before long we came down out of the mountains into a lovely valley full of pasture, enormous oak trees and old barns, with a small town in the middle. The town, at first sight, seemed only different from the others for being well away from the big highways and heavy traffic, and free to stretch itself a little. The buildings were mostly single-storeyed, and some had facades characteristic of frontier towns. Above one of them I saw the word GUNS in immense letters.

Francesca pointed to another store a little way along. It was a farm producers' cooperative with a nicely made carved wooden sign. Next to it was a small restaurant called Wild River Cafe. Both belonged unmistakably to a different culture altogether from the brash gun shop, but both were closed.

We turned up a side street to see several big wooden buildings. One had apparently been a cinema, and another might have been a mill. They were both shut. Then came a short row of low buildings leading to another restaurant and it was among these, as we made our way past for a coffee, that we struck gold.

It was called the Yolla Bolly Bookshop, and we glanced idly at the window expecting to see the usual racks of best selling pulp paperbacks, greetings cards and souvenirs. But this was a real bookshop, a shop either one of us would have been pleased to find even in London or San Francisco.

I looked at Francesca.

"Are you thinking what I'm thinking?" she asked.

I nodded.

"It's incredible," she said. "Let's go in."

We were welcomed by a petite woman with blonde hair and a grave but charming smile who demonstrated her judgement immediately by leaving us to look around quietly on our own.

The more we looked, the more we were impressed.

"This place is far too good," I whispered. "Do you think she sells anything?"

We were both wondering what sort of people would be living here to justify such a shop. There were books from publishers all over the world. Poetry, fiction, biography, art, much to do with natural history, and a good deal about homesteading, self-sufficiency and the associated crafts. It was a big stock, in two rooms, and all of it was carefully chosen by someone with not just a love of books but a real understanding of them. A clue to the mystery appeared when Francesca picked up, by chance, a printed sheet entitled 'Book Farm', issued by the Yolla Bolly Press.

"Do you have a press, too?" I asked the woman at the counter.

"Yes, we do," she said. "It's over in the corner of the valley."

And then it all came out. We had found the one cowboy valley in the middle of nowhere with a press which designed and produced books for publishers on the East and West coasts of America, including the prestigious Sierra Club of San Francisco.

"And the bookshop?" I asked. "Is that just a hobby, or do people round here read books?"

"You'd be surprised," she said. "There are some pretty interesting people in this valley. Actually, we're not even the only press here. We're just the biggest." And she laughed. It really was a fine joke.  '

"I see you've got electricity," I said, still laughing. "There wouldn't happen to be schools here too, would there?"

"Sure," she said. "Why? Are you thinking of moving in?"

"Maybe," I said.

"Yes," said Francesca.

"Well, you couldn't find a nicer place," she said.

Soon after we got back to Tee's house I had to fly to Paris for a TV show. It was an odd, unsettling experience. Only in France could a programme about books and authors command an audience of millions for more than an hour of prime time. To be chosen to appear on *Apostrophes* was a stroke of great good fortune. I was quite nervous of having to compete, in French, with a group of literary wits, but it turned out to be very enjoyable on the night. Thanks to Bernard Pivot, the expert host, I talked happily and fluently about my feelings on the journey, realizing as I did so how far I had had to suppress them.

I got a measure of the influence of the programme the following evening, when friends took me to dinner near the Pantheon. As we left the restaurant, various people at different tables rose in their seats to applaud. I was astounded, suspecting that some kind of trick was being played on me, but there was no doubt about it. I had become, as the romantic cliché has it, an overnight celebrity. And if it was true here in Paris, then it was true throughout the country. I toyed for a while with dreams of stardom, and then reluctantly let them go. How ironic, I thought, that I should have chosen just these weeks to leave France and live seven thousand miles away, where I would soon be forgotten.

But that was not the only irony I detected. A much more significant one hovered all around me at that time. On the programme I talked most about the importance of vulnerability when traveling. Only by making himself open and available to whatever comes along, good or bad, could a traveler ever hope to benefit personally and permanently from his journeying. Without vulnerability there could be no real change. Yet once he begins to discard his defences he realizes how much lighter and easier each step forward becomes and how overburdened he still is with the protective armour supplied by his sophisticated upbringing.

The greatest joy and reward of my four years of traveling, I said, was to learn how to be truly and fearlessly myself in all kinds of situations, and to find that this always brought out the best in those around me.

As I talked about it I had for a while the same thrilling feeling I was describing, only to realize then how far I had fallen from grace. Ever since my return I had been forced to burden myself with one piece after another of that same armour plating which I had just learned to cast off. In marriage, where I had hoped to find a new growth and freedom, I had become more cautious, more defensive and more stultified than ever. Just when I wanted to put all the lessons of the road into glorious, liberating practice, I was flung back instead into the old social barbarisms.

At my most pessimistic, I felt most sorry for Francesca. Her intuition had warned her.

"I know, one day, you'll have to go off on another long journey," she had told me when we first married.

"Nonsense," I said. "I've done it, and that's enough. I won't be a Flying Dutchman."

She was not impressed.

"I just hope it won't be too soon," she said.

Now my confidence was shaken. Perhaps she had known all along that the qualities which attracted her to me were the very ones which should have disqualified me from marrying at all. Perhaps she had perceived a simple truth, which I stubbornly refused to accept: that a man goes around the world because he cannot comfortably stay at home.

Francesca came to San Francisco airport to fetch me, driving the old Valiant we had bought for six hundred dollars before I went away. She stood there, trembling slightly, hardly daring to move as I came through the door, almost as though she expected me to appear with a starlet on each arm. She was carefully dressed and wore make-up which was something she generally did without. I hugged her, and she sighed.

"Do you love me?" she asked. "Do you really love me?"

"Oh yes, I do. I really do. Don't you know I do?"

"Sometimes I wonder whether you'll come back. I always think you'll find someone glamorous and fall in love."

"I love you. How could I fall in love with anyone else? I don't even see anyone else."

"It's just that I feel rather fat and unlovable. Oh, I'm so glad you're back. It's been getting a bit hectic at the house. Seamus and Sioux have been there most of the time. And then there's the coke business."

"Seamus isn't drinking Coke?"

"No, no. Cocaine. Anna deals in it. It's funny really. I didn't know what was going on at first. All these bright, smartly dressed people would turn up at the door, people I'd never seen, and they'd wave across the room at me, saying "Hi!" as though we were old classmates and disappear into the kitchen with Anna. I always wondered why anyone would want kitchen scales that weighed to the nearest milligram. I think Tee's a bit pissed off with it. She doesn't like it in the house. That, and the beer cans, and the strained voices calling Seamus long distance from Washington state."

"Maybe we should start looking for another place."

"Well, I wasn't sure whether you'd want to. I half-expected you to come back from Paris saying you couldn't bear to leave France after all."

I took a deep breath.

"No," I said firmly, "I like it here. How about you?"

"Yes," she said. "I want to stay. I think it will be good for me. Good for us. I'd like to make plans for the baby, to sign up with a doctor. And can we go back and look at our valley again? But you probably want a few days to recover . . ."

"That's the last thing I want," I said. "We'll start tomorrow."

We decided a lot of things on the drive from the airport, and the positive mood made us both feel fine. At such times I forgot our difficulties and foresaw only happiness. And the important thing, I realized, was that such times were becoming more frequent.

We went out next morning in the ineffable sunshine to find a house. We looked in the newspapers and visited all the agents as we found them by driving around. Houses were scarce and expensive. Agents had difficulty controlling their laughter when I told them what I wanted to pay. Four hundred dollars a month seemed like a fair price to me for a small place, but not to them. They said they'd let us know.

There was a small office on East Blithedale we hadn't tried. A smart-looking woman sat inside the window. Her poodle greeted us first, then she did. Her manner was very sweet and tough. We sat down and I told her what we were looking for. She was as amused as all the others, and said there wasn't much hope. It was our cue to raise our offer or leave, but I just sat there and looked at her in silence. She began to riffle through a card index, and then said, just the way they do it in the movies:

"Now wait a minute. There's just a chance. This place came in this morning. Of course, it's out to all the agents. It's most likely gone. They'll be standing in line all around the block for this one. A small house on Laverne. They want three seventy-five. You wanna go for it?"

She reached for the phone and pushed the buttons. Then she introduced herself to someone called Oscar. Her voice was like a honeyed buzz-saw.

"Thank you, Oscar, I'm fine. Now, are you still looking at people for Laverne, because I have a very sweet young couple here. You are. Good. I'll show them up there. Now, Oscar, I want to ask you as a very special, personal favour to me - and, Oscar, I do think you owe me one – I want you to extend the loan on that block over at Tryon. You won't? Good. 'Bye now, Oscar. Have a nice day."

Her equanimity was marvellous.

"When would you like to see it?" she asked. "I'm busy now. After lunch?"

We went back at two and followed her enormous brown estate car to a pleasant street uphill from Miller Avenue. She drove along it and back again, obviously lost, and then stopped and beckoned to us. I got out to talk to her and she pointed at a narrow tarred driveway which shot up from the road. It was the steepest drive I could ever remember seeing. There was nothing at the top but big redwood and eucalyptus trees.

"I guess it's up there," she said, doubtfully. "Do you think I'll make it?"

That was the only hint she ever gave that even her life might have its uncertainties.

"I don't know,' I said, 'but you may as well try. I don't suppose you'll fall off."

When we were halfway up, the house became visible on the left. It was a small wood-framed cottage, square, white-painted and unpretentious. The manoeuvres when we reached it were hair-raising. A small truck was already parked on the little spur that ran off the drive in front of the house, and we had to turn our cars on what felt like the side of a pyramid, but we managed it and walked up a few crumbling brick steps to the front garden.

Standing for a moment in the hot sun on a lovely little lawn we looked around us. The view was incredibly rural. Even though the valley was crammed with houses and streets, we could see only two or three houses on the hillside opposite. The rest was trees and magnificent flowering bushes, surrounding us on all sides.

We were both excited and trying to keep a straight face. I already had that breathless ache you get when you know your good fortune is going to follow through. First our cowboy valley, then this. Even without looking into the house we knew it was right, and the rightness of it was of the utmost importance to us. The coming of Iswas gave our every step a luminous significance, as though we were looking through the eyes of an unborn child – as though our emotions were already making themselves felt in that dark, fluid world where the future was taking shape.

The agent was in a hurry, and we were not allowed to dawdle. The interior of the house was very simple. The front door opened directly into the living area which stretched the length of the house, about twenty-five feet, with a brick fireplace at one end. Off to the side were a kitchen and a bathroom, and above these was an open gallery, long and narrow. The roof rose in one steep slope from the living room wall to the gallery wall. We found out later that it had been built as a summer cottage for a San Francisco family in pre-war days when Mill Valley was a small hamlet, but only half the house was finished, accounting for its lean-to shape. If the roof had been made of glass it would have been like many Paris studios, but there were plenty of windows, and the feeling was light, airy and spacious.

A bulky man in white overalls and a white cap was touching up some paintwork in the kitchen. I told him how much I liked the place and asked him about the heating. He had ginger hair and a trim ginger toothbrush moustache, and spoke with an extraordinary pedantic precision.

"The gas convection heater should provide for most requirements," he said, "and it can, of course, be supplemented by use of the open grate, subject to prevailing weather conditions. The wind may sometimes cause unsuitable down-draughts."

The words were as soulless as a manual, but there was an underlying awkwardness and diffidence which intrigued me. I had no chance to pursue it. The agent dragged me away with her brusque, commanding voice.

"If you have any questions, Mr Simon, you should ask me. The owners don't like to have their workmen distracted from their work. They are paid by the hour."

The painter went back to his work, seemingly unaffected by this loud announcement, and we left the house agreeing that if there were any chance of our renting it we would be delighted.

We had some tedious forms to fill in at the agent's office and our lack of local references was an obvious handicap. I produced an American copy of Jupiter's Travels which had just been published with my picture on the flap, and she admitted that it might serve. I said we would be going north for the weekend, and she said to give her a call Monday morning in case, though we shouldn't expect anything because there'd be a line as long as Miller Avenue for this one and we didn't really have a chance.

The next day was Friday and we got onto the freeway early. The Valiant, old as it was, took the journey without a murmur of complaint, its famous 'slant six' engine delivering a smooth power that was a thrilling change from small European cars.

That weekend a solemn, avuncular estate agent took us around in his four-wheel-drive jeep. We saw pieces of land all around the hills, some of it too expensive, some too precipitous, some too remote, some too dry. When we were out there I saw Francesca shrink from the savagery of it, and when we returned to the valley I saw her relief as she recognized in the flat pasture studded with mighty oaks a resemblance to the parks of England.

There was one piece of land in particular, with meadows, woods and a river which we passed several times and which she always pointed to. There was no house on it, only a well. We asked around and found it belonged to a retired couple who had moved to another town. Everybody told us there was no chance. People had been trying to buy it for some time because it was a 'choice piece'. But the owners had a daughter still living in the valley and Francesca, who was determined to play a part in this, went to visit her. She came back triumphantly with the names and telephone number of the owners, in a town called Red Bluff. I rang them. It was the wife who did the business.

"Well now," she said, "it just so happens we just figured maybe it was time to sell."

Even the price was right.

I began to get scared. It was too easy, and after all this wasn't what I had wanted at all. My dream had always been of hills and streams tumbling through rocks. She said she sure would give me first chance, and I promised to call back.

On Sunday we went back to the piece of land in the hills I had liked the best. It was steep, with a shelf at the top and some flat land at the bottom where two year-round creeks met. The view from above was splendid, and you could just see some of the roofs in the valley to the south. We walked down to the river, Francesca struggling a little with the extra weight of Iswas who was already a formidable presence. The water gushed and swirled deliciously round the honey-coloured boulders. We found a pool among the rocks deep enough to swim in and we took off our clothes and splashed about happily for a while. Then I left her sprawled in the sun, and scrambled back along the river bed and up one of the tributaries that flowed between two steep hills. The overhanging trees formed a cool, green-glowing cavern of light and shade. The water trickled and spurted among mossy stones and ferns and fallen alders. I came back and talked about a dam I might build, a turbine to generate electricity, a hydraulic ram maybe to pump water up the hill, solar energy heaters, fish tanks to breed trout, catfish, even lobsters, methane generators, wind chargers; all the fine schemes I had learned about and stored up from Africa, America, Australia, India, waiting for the time and the land to come together.

As I talked, all those dreams became as real as we were. She said she would never forget how happy I looked in that river, dreaming my dreams, and I said I would never forget how beautiful she looked. It was true that I had never seen her so freely at ease with her own body as she was that day on the rocks in the river, and for a while it seemed that we might have a chance at those dreams, but they were my dreams not hers. The long climb back to the top reminded her, and the long drive back to the valley underlined it, and that evening I knew it was too much to ask.

We passed through the valley land again, at dusk, under a brilliant red sky, and I had to agree that it was beautiful down there as well as handy for town. On Monday morning I called the agent in Mill Valley and she said:

"Good news. You've got it. I never thought you would. Come back soon and sign up. Have a nice day."

An omen like that is irresistible. We had both felt so sure of the place. Here was the evidence that our feelings were in tune with our fate, that this was a time for bold decisions.

"Let's go back and look at the piece on East Lane," I said.

We parked the Valiant outside the gate, flicked up 1-2-3-4 on the old brass combination padlock, and went in. Immediately in front of us was an area shaded by oaks and walnut trees, with big blackberry bushes spreading between them. As we came near a flock of quail startled us as much as we had startled them by whirring off suddenly, followed by a small deer streaking for cover in the woods.

Some way over to the left were the fences and loading ramp of an old corral built of grey, weathered fir and redwood. The grass everywhere was long and still green. Soon the sun would begin to dry it, and it would be ready to cut for hay. Then the cows would come on for the summer.

The rains had stopped now and there would be no more until late September. The creeks still had water in them but there were places where we could ford them and we walked all around the land. There were several meadows, big and small, separated from each other by some acres of woodland, a mixture of oak and ash. We found many lovely spots among the trees, on the edges of the creeks, which stirred my feelings almost as much as the mountain land did, while the mountains themselves were always there and visible at the edge of the valley, beckoning but not oppressive. I had to admit it made sense to come down here. There would be no long time-wasting journeys into town over rough roads. The soil was fertile and the land would increase its value more rapidly. Anything would grow on it, and a child might be safer here.

At one particular place under the trees we stopped for a long time. It was a broad, shallow gully where the usual scrub was supplanted by a carpet of emerald grass as fine and delicate as silk threads. The trees reached across it to form a cool, green bower. I took a picture of Francesca standing in the grass beneath the leafy arches, a small and infinitely touching figure in black gum boots, a loose cotton dress, dark hair with a trace of copper framing her pale, shy face and her fingers lightly clasped in front of her. The sunlight fell on us as though filtered by stained glass and I recognized a recurring theme in the life of my imagination, a haven of translucent green in dappled sunlight which aroused in me feelings of deep relief and joy. Where the image sprang from I could not say, but it came to me in dreams and enticed me on my travels, and it was a conclusive element in my own decision that day that I would sacrifice my mountains for this piece of valley land.

Before we left the valley that afternoon I telephoned the people at Red Bluff and told them I wanted to buy their piece.

"Maybe one day," Francesca said, "you will be able to buy your mountain land as well. I would love that."

Every new decision committed us more firmly to California, yet we had been there scarcely six weeks, and two of those I had spent in Paris. We were rushing with the tide again. Often something would remind us of life in France and cause us both to feel deep pangs of loss. The trigger was usually trivial, and almost always something to do with food and drink. Just a glance at the cheese counter in a Safeway store was enough to precipitate remorse. We both loved the great French country cheeses, and Francesca's feeling for Roquefort amounted to an obsession. Pregnancy had played a strange prank on her palate and she could no longer bear to eat it, but the *thought* of it was still enough to revive old longings.

No supermarket could hope to compete with the provincial food markets of France. Every Saturday, at our nearest small town, the wine growers poured in from the hills and plains to buy provisions for the week, to choose some specially succulent beef or lamb for the Sunday *grillade,* to pick up seedlings for the garden, feed for chickens, fertilizer and herbicide, a pair of boots or a new handle for the *pioche.* Whole families came to mingle with the townspeople and crowd around the stalls. And the merchants drove through the night and the dawn to have their stalls open on time. Fishmongers rolled in from Mèze and Séte; the *charcutiers* came down from the cold uplands of Lacaune with their cured hams, their myriad sausages, *pâtés,* briskets and brawns; the cheese merchants came from even further and higher, the mountains of Auvergne and Cantal, bearing cheeses of every origin, varying in size from pillboxes to millstones.

Market gardeners abounded, there was fruit from Spain and North Africa as well, and because of the important Arab element in the population the market had a strong exotic appeal too. The merchants displayed their foodstuffs with the loving concern of connoisseurs, showing their wares to best advantage in a way that emphasized the beauty of food and its importance in life, rather than dwelling on such negative matters as hygiene and packaging, so that we were surrounded by bounteous arrays of beautiful food that stimulated the appetite and the enjoyment of life.

Every merchant was the proprietor of his stall, and his or her presence and personality was as important as the food on the counter. We could not think of cheese without thinking of Charley, the plausible and slightly roguish merchant, who acted out a comic rivalry with his wife, and tempted us with plugs of Roquefort drilled out of the great foil-covered slabs labelled 'Société' and 'Marie Grimal'; this one strong and salty, this one sweet, this one creamy and mature – oh, that Roquefort! It was made in the mountains only a few hours away and has never tasted as good anywhere else in the world. And then, by association, we thought of Raymond the fishmonger from Mèze, a gymnast and juggler, who flew and twirled behind his loaded, ice-strewn counter. He wrapped his fish in paper printed with recipes for fish soup and *rouille de seiches,* and the packages vanished and reappeared in his hands to win a reluctant grimace from the beady-eyed matrons jostling each other to get a good look at the *baudroie* and the big, shiny black mussels.

There was Fernand, and the laconic *charcutier* who used to josh me with his attempts to pronounce English. There was the herb lady, and the live-chicken man, and the family from Marseilles with the incredible displays of olives, pickles, nuts, oils, vinegars, salted fish and dried fruit and, I always suspected, a hundred other things I had not yet discovered, set out on barrels and boxes under an awning behind the market building.

How could the anonymous shelves of a supermarket, with their cans and boxes and sterile plastic slabs, begin to compare with the sensuality and the sociability and the visual feast of such a market? Thinking about it, and going on to wallow in memories of restaurants, hotels, country roads and beaches, we were soon swallowed up by an orgy of nostalgia. It seemed to us then that nowhere in the world were the true satisfactions of life better understood and provided for than in France, and that we had been insane to leave it. And only after a while would we return to our senses and remember just how unhappy we had been there. Then I would think about the land we were planning to buy and the great open spaces around it, and I would recall how cramped I had begun to feel, not just in France but in Europe, how controlled and regulated life had seemed, and how often the response to an idea was 'No'. What if you wanted more than to slip, unprotesting, into a ready-made off-the-peg life, pre-tested, taxed, insured and guaranteed for twenty years?

So we were often buffeted between our love of the old life and our hopes for the new. And I, who had tasted and admired a dozen lives all equally attractive in their quite different ways, had to resist them all fiercely as they were brought to mind by one thing or another during the course of every single day. I did it by concentrating on the virtues of America as we discovered them.

The simplicity and flexibility of life in America struck us as soon as we started to fix up the house on Laverne. Almost the first thing I tackled was the telephone. We wanted one quickly, and I imagined that it would be a lot easier and quicker to get one here than in England or France, so I guessed that at worst we might have to wait a week or two.

I called the company to find out.

"Do you have a phone?" asked the trained, polite voice.

"No, of course not," I said, bewildered. "If I had one I wouldn't be asking you for one."

"Yes, sir. I know, sir," she said, patiently, "but do you have your own phone to plug in, or do you wish to purchase or hire one?"

"You mean people own their own phones?" I asked, amazed.

"Yes, sir, they sure do," she said. "Now since there is already a line to your house, all you have to do is come down here to the phone store and choose a phone."

"How long will it take? I mean, how soon can I come?"

"The store is open from nine thirty in the morning through five thirty in the afternoon, sir," she said.

That's all there was to it. We took our red telephone home in a plastic bag the same day, and before we got there the line was live and had our number. Anywhere else in the world at that time, such facility would have seemed miraculous.

The landlord was there when we arrived. He was the same man we had taken to be a housepainter on our first visit with the agent. Remembering the agent's remarks I wanted to laugh and joke with him about it, but he received us very formally, in the same stiff and pedantic manner as before, without a smile. If he had been merely taciturn I might have chanced it, but there was some great unease struggling inside him which put him at odds not just with the smiling culture of Mill Valley, but with the world at large. He was too concerned with keeping the lid down on himself to risk a spontaneous chortle.

All the same, he said we had got the place because he had happened to be there when we came and had liked the look of us.

"It will be quite satisfactory to have a writer in residence," he said, but when I tried to explore his interest he rebuffed me bluntly, saying his studies in theosophy left him no time to read ordinary books. His awkwardness was so evident that I was not offended, and he was nice to us in his way. When I realized how much more at ease he was with Francesca, I left the talking to her.

"We like your house so much," she said. "It's very important to us because we are going to have a baby in September."

Then the first smile appeared, slight but unmistakable beneath the ginger moustache.

"Are you really?" he said. "My mother will be interested. There is a lot of fruit here which you may pick and use."

He began to point around the grounds.

"Those are apple trees. Over there is a pear. There are Japanese plums in back of the house, and up there you will find cherries."

"Everything is so fertile here," she said. "It's really incredible to see all these trees and bushes shooting up everywhere. We've been living in a small village in the south of France and the ground there is so barren and rocky, all that will grow there is vines."

"Is that so?" he said, almost eagerly.

"Well, not exactly," I murmured, but he went on, paying me no heed.

"Since you come from France, you will have something in common with the gardener. He is supposed to come once a week to improve this lawn and keep things in order. I would like you to let us know if he fails to come. He is a Basque, from France."

"How extraordinary," I said.

"Not at all," he told me, reprovingly. "There are many Basques in San Francisco. Now, so far as the garden is concerned, we ask you only to keep these shrubs watered. You may use the garage, but I have quite a stock of automobile parts there which it is not convenient to move. That is another of my interests. You may like to see them."

"By all means," I said, anxious to ingratiate myself.

He had fenders, doors, radiator grilles, and other large pieces of bodywork from a car dating somewhere around the fifties. I thought I had recognized the model they belonged to.

"Aren't those from a Dynaflow?" I asked humbly.

"No, sir, they are parts of a Cadillac I intend to reassemble."

He went on to talk about them for a long time, and it was obvious they had a calming effect on his spirits. I learned my lesson and did no more than grunt as he spoke. Then between us we brought in another piece, the hood, from his pick-up, and placed it carefully on the pile. By the time we had finished I felt we were almost friends.

"I shall tell my mother about your wife," he said as he climbed into his cab. "I'm sure she will want to know you are comfortable."

I went back up to the house where Francesca was waiting.

"What a peculiar man that is," I said. "Don't you think so? What is it about him?"

"I don't know," she said. "I think he's rather sweet. Isn't it wonderful about the fruit?"

"It's weird," I said. "I feel as though we've been visited by a gnome, or a dwarf. That's what he is. An outsize dwarf. A crusty, humourless dwarf with a heart of gold who hammers on old motorcars in underground garages and distributes jewels in the form of apples, cherries and plums."

She was looking down at the floor. Her face had gone dark and pensive.

"What's the matter?" I asked "Is it the lino?"

The floor was covered with green linoleum. It was the only ugly feature of the house.

She didn't speak.

"What is it?" I insisted.

"I wish you didn't have to go away," she said.

My heart sank, resentfully.

"Why do you have to think about that now?" I said.

"I think about it all the time," she said.

"Well, it can't be helped," I said abruptly. "We always knew I would have to go. Anyway, it won't be for very long," I added, defensively. "Then I'll be back for good."

"Hah," she exclaimed bitterly. "You'll always be going away. You're a gypsy. Admit it. But you shouldn't be leaving your wife at a time like this. It's cruel."

I didn't know what to say. It was true that I had to go back to England, to promote the paperback. The dates had been fixed long ago. There was nothing I could do about it, even if I had wanted to. It was too important. And because it was inevitable, I could forget about it. But she couldn't. I wanted to help her, but I didn't know how. My frustration made me angry.

"For God's sake," I said, "why do you always have to choose the best moments to drag up some misery or other? You know I've got to go. You know I'll be back in plenty of time."

She looked at me then with the venomous expression that I dreaded.

"You might at least say you're sorry. Why don't you say you're sorry?"

"I'm sorry," I said. I didn't sound sorry.

"You're not sorry. You'll be glad to get away from me. You'll be glad to leave that fat old frump you married by mistake. I can see you now, swanning around the country meeting glamorous women and talking your silly head off about your bloody journey – and all those bloody women you made love to. All those famous love affairs the whole world knows about . . ."

She was in a frenzy of hate and I was paralyzed with fury, incapable of doing anything to stop it, and even as she heaped on the abuse and I fought back, I was asking myself: How does it happen so quickly? How can I be so helpless? Why can't I do something to stop the pain? Didn't I learn anything, after all?

"I'm getting out of here," I cried. "I can't stand any more of this."

"That's right," she said. "Run away, just as you always do. Just as you always have."

I turned and made for the door.

"Help me," she screamed.

"I can't," I shouted, and ran straight into the man from the gas company.

He was in blue overalls and carrying a bag, and he almost fell backwards off the stoop, but his face registered no surprise. They must have trained him well down at the PG&E.

"Hi!" he said. "I've come to check out your connections."

Every vestige of emotion disappeared from Francesca's face. The livid skin blushed. The deep, tortured creases in the forehead smoothed out. The bitterly bunched lips unpursed themselves. She smiled her nice smile and said, "Come in."

"Go right ahead," I said, and walked out into the garden, still churning inside. It was a horrible feeling that made me gasp for breath. After a little while she came out too. She tried a little smile, and I tried one back.

"Do dwarves have mothers?" she asked.

"They certainly do," I said, "and they're nuts about theosophy."

She came over and touched my arm, and I held her very tight.

"Saved by the gasman," I said.

"Oh, my love, I'm so sorry," she said, crying. "I don't know where it comes from. It's not you I see standing there then, but someone very cold and remote. I'm sorry about the things I say. They aren't true. You do believe that, don't you?"

"God, I really want to."

The gasman came out of the door and looked straight at us. He said: "You're okay. I'll turn you on."

Then he walked round to the back of the house.

"That is a hell of a gasman," I said. "One day I'll learn to do what he does."

"One day you won't need to," she said. "Soon, I promise."

**18**

We must have seemed a strange and lonely couple, so many thousands of miles from our origins, with no family to call upon and no roots to sustain us at such a critical time. It's true that all our friends in California were immigrants from somewhere. Joe was from Alabama, Tee from Georgia, Anna from the East, Seamus from the Midwest. It was rare to meet a Californian in California, but at least they were Americans.

If our isolation was a predicament I was blind to it. I had not lived in my own country for twelve years, and I had spent four of those years on the road, proving that I was equally at home anywhere in the world.

"Perhaps you'll never be at home anywhere," people suggested, but I rejected this idea and refused to think about it. How could I entertain such a thought when I was married and had a child on the way? As long as I wanted a home (and I fervently believed that I did), why shouldn't it be wherever we chose to have it? There would always be good people around anywhere. As long as we loved and cared for each other, as long as we got along, surely everything would be fine ?

So I unconsciously extended the philosophy of the solitary traveler to include my wife, and forgot the lesson of Penang.

My idea of getting along was to be in charge. It was an easy mistake for me to make, so ingrained was my habit of solitariness. As an only son, with a father long since dead and a mother inevitably distant, however much loved, I knew little about the comforts and duties of family life, neither as the beneficiary nor the donor.

Oh, my method of control was nothing so crass as the giving of orders or the administering of reproofs in the Victorian manner. On the contrary, I was the mildest of husbands and the most eager to please.

"All I ever need," I said, "is to know you're happy."

It was not Francesca I wished to control, but our relationship. I would do almost any job rather than ask her to do it if it might provoke a disagreement. So I cooked and shopped and packed and did a thousand things that she would normally have done, and no doubt, had it been possible, I would have had her baby for her too.

And of course I consulted her at every turn and won her agreement to my suggestions by force of a lifetime's experience of doing all those things for myself, while insisting that she was naturally free to choose. So, sweetly and innocently, I forestalled every possibility of reasonable complaint. And that was my idea of getting along with my wife.

Then, when her frustration became intolerable and she exploded in misery and resentment, when the terrible out bursts of irrational fury swept over us, I was shocked and horrified and didn't know where to turn, because after all I had done everything a man could do, so how could I be to blame? And she deferred to me, as a hero and an older, wiser man, until once again her sense of impotence and futility burst into flame.

We were engaged in a desperate venture and, despite our love for each other, we would probably have been lost but for Iswas who, like the US cavalry, came drumming and kicking to the rescue. Francesca's own body went through profound physical and chemical changes to allow her to sustain another life, and her strength and optimism grew as Iswas grew inside her. Our life centered more and more around our preparations for a child, and in pregnancy she had a role I could not undermine, which restored her pride in herself. So gradually, as the weeks in Mill Valley ticked past, our crises diminished and we knew that, after all, we were going to win through.

Making the house habitable was wonderful fun. It was Tee who told us about Cost Plus, a store that imported traditional goods on a vast scale from the poorer parts of the world. Released by this happy discovery from the dire dullness of Sears and J. C. Penny we wandered around their emporium in transports of delight. We bought

Japanese crockery, Mexican glasses, Chinese baskets, and two Indian rugs, one almost big enough to hide the lino. We had a Romanian table, chairs from Taiwan and saucepans from Korea. All of it seemed, to us, phenomenally inexpensive. We were not looking for costly things to last a lifetime. Most of those we already had waiting for us in France. We wanted an absolute minimum of simple, economic stuff to live with now, through a warm summer.

It was a revelation to discover how little we needed, and how little we had to spend. We added a foam mattress from Berkeley to put down in the gallery, a chic standard lamp from a design shop in Sausalito and, our major investment, a sofa from Macy's.

We were infatuated with our little home. We wanted everyone to see how lucky we were. We bought wine and good food and invited everyone to come and see. Joe and Pamela, Tee, Anna, Seamus and Sioux all came and sat on our big rug or out on the lawn to congratulate us and admire the view.

They were all interested in our plans for Iswas. Which hospital were we going to? Had we chosen a doctor yet? About childbirth we were both practically ignorant. Neither of us had ever seen a child born. Now that it had become the only important thing in her life, Francesca was greedy for information.

Apart from Seamus, none of our immediate friends had children, but some of their friends did, and we quickly picked up all kinds of information about how things were done, or could be done. We found out which were the good books. Older women told us about the barbaric days of the fifties, when mothers-to-be were drugged unconscious and had their babies extracted like corks from bottles. Equally improbable seemed the ultra-avant-garde ideas of pioneers who were delivering their babies underwater, but there was a broad range of possibilities in between, all of which were practical in their different ways.

A surprising amount of information came our way quite casually in the streets and shops. Other women would notice Francesca's shape and say 'Hi! When're ya doo, honey?" and say it with such kindness and convincing interest that she found she liked it. And they would talk unashamedly about problems of labor and birth and breast feeding. People lent us books about the Le Boyer method, and the La Leche League and the Lamaze technique, and pretty soon we saw that having a baby in this day and age meant being caught up in a raging battle, swept hither and thither by rival ideologies, until we would be forced to become militant supporters of something or other.

The most vociferous were the Earth Mothers, who made 'being a woman' into a religious crusade. For them, every drug and device invented since Paracelsus was an instrument of man's repression of women. From them we got all the alarming statistics about the percentages of Caesarian births in this or that state or hospital, where babies were whipped out with the knife the way they once used to whip out the appendix. They talked about the evils of the epidural, the sin of episiotomy, and about the whispered side-effects of various drugs.

They were unnatural allies for Francesca, who found them embarrassing.

"I would hate to be one of those women in cast-off crinolines with breasts and babies dangling round their waist, prattling on about how beautiful it is to be a woman and a mother," she said, but even so some of their points went home, and she became quite keen to be delivered by a woman.

For myself I took it for granted that I would be there at the birth of Iswas, but that was as far as I went. I did not want to influence her decisions, and I was reluctant to take it too seriously so soon.

"The way people go on about it," I said to anyone who would listen, "you'd think childbirth was a disease, and that unless we find the right cure it will be a disaster. I can't take that view. It seems to me the odds are all on our side. Women are giving birth every second of the day in every conceivable kind of circumstance; standing, squatting, lying, swinging from branches, in grass huts, in the backs of taxis, in igloos and dugout canoes, and by and large it works out. So why should we, with all the advantages of affluence, civilization and expert medical help, have anything to worry about?"

This was not a popular speech in many quarters, and eventually I thought it was pretty stupid myself and dropped it. By the time we decided to go shopping for a doctor in earnest, I was quite ready to take the whole thing as seriously as anyone

Magde Girgas was too far away, in Oakland, to be our regular doctor, and we had to find one. We could have shopped in the yellow pages of course, but the need for a more human connection kept us asking around. Soon enough someone came up with a name. She was a female obstetrician at the hospital at Greenbrae only fifteen minutes away from our house. We made an appointment, and met a fat and jolly woman in a white coat. Her office was in a fine modern medical building which we took to be a wing of the hospital next door. She told us what the routine of pre-natal care amounted to, and I thought her very competent and likable. If we signed up with her, she said, it would cost eight hundred dollars.

That seemed very little. I had been bracing myself to meet the high cost of medicine in the United States. Were there no other costs? I asked.

Yes, there would be lab fees.

How much would they come to?

Well, they varied, but might be twenty or thirty dollars a visit. Say two hundred all told.

"But that's still only a thousand dollars," I said. 'Forgive me, but we don't want too many nasty surprises. I did think it cost more than that to have a baby over here."

"Well, you have the costs of the delivery," she said. "That's charged by the hospital."

"Aren't we in the hospital?" asked Francesca.

"Oh, no, this is the medical center. The hospital is separate."

Francesca and I grinned at each other to hide our confusion.

"So who would do the delivery?" I asked.

"I would hope to, of course."

"And how much is that?"

"The fee is five hundred dollars."

"But that doesn't cover everything?"

I was feeling hot under the collar conducting this mercenary interrogation, but she seemed quite happy, if a bit slow to anticipate my questions.

"No," she agreed. "You have to pay the hospital daily rate, and then of course there are ..."

"The lab fees," we chorused.

We were children of the British National Health system. In a world of private medicine we were like babes in the wood. It felt very strange to be questioning a doctor about her fees and expenses. It had the flavour of sacrilege, at first; a bit like bargaining with a priest over the price of salvation. Then I thought, to hell with this. Even in England doctors have to be paid, and drug companies make their profits. If it shocks us to discover just how much we have been getting for nothing back home, then maybe the shock will do us good. And at least, if we're paying, it gives us the right not to be apologetic.

From then on I found the whole process quite invigorating, and enjoyed the novel view of a doctor as someone who did what you paid for, like a plumber or a garage mechanic. But then, for once in my life, I could afford the luxury.

The total added up to around two thousand dollars for a normal birth, and that was less than I had feared. I sat back, my grim duty done, to let Francesca get on with the creative work of the day.

She wanted to know more about the delivery itself. What drugs were used? Could she refuse them if she wanted to? How close to natural childbirth could it be? Was it all right for me to be there? Did they use a foetal monitor?

The foetal monitor! That one always rang the alarms. Of all the trappings of male chauvinist dominance, the foetal monitor was what the Earth Mothers hated most. A wire was fastened to the head of the foetus while it was still in the womb, and connected up to an oscilloscope. Not only was the physical intrusion an unnecessary outrage, they said, but it turned the whole experience into a computer game.

Instead of everybody focusing on the Earth Mother and feeding in their psychic energy as she labored to bring forth, they were glued to little green lines on a screen. If any hospital sticks the 'fatal' monitor into me, said one super-disgusted Earth Mother, then they'd better damn well serve popcorn.

But yes, this doctor did use the foetal monitor. In fact, she said she was in favour of using all the help she could get Why not make it as safe as possible? she asked, and she made it seem all too reasonable.

There was a short silence. Francesca seemed to be struggling with her thoughts. Then, almost casually, but in a deeper voice which I knew indicated the effort she had to make, she asked:

"Would you be . . . er, do you ever deliver babies at home?"

I sat up then. The doctor did her best to conceal the severity in her voice.

"No. Some doctors do, of course, but I have to say that I don't approve of home deliveries. I feel that it involves an unnecessary risk. The hospital allows so much freedom and informality these days, and we have everything right there on hand in case of difficulty."

"Can you recommend any doctors in this area who do?" asked Francesca. I thought it was a brave question, and applauded her silently. The doctor was good about it. She gave us the details of a practice that was hardly more than a five-minute walk from our house. We finished the interview on a friendly note and said we would call back when we had decided.

We walked down the stairs to the lobby in silence. Around us was a gallery of bright, clinical offices. White-coated doctors and technicians moved purposefully between them. There were glimpses of equipment and glossy filing cabinets. As we walked out of the swing doors into the sunshine Francesca said:

"I hate hospitals. I've always hated them. I'd like to have Iswas at home. Do you mind?"

"No," I said. "Of course not. It sounds like a wonderful idea. We'll do whatever you want."

She took my hand and held it tight. Then I put my arm around her and hugged her. I felt very good about her decision. I realized it was exactly what I would have wanted.

**19**

I don't share Francesca's dislike of hospitals. In all my life I can only remember being put to bed in three of them and, oddly enough, in every case I was just left to lie there until things got better of their own accord. The first time I was only nine years old, and had some mysteriously swollen glands. The doctors had no idea what had caused the condition and they watched me for two weeks until the swellings went away. There was no pain. The nurses called me "Sunshine", and most of the time I was quite happy there, in a ward with a dozen or so other children. Still, it was my first brush with death. I had been given a really exciting story book, with pop-up illustrations, and the boy in the bed opposite asked to borrow it, but he found his eyes wouldn't focus on the print. I remember feeling quite sorry for him. The nurse said this could happen with appendicitis. The next morning the curtains were drawn around his bed, and they told me he had died in the night.

Eight years later I caught polio. Again I was spirited away to a hospital bed, this time with my own room, isolated from the world. Since there was nothing to be done about polio, everybody just waited with fingers crossed to see what would happen to me. Fortunately nothing happened, and I came out six weeks later with my puny muscles intact, having read a lot of good books.

The third and last time (I hope) that I took up residence in a hospital was in Penang, as you have read, and once again all I did there was lie still and get better. Despite the theft of my papers, and the frustration I suffered, I have only kind thoughts about Penang

General, and the same is true of the other two. They didn't interfere with me, and I got a lot of rest.

By present day standards I may seem to have had more than my fair share of childhood illnesses, but I don't recall feeling hard done by, and they were all squeezed in before my eighteenth birthday. I had rickets (a severe calcium defficiency that bends bones) when I was three. Then I went through all the usual childhood diseases – mumps, chickenpox, and both kinds of measles, as well as yellow jaundice before it got the grander title of hepatitis – but in those days many grave monsters, like diptheria, scarlet fever and whooping cough, lurked everywhere and penicillin was not yet in general use. Polio was my last, and luckiest escape, but in spite of that history I never thought of illness as playing much of a part in my life.

However, when you feed the key words "Africa" or "India" into any western mind one of the first images that pops up has "loathsome disease" written all over it. My mind was no exception. Just reading through the list of the more likely medical hazards would give any traveler pause. Amoebic dysentery, tuberculosis, cholera, malaria, bilharzia, meningitis, sleeping sickness, typhoid, yellow fever, all of these haunted my prospective path around the globe, and a fertile imagination can add many more. With dread fascination I read in my South American Handbook about the Rhodnius beetle which ventures out at night from cracks in mud walls in the Brazilian interior, and transmits a progressive affliction to the heart which is invariably fatal. It's called Chagas' Disease, and I nicknamed the beetle Rodney. And then there's elephantiasis, and swamp fever, and leprosy . . .

Of course there are different ways to deal with these threats. Most travelers go to great expense to protect themselves. Inevitably. Think of those members of the Iowa Farm Bureau I met struggling around the ruins of Macchu Picchu, or the tourist group from Colorado that I bumped into on the Amazon. They fly into Peru or Brazil with two or three weeks to catch the sights, but no time at all to adjust to the culture, the climate, and the food – let alone the drink. Obviously they are going to look for western-style hotels, brush their teeth with Evian water, eat imported food and view the natives from afar, with tour guides to tell them whom they can trust and whom they dare touch.

Most westerners who did not take these precautions would be hit, at the very least, with a seriously inconvenient tummy upset and run the risk of ruining an expensive vacation. That's tourism, and that's why my whole life is designed so that I don't have to be a tourist. I pay quite a price for the privilege. I haven't been employed for a very long time and I would not encourage anyone to take me on, as I have become pretty much unemployable. My income is as unsteady as a brick chimney in an earthquake, and frequently collapses altogether. I contribute very little to consumer confidence statistics, and my overheads are abject. When I travel I am not encumbered by expectations of comfort and convenience. But best of all, I am never due back at the office.

Why this life suits me so well I don't know, because I can't imagine that it wouldn't suit everyone. To be free to act on impulse and intuition, to be able to go whichever way the wind blows, has always been for me the most exhilarating and stimulating way of life imagineable. Having tasted it, I became determined to hold on to that freedom. It's more than thirty years since I began gradually easing my way out of the kind of organized life that demands regular appearances in the work place. From being a cog in the machinery of a big newspaper (and that, I admit, already offered more freedom than most people experienced in their working lives) I became my own boss. From being a dutiful rate and tax -paying citizen of London, I became an all but invisible troglodyte hiding out in a rural ruin in France.

So even before the journey began I had weaned myself off the great machine that keeps most of us pinned down in our places. When I proposed my plan to various sponsors I genuinely believed that the adventure might take a year or two to accomplish, but I never for a moment felt I was committing myself to doing it in a fixed time frame. It would take as long as it took, or as long as I could keep going, whichever was the shorter.

Even so, it was fairly well understood that I would have to finish it, meaning of course that I intended to survive. So just a glance at that imposing list of dire diseases had me rushing off to my medical friends for advice. They armed me with a formidable array of pills, potions and portable apparatus to fend off the beastly tropical bugs.

Eventually all of it got used, in one way or another, but hardly any of it on me.

I was protected, part of the time, by vaccinations and inoculations, but I learned as I went that these precautions were proving to be increasingly unreliable. In retrospect the seventies may have been the decade when man's battle with sickness crossed a watershed, and diseases began recovering lost ground. Malaria, I heard, was mutating, and had revealed a lethal form that attacked the brain. Hepatitis was branching out too, from A to B and on, no doubt, through the alphabet.

Fortunately I didn't have much time to dwell on the subject. I did take the anti-malaria pills pretty regularly, and once, in Sri Lanka, I treated myself to my own antibiotics to get rid of what was probably not a very serious fever. Otherwise I dispensed my miracle drugs mainly to needy natives. The disposable scalpels, provided by a nursing friend so that I could perform my own appendectomies, I used to cut leather for my new pouch. The famous jock itch remedy of cod liver oil and glucose became too troublesome to transport.

In fact, during those four years I was remarkably free of illness, and this has always been a great source of satisfaction, even pride. I didn't take exceptional precautions. I ate and drank most of what was put before me, and I mixed freely with people in all circumstances. As I moved around I encountered enough people who had been sick to realize that I must be doing something right, and eventually I became convinced that there were two major factors keeping me healthy. They were pace, and motivation.

I was very fortunate in the support I received. At one point, near the halfway mark, there was some grumbling from the *Sunday Times,* my principal sponsor, but nonetheless they continued to keep me on the road. Occasionally there would be shifts in the power structure of that august institution. Some new person gaining influence would wonder openly why a newspaper of such importance was associating itself with anything so plebian as a motorcycle, and then for a month or two my pieces would not get published. Sour notes would emanate from London, and I would feel under some pressure to hurry, or to cut the journey short, but they were few and fleeting, and easy to resist. If I have a real claim to be entered in the Guinness Book of Records it is probably for the longest sustained sponsorship in the history of newspapers. Almost all the time I simply governed my own pace according to how I felt. And that I think is what saved me from a heap of trouble.

It is obvious really. Human beings are made to adapt, but it takes time. Going south into Africa from Europe I must have moved through  many strata of microscopic flora and fauna.  I had a head start, having already lived in the Mediterranean basin, and whatever immunities that conferred upon me must have been added to as I went. My days were extremely eventful,  but all the obstructions caused by the war in the Middle East meant that I had necessarily to travel slowly at first.  I became involved in the lives of the people I passed among, and that became the pattern for the rest of the journey.

Just as a traveler is always picking up information from chance meetings with people coming the other way – tips about borders, money changing, the state of the road – in the same way, I am convinced, the body is also alerted to approaching changes in the environment.  How otherwise to explain that nowhere in Africa can I recall having any health problems at all. And it is no coincidence, I'm sure, that my morale was high, and rising almost all the way. I started with many anxieties, and as they were revealed to be baseless, my confidence grew. I was so full of good stuff, so amazed and excited by my good fortune that sickness was just not in the cards.

On a purely physiological level there can hardly be any argument; the better you are adapted to your environment, the better your body will be able to resist prevailing predators and parasites.  Clearly if you are moving between different cultures, there is a much better chance of getting used to what is in the air, the food or the water when you move slowly. Whether it is possible to build actual immunities in those relatively short times, I don't know, but simply feeling at ease with the temperature and the humidity is a great advantage.

I speak from direct experience. I came to Madras, in southern India twice. The first time, I was completely conditioned to the heat and the moisture, having arrived by ship from a very similar climate. The second time I flew in from Europe, and was completely off balance. I was uncomfortable, irritated, made poor judgments, and was much more critical of everyone and everything around me.  Soon afterwards I caught a fever.

Much the same sequence of events occurred in Brazil. I sailed from South Africa, and one of the world's most pleasant climates, into a steamy tropical port, Fortaleza. The customs seized my bike and set up frustrating bureaucratic obstacles, which added to my physical discomfort. I refused to accept the indolent pace that was natural to that environment, tried to hurry things along, made unwise choices, and got myself locked up and in fear of my life. By the time I finally got out of that Kafkaesque hell-hole, I was in a pretty vulnerable condition. I was physically depleted through being made to shiver through cold damp nights without clothing or bedding, but worse still, my morale was deeply dented. And for the first time I find, in my notes, references to minor ailments and discomforts.

Altogether I was a month in Fortaleza, and many of the troubles I had avoided in Africa, descended on me there. In retrospect I am hardly surprised. Looking back on it, Fortaleza seems like a suitable place for sickness. It was originally a Portuguese fort, as the name implies, and fragments of the old colonial city still remained. There was a park, a plaza (or *praça*, in Portuguese), a palace, and a prison. One or two of the old houses had survived and a few of the sidewalks were still paved with marble, but the city had grown and spread enormously to house, after a fashion, more than a million people.

Most of the population lived in poor patchwork suburbs, rows of long, narrow single-storey houses where renovation chased hopelessly after decay. The city seemed to be built on sand, which erupted through the cobbles and cracked cement, spilling everywhere in the heavy rains. Cars crashed and squirmed over rifts and ridges, and the earth seemed to be shaking the city loose. From prison I went back to where I had been staying before, with some Irish missionary priests on the edge of the city, and tried to recover my confidence and interest in life by getting involved in whatever came along. One evening I joined Father Brendan Walsh, one of the priests, on a visit to the poor Bella Vista district, where the diocese was fostering a community development project.

The people, friendly and peaceful, were grouped outside their front doors watching the children dash about in the humid warmth. Brendan – or Padre Brendão, as they knew him – was dressed like all the other adult males in a colorfully printed short-sleeved polyester shirt and pants. He was there to see how many youngsters had come to dance in the club he had encouraged them to build. There was a nutrition center too, where a girl from the neighbourhood passed on information about diet, and distributed food donated by aid agencies, like Oxfam.

A thin worried woman came to ask for Brendan's help and we followed her to her house. She and her family lived behind their small store, which was a hand-built shack. They sold staple foods like rice, beans, manioca flour, maccaroni, and also single cigarettes, cane liquor *(cachaça)* by the glass, and other small necessities. The spaces were lit by kerosene wick, and the mud and wattle walls pressed in close from the shadows. Several hammocks were slung in the far corners. Children dozed in two of them, and a small, middle-aged woman lay in a third hammock with a cloth pressed against her face.

She took the cloth away to show us her nose, which had distended in a black and shapeless mass on the left side. The younger woman explained that this was a relative who had come up from the country for help. In a whisper she confessed her fear that the relative's trouble might be passed on to the children. It was plainly a cancer. The priest tried to reassure them, and said he would arrange to have the woman seen and treated at a hospital.

It was a miserable scene, particularly when one imagined the invalid's long and lonely journey from the interior, not knowing what was wrong or whether she could be helped, and probably now sensing the alienation that her malignancy aroused even in her own family. The cramped dark spaces seemed like a materialisation of the gloom and confusion in their minds. The priest's readiness to take a practical initiative was worth more than a truckload of rice.

After my own recent imprisonment, my continuing struggles with the bureaucracy, and my physical discomfort, it was easy for me to identify with these people and feel their vulnerability. Fortaleza did have a public health service, and it was possible to get free treatment and medicines, but like most such services it was organized to suit the convenience of the staff. Peasant families had to mount long and exhausting campaigns to gain access to its remedies. A day could easily be spent in a state dispensary simply waiting in line with a prescription, not to mention the time spent getting there and back.

Officially the minimum salary stood at 320 cruzeiros a month, or about $46, but virtually no farm workers earned that much, and few had consistent work. Although it was an offence to pay less, in rural areas the law was easily evaded. Unskilled laborers – and the vast majority were in that class – could afford to buy staple foods when they were working, and little else.

One of the most disagreeable accompaniments to poverty (by no means unique to Brazil) was subservience to the caprices of minor officials who exploited their powers of procrastination and sought to strengthen the myth of their omnipotence. Documents were sacred, and without a supply of cruzeiros to smooth the way each paper, signed and stamped, represented an immense investment of time, anxiety and obsequiousness. The bureaucratic process was steeped in ritual. The importation of my motorcycle absorbed the attentions of at least ten men, and my bill for the formalities came to $125 – or about $600 in 1997 dollars.

And then, of course, there was corruption, the other scourge of the poor. The military dictatorship, for all its horrors, made an attempt to attack corruption at lower levels. Low ranking police and other officials were heard to complain that they no long knew whether it was safe to take bribes and tips. But where low-paid government employees took jobs on the understanding that their incomes would be eked out by "contributions" it took more than pressure from above to achieve reforms.

This kind of exploitation would not have been possible if the natural environment of Brazil were not so generous. Fruit and vegetables grow rapidly and abundantly. The sea and the rivers are full of fish. Shelters can be constructed quickly and cheaply using mud, bamboo, palm fronds and so on. The people on the whole are hardy and good humoured. With everything going well, a peasant family would subsist in a way which had its own rhythm and logic, but all these benefits were wiped out as quickly as they were bestowed by frequent harsh droughts and raging floods. The land belonged to a few, and only they could build up the margins of security needed to survive these natural cataclysms. The others were driven, destitute, to look for help in the cities.

It was so obvious that with just a little lift, a little vision, the smallest cushion against disaster, these people's lives could be transformed. No wonder they engaged the attention and the passions of aid workers from the west. Oxfam was a presence there, along with other charities, but they were viewed with hostility by the big land owners and vested interests. It did not take much to excite the suspicions of a paranoid military dictatorship, suspicions which were the cause of my own incarceration.

I reflected often upon this tragic contradiction – a people having to endure such misery in a land that offered such wealth. I had a great desire myself to live simply in a house constructed of naturally available materials, and to use my ingenuity to work with my environment. It was a dream that had begun in France, and it grew all the way through my journey. Ideally I would have liked to do it in a place where the people around me might benefit from my ideas, from what I had seen and learned on my travels, but that proved to be impracticable. At best I would have a chance to try it out in our valley in Northern California. Meanwhile I always took a great interest in the hundreds of ways that buildings were put together, and how their proportions worked for the benefit of the human spirit.

O ur house in Mill Valley was built on a shelf on a steep hillside. The way it seems to have been done was like this. First they made a driveway to go about halfway up the one-acre plot. Then they turned it across the hillside to make it level so that cars could park. To do this, of course, they had to cut a step into the hill. At the end of this step they built a garage, and along the cut-away side they built a red-brick wall. Then I guess they used the earth they had dug up and heaped it above the brick wall. This way, they could make another shelf to hold the foundations of the building without having to cut into the hillside above the house.

This was a simple enough idea, but I appreciated it, because many sites are cut into the hillside, leaving a high wall along one side, and the hill comes down too high and steep above the house. And like as not they will have drainage problems too. Instead we had a nice flat lawn next to the house, which joined up naturally with the trees and bushes rising above it.

When you came out of the house there were a couple of steps down to a cemented area alongside the house with a verandah roof over it. Then you could walk across the little lawn to a rustic shelter that faced the house, or you could go left past some flowerbeds and down a flight of steps built into the brick wall to the drive and the garage, or you could walk around the house to the small yard at the back where the other half of the house was supposed to have been built.

In the middle of this yard grew a plum tree. In front of the house, above the brick wall, stood one of the apple trees, the smaller one. The other apple tree was planted below the house beyond the drive, and the pear tree was behind the garage. The cherries grew above the house in the woods, and they were ripe in June even before I went away. The woods seemed quite dark when you went in from the bright sunlight. There was dense ivy growing all over and you had to watch for poison oak.

There were many smaller eucalyptus trees up there and a lot of dead wood which I hauled down for the fire. We liked watching a fire at night, even when it was warm, but I found the eucalyptus hard to burn on its own. I had to take the Valiant into the city to an abandoned school on the Panhandle where some black fellows were selling firewood from an old apricot orchard somewhere the other side of Oakland. It cost me twenty-five dollars to fill the trunk of the Valiant, and that seemed like a lot of money, but the apricot had a lovely fragrance which lingered round the house, and we could mix it with the dead eucalyptus.

The fire didn't do much to warm the house, because there was no insulation at all in the walls or the ceiling, but it was fine for the summer, and by winter-time we were already planning to have moved to our valley.

Apart from the fruit trees there was an abundance of blackberry bushes along the steep sides of the drive coming up from the road. It would be hard to imagine a more benign and reassuring spot in which to heal our wounds and rediscover our pleasure in each other. When I returned from Europe in July the apples were waxing large and green, the plum tree was laden with promise and the bushes were proliferating with berries already tinged red by the unfailing sun. All this burgeoning fruitfulness around us was the natural expression of our own happy expectations. We could not look at the soft and glossy grass without seeing a baby chuckling and mewling on it. Iswas would ripen and fall with the apples in the first days of September and soon after might even taste their sauce.

That summer bore fruit in every way. My tour of Britain was impeccably managed and gloriously successful. The old Triumph motorcycle (old in experience if not in years) was brought out of the museum and traveled with us, and every time I sat astride it with its original panoply of boxes and bags the memories rushed back and I was able to talk fluently and tirelessly about my adventures and the feelings they evoked. The book was reprinted, and reprinted again, and I could believe that I was at last pouring back into the world some of the riches I had harvested.

And still that was not all. Already before my departure Francesca had uncovered in herself a passion for textiles and weaving. It took her entirely by surprise because it contradicted all the academic abstractions she had been immersed in since childhood. With the extraordinary burst of energy and enthusiasm which comes in the middle months of pregnancy she threw herself into this new challenge. During the weeks I was away she took the old Valiant, with Iswas jammed up against the steering wheel and her feet barely touching the pedals, and charged across Richmond Bridge to Berkeley four or five times a week. There, in a big room that thumped and rattled with the din of beaters and harnesses, she lost herself in the gear, tackle and trim of one of the world's most ancient crafts. Combs, heddles, lease sticks, shuttles and shafts were her daily bread, and at night, prompted perhaps by Iswas's busy feet, she wove warp and weft into the fabric of her dreams.

When she fetched me at the airport that time she was glowing with health and confidence. There was a bottle of champagne waiting in the fridge, and all sorts of nice things laid out to eat. It felt marvellous to be back.

"Do you feel like I do?" I asked. "It feels like a real home. More like a home than we've ever known."

"I'm very happy here," she said, and we hugged each other.

"There," she said, "did you feel that?"

"I noticed there was something coming between us, if that's what you mean."

"The kick!" she said. "Didn't you feel the kick? He's at it all the time now."

"Careful how you talk about my daughter," I said.

"Isn't that funny? I never think of Iswas as a girl. Well, I don't think I do. Would you like a girl?"

"I really don't mind. I can honestly swear that it makes no difference at all, as long as it's one or the other. Do the kicks keep you awake at night?"

"Well, it's funny but you know how nervous I get alone. The house is full of creaks at night, but now it's like having someone there with me. I hardly get scared any more. Except one night. I got really frightened. I called the police."

"Jesus! What was that about?"

"I was in bed. It was dark of course. Then there were footsteps outside, sort of stumbling, drunken steps. That's what always frightens me the most – that some drunks are going to wander off from a bar, too pissed to know what they're doing. Then the dustbin fell over. I was really scared to death. I shot out of bed and got the police. You know, I was amazed. They were here so fast. I didn't think they'd pay attention to some silly old bat ringing them up in the night. I was still looking around for the poker when the policeman came to the door.

"He was very nice, really sweet. He said 'I think it's all right ma'am. We found a deer outside – one of the four-footed kind'. "

She burst into merry laughter.

"He was smashing. He said I had done the right thing. I was to call them any time. They didn't care how often. I was really impressed."

I was pretty impressed myself. I wondered how long it would have taken me to find the police in a strange phone book with a demon at the door. And deer! I would never have thought to find deer where there were so many people.

"He said there were a lot of deer around. They have them here the way London has cats. I've seen some since. They're lovely, but they make an awful mess of the rubbish."

We were sipping champagne. The Earth Mothers said that if she drank a glass of wine it would give Iswas permanent brain damage, but coming from France we refused to believe them. She was looking animated and charming.

"I've never seen you so rosy-cheeked," I said. "You look wonderful. Can I see what you've been doing while I've been away?"

So she brought out the samples she had been weaving and I admired them. Then she brought out rolls of material and went up to the gallery while I stayed down below finishing the champagne, and she hung them out over the rail one by one – sheets of cotton that she had printed with a silk screen – lovely intricate patterns in many colours. And I applauded noisily and she curtseyed, or tried to, and came down again flushed with pleasure.

But it was the weaving that had really captured her. After a bit of coaxing she declared that she thought she had discovered what it was she was meant to do with her life. And that is no mean discovery to make, so in that way it really was a very fruitful summer.

**21**

Until that afternoon at Greenbrae, having the baby at home was just one of the more unlikely ideas that got bandied around. Or so it seemed to me. Francesca said nothing to contradict that impression, and I was anxious not to interfere with her choice. Yet it was much more in harmony with my ideals than any other way. My concept of a good life was one in which we would learn to do everything that it was humanly possible to do for ourselves.

I was not strictly an advocate of self-sufficiency, an idea which was particularly popular at that time. The emphasis for me was on the learning, rather than the doing. I resented having to depend on specialists and experts for goods and services which it should be within the competence of any human being to provide.

If people did not know how to provide for themselves, I thought, then they would never learn to value and protect their natural resources. Their judgement would be shaky, and they would be too vulnerable to blackmail and bribery. While the specialists, if they were allowed to establish a monopoly, would become monstrous and lead us ever deeper into temptation. I was suspicious of technologists, and felt that like every other human elite they would be self-serving and convince us, as they have done, that the ever increasing problems of their making can only be solved by ever greater amounts of technology.

Some of this philosophy was already formed, and of course widely shared, before my journey began. In my French village I did my best to practicee it by learning the most elementary techniques of building with the most primitive materials: stone, wood, plaster, tile, lime and cement. I found out about gardening and some simple forms of architecture. In that same village an old lady told me that only fifty years earlier they had been able to provide for all their needs, other than coffee, sugar, salt and cocoa. When I first arrived some of those traditions still survived; in the way things were repaired and maintained, in the productivity of the vegetable gardens, and in the use of horses which were essential to maintaining a natural cycle that avoided the importing of fertilizer and the exporting of sewage.

Spinning and weaving had ceased, the last of the sheep had been sold, and nobody soaked and beat the fibers out of the broom plants any more, but the culture was still alive. Yet during the few years I lived there, it died. The horses went, replaced by tractors. Fertilizer came in plastic sacks, and the sacks found their way into the river. Houses were sold as holiday homes to richer foreigners than myself, and this sudden wealth generated a torrent of refuse from hasty rebuilding. Everything old was thrown out, regardless, and the river banks were lined with rubbish. The absence of the horses meant the loss of the mucking-out sheds, which had always served as a useful, if uncomfortable, office for the natural human functions. Toilets and drains were installed, the cobbles were ripped up and cemented over, and the sewage made its way into the river to join the fertilizer bags in an ironic dance of pollution.

Television entered the homes, and people relaxed from the drudgery of the old life to see how things were done in Paris. Clothes were thrown out rather than repaired, less food was grown, more bought, tin cans and plastic bottles joined the avalanche of garbage, incongruous building materials changed and spoiled the face of the village, and cars sped through it.

Within five years I saw the destruction of a way of life which had survived for centuries. And yet, I could not honestly begrudge the inhabitants of that village a single one of their new comforts and improvements. The tragedy, to my mind, was that none of them had been conceived or designed for rural life. From the blatant rubbish on their TV screens to the hopelessly inappropriate sewage systems, they imposed urban patterns and ideas on a profoundly rural community and degraded it. Just as chicken-pox decimated Polynesia, the urban bug hit my unprotected village and hundreds, maybe thousands, of others, and swept all before it. Stores of knowledge and wisdom were rendered useless, something harmonious and enriching to the human spirit was wasted. The external forms of beauty were preserved – a further irony – by the city-dwellers who made the village their holiday retreat, but the life of the village has long since died, and virtually all but the aged have fled to the cities.

It was this sad example that I carried with me around the world, and everywhere I saw the same travesty in the making. In tribal Africa, from one end of Latin America to the other, on Kata beach, in the villages of India (perhaps last of all there) the process of spoliation was either accomplished, or happen astonishing, or an inevitable future event visible to those who, like me, had seen the blight and recognized it elsewhere.

What was the good of railing against changes which brought to people antibiotics, food, education and relief from drudgery? Of course, everyone should share these benefits. But must the world be sold up to provide them? Feeling helpless before the tide, I could only hope that somewhere, one day, I would make my own stand. Now the time had come.

I knew I was ready to take risks, to accept some hardships and deprivation to find a better way, and I knew that Francesca was ready to share them, but we had learned some bitter truths about ourselves. Without peace and understanding between us we could not hope to live such a harsh and demanding life. The land we had bought was our first, timid step back on to that path. Perhaps a home delivery seemed like a cranky and foolish thing to risk here on the outskirts of San Francisco, but it fitted closely with the kind of life we still hoped to find in our cowboy valley.

Once Francesca had made up her mind, the idea fired my imagination as nothing else could have. It was the bravest pledge she could have made to the ideals we had talked about. It proved that we were still on the same road, and we became fanatically determined to make a success of it, as though it were some kind of fitness test, as though it would qualify us for the life ahead and the other children we hoped to have in the future.

Unlike most of the other couples we met neither of us had jobs to go to. We were free to do as we pleased. It would have been better, though, if we had had employment. After the concentrated excitement of Francesca's classes in Berkeley, with her fingers itching to pursue her new-found vocation, time lay as heavy on her as Iswas. With an old sewing machine, bought through a supermarket advertisement, she made a duvet cover and pillowcases. We bought a rush baby basket from Cost Plus, and she lined it with some pretty quilted fabric with a brilliant mosaic design that made it seem like a tiny Byzantine chapel. She had never sewn, nor knitted nor crocheted in her life, but she began to do them all, and everything she touched became beautiful under her hands.

Then one day after visiting Tee she mentioned, in an offhand way, that there was a loom for sale. The more she deprecated it – it was too big, too expensive, too good for her – the more clearly her yearning for it showed through. We went to look at it together. It stood in a small, sunlit room overlooking Tee's house from across the street, a wondrous looking thing made of pale, varnished maple. It had a forty-eight inch reed and eight harnesses, with room for another two. There was almost nothing one could not attempt on such a loom.

A loom is not to be trifled with. Lovely as the finest piece of furniture, it would grace any room, but to buy it as an object of beauty alone would be the utmost foolishness. Just as an unplayed piano is a constant reproach to its negligent owners, so an unused loom would glower in the corner and radiate thoughts of failure and incompetence. A piano and a loom are remarkably similar in the demands they make, in their solidity and permanence, and in their response. Weaving, even more than architecture, is frozen music, and to bring either a piano or a loom into the house is to accept a serious responsibility.

When Francesca decided she would have it after all I knew what a heavy commitment she had made. Seamus and I heaved it into an old truck and brought it back to our house. For a moment it teetered dangerously above his head as we struggled up the cement steps from the drive, but his strength overcame its massive weight. We installed it triumphantly by a window and drank to it in beer.

For days we gazed at it in admiration. Francesca sniffed around it like a terrier at a fox-hole, dying to get at it, but intimidated by its sheer size and complexity, fearful of starting something she couldn't finish. Finally, she warped it up for a sample and got going. It was hard work. She made mistakes and undid a good deal as she went. She spent hours tangling with her books, trying to recover what she had already forgotten from her studio days.

She was not a calm worker. She became infuriated, frustrated and desperate at times, and as the weeks of August passed Iswas became more of a handicap. Her energy deserted her, the summer heat tired her, and when she had finished a small chaircover, good as it was, she knew she could do no more.

As for me, I found it more difficult to work too. I had a commission to write a short article, normally something to occupy a few days at most, but I labored over it for weeks, and eventually had to take refuge in the library at the other end of town to get it finished.

There were other little jobs to do and things to get: sheets of plastic to protect the bedding, a thermometer, a special tube with a rubber bulb on it to suck the mucous plug from the baby's nostrils. Francesca went out too, of course, to get the nicer things like the mattress for the basket, the receiving blankets and some tiny cotton shirts, but she found the car increasingly awkward to handle.

Pregnancy made her unusually nervous of accidents and when I drove she became very scared. In San Francisco, on the switchback roads, she was in terror, screaming 'Stop' every few yards, and we had to give up going to the city.

I found a mirror that had YOU'RE GORGEOUS printed on it. We ate nice food and were always happy when friends came, but between us alone there was still an underlying tension which was hard to dispel.

Some of our difficulties were no more than any couple would face while waiting for their first child to arrive, but we had others which put a much heavier burden on us. All our hopes for the future depended entirely on an act of faith: that we would be able to find on our land a life that would bring us together. And really we had very little basis for that faith except a stubborn desire to make it work.

We found it difficult even to talk about the future. I was scared to describe the ideas which kept buzzing in my head about what we might build, or grow, or do in our valley, for fear of pre-empting her own less tangible dreams. While she, too, began to feel very exposed, uncertain about our prospects, and exhausted not just by her physical condition but by the effort of maintaining the faith. Unable to toy with the future I toyed with the past.

Only a week after I got back from England the letters began to follow. Some contained reviews of *Jupiter's Travels,* others were from readers. Every day there was something. Francesca encouraged me to write back to readers and I did it gladly. I was astonished that so many people had taken the trouble. Most of the reviews were good, and one or two reviewers had tried to find something useful to say, but many of them seemed more anxious to excuse themselves for liking something that they felt was vaguely beneath them.

'It's no good looking for his politics, because he hasn't any,' wrote one lady, betraying a rather narrow view of politics.

'Humourless and self-obsessed,' wrote another. 'Bursting with moments of sudden hilarity,' wrote a third, while a fourth complimented me on my humility. So they came, tripping over each other, and I beamed with pleasure, fumed in rage and spluttered indignantly by turns. One editor devoted an entire page of his magazine to confessing a strong dislike to me personally and advising his readers to read the book although it wasn't very good. Another said I had written so little about one section of the journey that he suspected I hadn't made it. Another said the account was so detailed that I must have made it up.

Of course I read them all avidly, searching between the lines for what was not there, but on the whole they offered little enlightenment. The readers made up for that. A few were outright fan letters, but almost all of them made great efforts to say something worthwhile from their own experience to explain why I had touched them.

The easiest one to like was the shortest of them all. It came scrawled on a piece of lined paper torn roughly out of a pad, and it said simply 'Thanks. I've finally had the inspiration to leave this fuck-awful job and do something worthwhile. Chrissy. '

Anything that touched on my journey and the book posed a dilemma for Francesca, and my heart bled for her. She was proud of me, proud of what I had done, proud of the success of the book, but it always seemed to take me away from her, to throw me back into a past where, to her mind, I had flourished so much better than now.

The letters kept coming, the sales figures soared, the sun became hotter, and it became ever harder to keep ourselves on an even keel.

Although I was hopelessly underemployed, I made the most of what jobs there were. In a frenzy of enthusiasm I turned an old sun-bathing couch from the garden into a delivery bed. It was a heavy wooden contraption with a wheel at one end, and an adjustable back-rest, and it proved to be hopeless in the end, but it kept me busy for a while.

The birth gurus recommended having something beautiful around to look at when the labor began, as an object of meditation. We had a lovely print of a primitive Garden of Eden painted by Buttercup Garrad, who was a friend of ours, and I said I would get it framed down at the do-it-yourself shop on the avenue. A perky young Canadian helped me to size up the mounts, and I explained what we had in mind to do with it.

"You're havin' it at home, are ya? Well, no sweat. You know, I delivered my first baby when I was thirteen. I was a farmer's boy in Canada. We lived way out, but close to the big trunk road. Our house was a little downhill from it, and a smaller road came up to join it there. I was at home with my kid sister while my parents were out for the evening. Well, I heard the smash all right. Some guy was bar-relling along the trunk road with his missus, trying to get to the maternity in time, and this other feller came up the fork and right into him. His car rolled over in front of our house, and the man was out cold, but his wife was giving birth in the back. I looked after it fine. I'd done calves and other animals, and it was a cinch. Human babies don't stretch the way some animals do. Boy, they can come out like an elastic band."

Whenever I got out of the house there was something like that. At the junction where we came down on to Miller stood a big deli-catessen called Jerry's with a pharmacy in one corner, and opposite the pharmacy was a hairstyling shop called Shear Fantasy. At least, that's what it was meant to be called. I looked up one day at the big, expensively carved wooden sign hanging outside and saw that it read SHEAR FANATSY At first I didn't know what to do with this priceless discovery. I didn't want to waste it by telling them in the shop, but when I was in the pharmacy later I could see the sign through the window.

The pharmacist was a tall, sleek man with an imperturbable smile. I thought nothing could shake him.

"Have they been in business long?" I asked idly, pointing through the window.

"Who's that?" he said.

"Shear Fanatsy," I said.

"You mean Shear Fantasy," he said, condescendingly.

"No, Shear Fanatsy," I said, trying to conceal my triumph. "You know, the haircutters, Shear Fanatsy."

He gave me a queer look.

"No, you mean. . ." Then he looked himself, and whistled softly. "Well I'll be damned. I must have looked at that sign . . . Hey, we'll have a bit of fun."

He found their number in the book and rang them up. He had the best poker style I've ever seen.

"Is that Shear Fanatsy?" he said. He was grinning at me, but his voice was flat as a pancake.

I could hear the tone of voice coming through the receiver. There's some nut on the line, it said.

"No, I don't want Shear Fantasy," said the pharmacist. "I want Shear Fanatsy, on Miller."

It was lovely to watch. He milked it of every drop before he said: "Well, I'm looking at the sign now and it says Shear. Fanatsy." Then we had the immense pleasure of watching them come out of the door, one by one, to stare up at their sign and turn pale.

Our last and best distraction from the perils of the past and the future was the fruit business. The trees produced a vast crop of apples, gloriously crisp and juicy. I picked hundreds of pounds of them, climbing higher and higher into the trees as Francesca stood nervously on the doorstep uttering warnings. I tried not to alarm her, but I couldn't leave the apples alone. We made endless amounts of apple sauce, but the brown paper grocery bags stacked full outside were hardly diminished.

We gave away as many as we could, but the apple mountain remained.

"We could try selling them," I suggested, doubtfully. "How about taking them all down to the flea market on Sunday?"

I had little hope of doing good business, but the Sausalito flea market was fun, and I thought it would be interesting to go there with something to sell. It would give us a different view of the people. We piled the apples into the trunk, put two folding chairs in the back and set out to compete for the great American buck.

We did not arrive at the crack of dawn, but it made little difference. Most of the best places were already occupied the night before, and anyway it wasn't going to matter much where we were. The first thing we saw as we drove in and paid our six dollars was a truck loaded with apples from Oregon. They were selling cheap, but by the crate.

'We'll undercut them,' I snarled, viciously. "It's rough, but that's the American way."

The market spreads out over a big area of open ground, far from the town. It's a real flea market, selling a lot of junk and a few nice things among them. People who are moving come and sell off stuff they don't want to cart along. People sell stuff to raise money for a vacation. It's a great, friendly place, a nice mixture of amateurs and professionals, one of the best flea markets I've ever known. It doesn't have anything like the fund of good things to draw upon that the European markets used to offer, but they are mostly in the past now, and Sausalito does very well with what's around. We had bought a leaded window, two elegant chairs and a clarinet there and we were very happy about it.

We found a spot and spread our best apples on the ground on newspapers, and put bags of them all around with ridiculously low prices. All we wanted was to have people eat our apples and get back the admission price. Then we sat in our canvas chairs and waited. We must have looked quaint and, to tell the truth, we rather counted on it. People grinned broadly at the sight of us, but they bought apples too, and we made a profit of two dollars which even covered the gas and a hot dog.

The man with the apple truck came by and laughed. "You must be kidding," he said. "Those apples are no good."

"Try one," I said, and he did. He said it was good after all.

"What kind are they?" I asked.

He said they were Jonathan's and that they went mushy real quick, but that didn't bother us. We had a really good day, one of the best, and went home tired and happy, feeling like characters out of Steinbeck. Whenever we did something like that together, a first-time try for both of us, we got on wonderfully well. But I'd been around too long, done too much, and it hurt me to pretend ignorance. I looked young for my age, and felt it, but I was old for her really and we both knew it. Too old for marriage and families. Too old for her.

Age had never seemed to matter to me before. It was the frustration and idleness that made me think about it, and I saw how marriage could put years on a man. With so much in the past to recall, and so little in the present to take my mind off it, I felt my life slipping away as I waited, and waited. And for what? The less I did, the older I became. The more I did, the greater the distance between us. As the 'due date' came closer, the waiting grew heavier, and then there were times when I was sure that the birth of Iswas would be the death of me. Already I could feel the strands of the web fall lightly across my limbs. Only a gossamer touch, but enough to make me squirm and panic. It was all a terrible mistake. I was no man to be caught in that web, like a fly, and sucked dry by a squalling baby and a distraught mother. I felt a powerful impulse to run, to disappear, to change my identity and never be seen again.

I had known men who had done that. Friends of mine, men I respected. It had seemed extraordinary to me then, but now I understood. One of them had never returned. How callous he had seemed, or how insane. Now all I appeared to lack was the courage to follow his example. The desire to escape was no less strong for being intermittent, but I let circumstance govern my actions. The precise moment never came, and if I ever thought about it in a practical, deliberate way – where would I go? – what would I do? – I knew quite clearly and coldly that sooner or later the circle of experience would bring me back to exactly this point again, but crushed by the burden of betrayal. The web was my fate. I had chosen it, and wanted it, but I could not help fluttering my wings pathetically as it closed around me.

For Francesca the birth of Iswas could only mean the most stupendous release. There was nothing in my own experience that would help me grasp what was in store for her. As the last days passed a new sense of resolution buoyed her up. She was ready for it as she had never been ready for anything before. At last it was over, the waiting, the weariness, the immense weight of it. She suffered from none of the symptoms that afflicted some of our friends at the birth classes she attended; the swollen ankles, the rising blood pressure and dizziness. She was proud of her health and fitness and believed absolutely that she would give birth easily to a normal, healthy child. Her confidence was unusual and inspiring.

Iswas had dutifully performed all the required acrobatics, turning upside down and dropping into position. We both now knew, or thought we knew, exactly what to expect. We had seen pictures of the odd distortions that babies suffer during those last momentous convulsions that expel them into the light. The pointy heads like ice cream cones, the bizarre colourings, fearful rashes and shocking hairy pelts would not frighten me. We knew when to call the midwife, when to expect the doctor. We had even been to the hospital with other couples to see the maternity wards where they would be going and the equipment that was waiting there, and Francesca was all the more confident in her decision to have her baby at home. She was determined to resist the temptation to take any drugs, and I had promised not to suggest it to her if things looked too painful.

"I'll know," she said, fiercely. "If I need anything, I'll tell you soon enough. Don't make it harder for me."

She was ready, and the day arrived, and passed – and the next day and the next – and nothing happened, and she began to wilt. Somehow we had not prepared ourselves for this most normal of all phenomena. First children rarely arrive on time, but we had been hypnotized by the calendar and I watched her confidence cruelly drained as the days dragged on, and still nothing happened.

The mail still flowed abundantly. 'Outraged' of Camberley wrote: "Why did you spoil what could have been an outstandingly interesting book with such detailed and boring descriptions of your bodily functions? . . . Do you really think that using the word 'fuck' made your book more readable or enjoyable? These aspects of your book made me consign it to the wastepaper basket."

From apples and plums I moved on to blackberries, making more jam than we would ever know what to do with. On Friday, six days after the 'due date', we visited the doctor for reassurance.

"It's my weekend off," he said, "my first in months. I'm going north to fish." He looked at us quizzically. "And I bet you have your baby this weekend. It's funny. I had a feeling I wouldn't be there for your birth. I even arranged for a friend to stand by. He's a fine doctor and I asked him to come and meet you."

We met a giant of a man with a gentle face. We both liked him immediately but by now we had become deeply resigned to waiting for ever. We couldn't bring ourselves to believe in it any more. Doctors could come and go, but Iswas had decided to stay where he or she was. We went home, resigned and apathetic, to sit it out.

The next morning she felt the first spasms, and all our lethargy vanished. Like sailors drifting in the doldrums we heard the look-out shout "Land, ahoy!" and our patient misery changed to feverish expectation. The signals came faint and far apart. We called the midwife to warn her, and she prepared herself cheerfully but counselled us not to be over-excited. We should call her, she said, as soon as the contractions were five minutes apart, but there was no point in her coming before that and it might be quite a while. She was right. The spasms faded away, and despite ourselves we felt let down. In the evening they began again, but too far apart to be taken seriously. We opened out the sofa downstairs to make a bed and I prepared it for Francesca.

"You'd better get some sleep while you can," she said to me. "You're going to have a lot of work to do. I'll sleep down here and wake you if anything happens."

I slept until six, without dreaming, and came down to make breakfast. She said she had felt something about every half hour through the night. She had not had much sleep. I brought the foam mattress down and laid it on the floor below, with the plastic over it and lots of padding under the sheets to absorb the moisture when the 'bag of waters' broke, another of those mysteries we had been initiated in.

We called the midwife again.

"I'll be ready," she said. "Don't worry. I'll be there as soon as you need me."

We were beginning to feel our loneliness. I was looking through one of my old notebooks and saw that it was just seven years since the army coup in Chile and the death of Allende. The feeling of that day came back vividly. The Chilean tragedy touched a raw nerve in Europe and caused pain out of all proportion to Chile's size and importance. Its very remoteness gave it a special poignancy.

My notebook entry read:

'Victoria jabs. Yank with DX. Good riddance to A.'

I remembered the incident very clearly. 'Victoria' was the London air terminal, a good place to go for inoculations. My journey was to begin in a month's time, and I was there waiting for my first cholera shot. It was a crowded room. The American was ahead of me, a big man, though not as big as he made himself appear. He was fastidiously groomed and looked prosperous. His black-and-white dog-tooth checked trousers were only a little too loud. Among his many accessories, all luxurious, were a gold watch, a ring, a tagged bracelet, cufflinks, a new umbrella and a woman. I fancied that he had a businessman's face and a gangster's eye which occasionally roamed the room looking for a gap in the market or a soul going cheap. He was reading a newspaper.

'DX' referred to the *Daily Express* he was holding, the old style broadsheet newspaper that I had once worked for. The front page displayed a sensational photograph of the Moneda, Chile's presidential palace, in flames after a bombing attack. The headline announced Allende's death.

The American spoke in a loud, lazy voice to his woman.

"From what I hear, it was a damned good thing they got rid of him."

The woman's manicured hand fluttered aimlessly in the lap of her peppermint-green skirt.

The boorish, over-confident voice rasped on.

"He really screwed that country. You remember Al – the other night?"

"Sure," she nodded, eagerly.

"Well, Al says that wasn't all he screwed. He was a hell of a ladies' man – you bet."

I was remembering my bitterness at those careless words when I heard Francesca make a noise, and turned to her. She let out a sigh.

"Something's happening," she said.

"What about Tee?" I asked, and she nodded.

I called Tee, and she said she'd be glad to come over. She had always wanted to be there, and Francesca wanted her to come.

"Nobody else," she said. "Tee and you and the midwife."

She was very clear and decisive about everything to do with the birth, and I was grateful for that. It was Sunday, another beautiful day. Around ten in the morning she gave a loud gasp.

"God," she said, "that was a big one."

And then it really began.

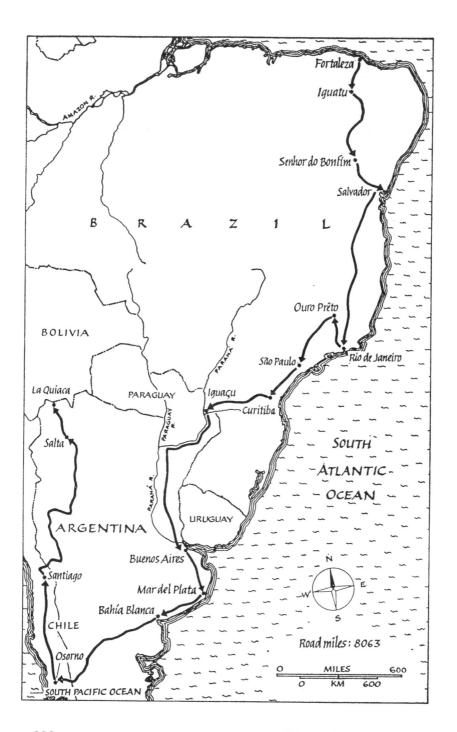

Fortaleza
Iguatu
Senhor do Bonfim
Salvador

AMAZON R.

B R A Z I L

BOLIVIA

Ouro Prêto

PARANÁ R.

São Paulo
Rio de Janeiro

La Quiaca

PARAGUAY

Iguaçu
Curitiba

Salta

PARAGUAY R.

SOUTH
ATLANTIC
OCEAN

PARANÁ R.

ARGENTINA

URUGUAY

Buenos Aires

Santiago

Mar del Plata

Bahía Blanca

Road miles: 8063

CHILE

Osorno

SOUTH PACIFIC OCEAN

N
W        E
S

O    MILES    600
O    KM    600

# 22. Argentina

The road to Chile began as soon as I entered Argentina. Brazil, so catastrophic and triumphant, so coherent and diverse, so powerfully soft, so grand as to be a virtual sub-continent in itself, stands hugely apart from the rest, nourished by separate roots, soaked in its own poetry and myth. In Brazil I wandered for four months among death and love, torture and music. Then, one September morning in 1974, I floated across the Iguaçu river, uncannily calm below the world's most turbulent falls, and rolled off the ferry into Argentina.

Argentina was a political no-man's-land of urban guerillas, fascist assassins and Peronista mobs, all muddling deeper into chaos under the confused and desperate presidency of Peron's widow Isabelita. It was then more than a year since the four generals had plunged Chile into its own peculiarly bloody catharsis. As I roamed through the Argentine wilderness of conflicting hopes and growing disorder, a lurid beacon seemed to glow from the far south. I felt myself drawn down that funnel-shaped land mass to the country where Argentina's own horrible fate was already mirrored.

Not that these distant views of nations and their troubles, the stuff of journalism and television documentary, have much to do with daily life. On the ground they are translated into pinpricks; perplexing shortages of toothpaste or cooking oil; a deeper suspicion of strangers; soaring inflation and irritating currency regulations.

I never came closer to the violence of Argentina than to see the bullet holes in a hotel letter-rack in Villaguay. The owner had been shot dead there the day before, by mistake. The target was a govern-

A small part of the colossal Iguaçu Falls that I passed on my way from Brazil to Argentina. Yet only a few miles downriver, where the ferry crosses, the water is so tranquil. I crossed into a region called Missiones, and found myself among blond, blue-eyed Teutons playing the latest hits from Germany, and eating Schnitzel

ment official traveling with two bodyguards, and it was one of his own bodyguards who shot at him. He had ducked behind the reception desk and saved himself, but the proprietor and the other guard were riddled with bullets.

That same day I had ridden carelessly into a deep rut of baked mud and lost control of the bike. I pitched over the handlebars and the bike somersaulted on top of me. I felt it land on my right thigh and was sure my leg must have been broken. "Christ,"I said, "you've really done it this time." I said it out loud, but I got up and the bone was intact. The bike lay sputtering like an upended beetle. I switched it off and looked at it. The lights were destroyed, the handlebars revolved through ninety degrees and, worst of all, the forks were twisted. Both boxes were badly damaged, and my belongings lay scattered over the road. Slowly, as my thigh muscles swelled to enormous size, I lashed everything together and limped on into town.

I stood stiffly outside the hotel that evening in the town plaza, watching events. The police station was buzzing with activity after the assassinations. Several fat policemen, tightly belted into khaki drill uniforms and carrying sub-machine guns, stood to salute the flag as it was lowered. After nightfall two of them mounted guard at either end of the building, whistling to each other occasionally in the dark. To the world at large, I thought, Argentina was a dangerous place where men and women were kidnapped and murdered daily, yet the only violence I sustained was a stupid motorcycle accident, which I had been lucky with. The repairs occupied me for several days. I scarcely thought about the bullets in the pigeonholes again except as a story to tell.

A Brazilian diplomat had given me an introduction to Mercedes de Menendez; that is to say he gave me her telephone number, and as soon as I arrived in Buenos Aires I called her. She was a university student and had a group of friends, and we went around the city together. I was lucky that they spoke some English, because at the time I was still hopelessly entangled in Portuguese and couldn't understand a word of Spanish.

They took a lot of trouble with me and treated me with great respect, which I found surprising but, naturally, rather pleasant. It made up for the fact that all the girls were spoken for, and perhaps it was meant to.

Mercedes was slim and pale with reddish hair. She came from a well-to-do family who lived in an apartment full of heavy furniture in the French style in a fashionable part of town. Given her background I thought her eager, unaffected curiosity about the world was a refreshing sign of true intelligence. She had chosen her friends well, for they were all free-spirited. She was with Jorge, a lean and dreamy man who sported a wispy light brown beard. There was his brother Pucci, willowy, slightly camp in manner, and Hebe, a majestic, dark and sultry girl. Raoul was small, intense and passionate. His girl friend was the only one of them who worked. Her name was Marta, a pretty, practical girl full of good-natured energy. They kept me up late at nights with coffee and barbecues and lots of talk about politics and life, and they taught me to sing the tango.

When I told them that I had to leave they all decided to come with me, and we met again 250 miles farther south on the coast at Mar del Plata, where the *Porteños* go to get away from the muddy water of the River Plate and enjoy the fresh, salty ocean. We camped among the sand dunes there and enjoyed ourselves immensely.

They were all passionately engaged in the political drama of Argentina, waiting for the next inevitable stage, differing wildly on what it would be. I told them about the assassinations I had almost witnessed in Villaguay, a typically confusing incident, and they did their best to explain what was happening, but I felt they were too much part of it themselves to understand. Just by watching them argue among themselves I maybe came to understand it better.

They all admitted, quite sadly, that every Argentine was more concerned with defending his own opinion than arriving at an agreement, but then there was so little in Argentina's history to inspire confidence in a compromise. I felt quite sorry for them as the arguments rumbled and exploded through the night.

On our last night it even entered my dreams, but I woke up to hear real gunfire. Soldiers were shooting at targets on the beach. Out at sea I saw a multitude of black figures apparently advancing on the coast, and thought I was witnessing some sort of frogman commando raid before I realized they were seals lying out on a reef.

The weather had been worsening and it was obvious we couldn't stay any longer. I'd had plenty of practice at saying goodbye, but I had got close to their hearts and I felt I was leaving them to bad times. We were all very sad. The sky was dark. The road followed the coast almost due west, and a powerful southerly wind blew up, with freak gusts that threatened to knock me over. Then cold rain fell in torrents, whipped up by the wind. After a short while the throttle seized. Then the engine lost power and before long I was forced to stop.

It was a bleak coast in the storm, and the only refuge I found was a small concrete bus shelter. The floor was inches deep in water, but there was a cement bench. I wheeled the bike in and perched on the bench, wet and cold. It crossed my mind that the bus shelter was exactly like the ones to be seen on the south coast of England, and that the scenery was so similar that I might easily have thought myself sixty miles from London in winter. The thought depressed me all the more.

There was some relief in work. Eventually I discovered that the carburetor main jet had unscrewed itself and dropped into the reservoir. I repaired it, cleaned the throttle slide, cooked coffee and changed my clothes. Halfway through this performance the rain stopped and a troop of little schoolgirls in white nylon aprons appeared from nowhere to catch a bus. They were in the charge of a serious señorita. They watched me gravely as I reassembled myself before their eyes.

A little farther along the road the throttle stuck again, this time at the twist-grip, and it was there in Miramar, as I worked by the roadside, that a middle-aged couple stopped their Morris Minor at the sight of my British number plates. "Where are you going?" called the man, in hearty English. I told them I was heading for Bariloche.

"Oh, you must stay with Teddy Wesley," he cried with great enthusiasm. "Here, I'll write it out for you." He gave me a scrap of paper with the address on it.

"He's a wonderful chap. Tell him George and Elsie sent you. Give him our regards."

Bemused and heartened by this unlikely meeting, because I was after all in Argentina and not in Kent, I rode on to cross the Pampa to the Andes, and Chile. It was a prospect of tremendous excitement to me, as much of a journey into the unknown as crossing the

Atlantic to South America, even as that first plunge into Africa a year before, but I faced it without the nervousness I had known then. In that year I had begun to find a sense of fitness and purpose to this traveling. It worked for me, it suited me literally down to the ground, and fulfilled some lifelong yearning that I had only guessed at vaguely.

It was not, as I might have thought myself once, the pursuit of adventure that animated me. The stuff that makes for heartstopping incidents in books was not what I was after. They happened, sure enough, along the way, and I guarded them carefully in my notebooks and memory for just that reason – that they would read well in a book – because I doubted my ability ever to convey the pure satisfaction of just moving along, easing through the landscape, moving with the flow from one culture to another until I could hope at last to see how they joined and mixed and separated and grew from what was common to us all.

A year on the road had given me a profession to follow and while I knew it might all come to an end at any moment, experience had given me a sturdy sense of confidence and viability. I needed nothing in particular to happen to make it all worthwhile. Just the daily ration of sights, sounds, smells, feelings and tastes was plenty to keep me healthy, to feed my mind and accumulate in my precious store of understanding.

Riding the motorcycle was second nature. Sitting on it was as natural to me as sitting on a chair, and more comfortable. Everything about it was customary, the passage of air across my face, the changes of temperature, the scents of hay, dust, sap, dung, diesel, stale urine, whatever was in the air, and though I regretted the loss of silence and my inability to hear birdsong and distant voices, the sound of the engine was comforting, in its way, and helpful to my thoughts.

I knew the bike well, believed in it and accepted its faults. I had everything I needed well distributed about me, and I knew that if anything went wrong it would be providence to blame and not me, and there was some satisfaction in that too.

Somewhere beyond Bahia Blanca, as I headed inland at last, the bike completed its first twenty thousand miles, and that was a sufficient sign of a healthy partnership, if I had needed one.

From the earliest moments of planning the journey, it was the oceans, mountains and deserts that gripped me most. I had crossed a desert and an ocean. Now the Andes were ahead. They had beckoned from thousands of miles away. I saw the world divided by two vast natural curtains of rock, the Himalayas separating north from south, and the Andes east from west. The Himalayas I could not expect to cross, though I hoped to get in among them one day, but the Andes stood in my way. They were the natural watershed of my journey, and I had always imagined them as a magic divide, beyond which, perhaps, lay a looking-glass world. There was always lurking in me an irrational hope that somewhere along the way I would stumble on a land where grass was pink, and trees were blue, and people stood on their heads. So I set off across the Pampa with a lively sense of anticipation.

It was a national holiday. Everything was closed, scarcely anything moved, and I had the Pampa to myself. At first there were thorn trees but they soon gave way to grass and scrub about three feet high. The road was slightly raised and there was barbed wire fence along each side. For three hundred miles the landscape was unchanged. I saw a few cows, and hawks hovering over a carcass or two. It was October, late spring in the southern hemisphere, and the sun rose high and hot and hazy. A constant wind blew from the north-west across and against me and sent tumbleweed rolling across my path, but the road was good tar and, stopping only to make some breakfast, I came out on the other side by mid-afternoon at General Roca.

The next day the landscape changed, becoming more barren and desertlike, but with the first undulations of rock breaking up through the ground. A puncture delayed me, and after 170 miles I got to Piedra de Aguilla and decided to camp there. The village was sited beneath a row of dramatic, jagged rocks; simple mud-and-brick buildings painted brilliant white. One door had a butcher's sign and I bought a few ribs and kidneys of lamb from a young man, then went next door to buy eggs and wine. The same man popped up behind the counter. It was like playing shops and it gave me a little childish pleasure. There was a law, it seems, that meat and dairy products could not be sold in the same shop.

I knew there was a river near by and I followed a dirt road about half a mile to find it. On a grassy bank, under trees, I pitched my tent. There was a steady cold wind, so I dug a shallow pit in the ground, built a fire in it, stuck some green, sharpened sticks into the earth so that they lay slantwise across the embers on the lee side, and balanced my ribs on them. The system worked well, and I planned a few improvements for the next time. The wine, cigarettes and tea made good company. One good evening like that, alone under the stars in a strange land, can warm the memories of a lifetime. The night was cold and peaceful. I woke early and ready to greet the Andes, now only 150 miles away.

The road rose steadily, and not far along they came into view. I stopped for a while and let the silence sink in. The country was marvellous in its strangeness. It was a land of semi-desert, cradled between peaks of rock and carpeted with a sparse sage-green scrub. Nearby the ground was brown and stony, but farther away the green deepened until it rolled up against the escarpments. I saw some horses running free, and heard them snorting and whinnying. Ahead of me the road dropped again to the valley of the Limay river, and there, far away, were the first snowy peaks of the Andes. A great exhilaration seized me, more than I could absorb, and I had to do something to expend it. I took some pictures of myself and the bike, something I rarely thought of doing. With the camera balanced on a rock and the delayed timer cocked I scampered back and forth laughing and playing like a child, while a horse, unaccountably roaming free, gazed at me with limpid eyes.

That ride from Piedra to Bariloche was altogether glorious. At Traful the road rejoined the river and ran with it through the Valle Encantado, a gorge guarded by rocks eroded into the most fantastic shapes. And then, finally, the first of the lakes appeared. Nahuel Huapi, a breathtaking blue among a rich green forest of pine, tucked in at the very feet of the snow covered slopes which soared up, young and sharp, to eight thousand feet.

Nothing had prepared me for the stunning beauty of that place. I avoided tourist brochures like the plague, and read as little as possible about the places I was to visit until I got there. Maybe I had once seen a lake as blue as Nahuel Huapi, or a mountain as tall and white as the Catedral, or forests as green as those around Bariloche, but to find all three together under a blue sky in that crisp, cold light was as outrageous as a vision of paradise; a poet's nightmare, for it made poetry superfluous.

I found the Wesleys the other side of Bariloche on a piece of land between two lakes. Teddy was not the cuddly figure one might have imagined. He was a strong, tough man with green, glittering eyes, a slow detached smile and the beard of a conquistador. Born in Argentina but descended from the Wellesleys, and therefore related to the Duke of Wellington, he was old enough to have fought as a commando in the Second World War and looked young enough still to conquer Peru, if it had been available.

He had a slight, fair-haired wife with a kind but distracted manner due, no doubt, to the effort of bearing and raising their four sons. They accepted me without fuss, and installed me in an empty caravan parked behind the house. So for eight days I was able to wander at will around this natural heaven, and return in the evening to pleasant company, and stories by the fireside. Bariloche was a famous resort,for skiers in the winter, and for walkers, climbers and anglers in the summer. It was also Argentina's center for atomic research, and the institute there attracted brilliant men of all nationalities. The mixture gave it a cultural and intellectual life that would be lacking in most holiday towns.

Teddy took me to meet Andrew, a Polish ski-instructor who lived a disreputable life on the shore of the lake. He was a born storyteller and told scurrilous tales about the people of the town, staring at me with faded blue eyes, defying contradiction.

"Suicides," he declared, "are all happening for sexual reasons. Take that woman. . . " and he named her ". . . who threw herself from the window. She did it because he couldn't satisfy her. You think I don't know. He stinks from far away."

According to Andrew many men stank from far away and, if one were to believe him, he was kept busy on a one-man crusade to save women from suicide, but there was no denying his vigour and his courage. He had been a sailor on the Polish ship Batory, and had seized life by the scruff of the neck by jumping ship in Buenos Aires to make his way across the continent. He had built his own house from fragments on a piece of no-man's land. It was that kind of place, and his stories were full of joy and vitality.

At the other end of the scale I met two Germans, Ruth and Alfred, who had built the best hotel in Bariloche, El Casco. They had built it more as a luxurious mansion than a hotel and they received us for dinner as friends in their splendid foyer. It was between seasons and there were no guests, so that it seemed indeed to be their private establishment, a recreation of pre-war baronial splendour. She had the full-blown proportions of a Wagnerian heroine, filling out her grand ball gown, while he was dwarfed beside her, a neat, small man in a correctly old-fashioned dinner jacket, with bow tie.

Theirs was a romantic story too. He was from Stuttgart, she from Berlin. In the war his wife had escaped to Sweden, her husband had been taken prisoner in Russia. Both marriages died through separation. They met, married and came to Bariloche, both anti-Nazis who now found themselves mixing socially with Nazi refugee scientists. But the old wounds had healed. It didn't matter any more. Gradually, their daughters had come of age and visited them, and both girls had married into the Institute.

Far from the political turmoil of Buenos Aires, Bariloche was like a world apart, living to its own rules, a fine place for people who were sick of politics and past sorrows and wanted to begin again. It had a great attraction for me too, and was one of those places I stored up as a bolt-hole for the future. Argentina was still a democracy, of sorts, and I was well aware that over the mountains I would be coming down into a police state as ruthless as any existing at that time. When it was time to leave the Wesleys, it was as hard as it had ever been.

I rode away from the them three times. The first time, just down the road, I realized I had left a part of my kitchen behind, and returned for it. The second time I had almost rounded the lake when it struck me that I didn't have my waterproof pants with me. I crept back sheepishly to fetch them. These embarrassing delays caused me a deal of trouble later on.

T ee arrived at Laverne Avenue with a big box of fried chicken
and a nice bottle of white wine. We already had champagne in
the fridge and lots of nuts and potato crisps, as well as steak
and soup and other good things. We were going to eat well and
make a party of it. Francesca was wearing a long white night
dress trimmed with lace, leaning back on lots of cushions.
Buttercup's picture was in a prominent place where she could
see it.

'You look good,' said Tee, and she did. She was vibrant and happy,
with that special alertness I remembered from when we had first
heard Iswas's heart beating. She talked and laughed with us as
though nothing was happening, and then every ten minutes or so
was swallowed up by the pain and effort of another contraction,. We
did breathing exercises and she followed my hand avidly as it rose
and fell, clinging to it with her eyes while the pain came to a peak
and died away. I was lying next to her and felt close and involved and
useful to her, and very glad to be there.

Then she would emerge and go on talking where she had left off,
and we got used to these curious intervals of frozen time. Gradually
they became more frequent, but it was early afternoon before they
were even five minutes apart and we could justifiably call the midwife. We were anxious to get her there, as a sign of hope and
progress, maybe too anxious because by the time she arrived the
intervals were greater again.

We began to realize we still had a long way to go, and Francesca was beginning to tire. She had been labouring now, more or less, for sixteen hours.

'It's such bad luck,' she said. 'Why do I have such bad luck?'

We were very lucky with our midwife. She was a young woman with a child of her own and a personality that inspired complete confidence. When she came in she seemed not in the least surprised to find us struggling, and put our minds at ease immediately.

'It's all right. I'm sure everything will go just fine. There are plenty of things we can do,' she said. 'Now let me just see whether you're dilated.'

Labour and birth are measured in dilations and contractions. Five-minute contractions – fetch the midwife. Two-minute contractions — fetch the doctor. Meanwhile, the pelvic girdle has to expand to let the baby out. That's what the labour is about. It's measured in centimetres, and ten centimetres is the target. Ten centimetres is what the baby's head needs to get through. It's just a figure, a perfectly ordinary fact of life, until you see someone lying there panting, racked with pain and drenched in perspiration trying to achieve it. Perhaps that's why doctors and midwives who deliver babies by the hundreds are still inclined to think of each birth as a miracle. We had two centimetres. No more.

'I'll tell you what,' said the midwife. 'Why don't you go for a walk?'

Of course! What a natural, sensible idea. We're thinking about it too much. If we get up and get moving, that should do it. If there had been a rice paddy outside, I would have suggested we go and plant some. Images of primitive life comforted me. Francesca got up, relieved, and put on a dress.

We tottered down the steep drive together. Every now and again she would grab me while I held her through another convulsion. We walked a long way round and came back over the top of the hill. By the time we got to the house things had speeded up somewhat.

Five minutes. Four minutes. Three minutes.

And four centimetres.

The midwife thought she'd call the doctor anyway.

We were down on the bed again and working hard. It was tiring for me, exhausting for her. She was very tired and her back hurt like hell. I rubbed it all the time. Then Tee took over for a while, and then the two of us lay there with her, one doing the breathing, the other rubbing to relieve the terrible backache.

But we were stuck at three minutes and four centimetres.

"Okay," said the midwife. "We'll try something else. We'll break the bag. It usually happens naturally about this stage, and that should move it along."

She got an instrument from her case, a long needle like a crochet hook, and did her bit to help nature. By now we were all as gripped and involved with the birth, its vagaries and anatomical imperatives, as surgeons at the front line. All niceties of modesty and reticence were forgotten. When Francesca said it was hard not to swear when the peak of the pain hit her, we all encouraged her with laughter.

"Go ahead," I said, "Shout it, and to hell with Camberley."

And she did. It sounded perfectly reasonable, and it gained us another centimetre. But no more.

The doctor arrived about six in the evening, and settled his massive frame in one of our canvas chairs to wait. He was quiet, if not entirely composed, and left the routine to our midwife who was still encouraging and enthusiastic. Her presence was so positive that, for all the dismay we felt as each new surge of progress faded and failed, we were sure that soon the wonderful moment would come. But it had been twenty hours of struggling now, on nothing but a dish of soup, and Francesca was dreadfully tired.

"Better give her an IV?" the midwife said. The doctor nodded.

"It's for dehydration," she told us. "Just to make up for all the sweating. Dehydration is very exhausting."

She brought out the bottle of saline and the tube, and hung it on the wall, on a lamp bracket. Francesca accepted it without a murmur, but she asked for nothing else. She knew the midwife would have all the drugs in her bag, but she was going to do it her way.

The doctor said it would be a couple of hours yet and thought he ought to have some dinner while he could. He gave the name of a Mexican restaurant in Mill Valley, and we didn't see him again for an hour and a half, but when he came back we had got no further.

It seemed impossible, intolerable, but I was so committed now to supporting her that I did not think beyond the next contraction. It seemed to me that the techniques we had learned were no longer doing much for her. She seemed unable to get on top of the pain, despite the breathing, and it just hit her every time. But I felt responsible for pulling her through, and I had to believe it would work.

Then the doctor stirred and said:

"I'm sorry. We've waited long enough, maybe even too long. It's time to go to hospital."

# 24. Chile

The ride to Villa la Agostura was sensational. For thirty miles I rode along the opposite shore of Nahuel Huapi with the blue water and mountains on my left, grassy slopes and pines on my right. It was grass to revel on, to roll in, to fall in love on. Then I climbed to 6,000 feet and Puyehue Pass. The road was dirt, but a good firm surface, with snow banked up on either side, and the conifers gave way to a tall deciduous tree with light green foliage. The Argentine border gave me no problems. Then, some way down the other side, came the Chilean immigration.

It was impossible to go in there without recalling the carnage that had engulfed Chile a year before: the bombs, the corpses in the streets, the wholesale arrests and massacres, the torture and brutality, and, ever since, the relentless hunting down of 'Marxists'. Then, for a moment, I wondered whether I had been foolish to come. There were rumours of a strong connection between the armies of Brazil and Chile. Perhaps they would have my name on their blacklist already. Would they let me in at all? Worse still, would they watch me, follow me, wait for a false move?

Well, it was too late for paranoid fantasies. I went in with my passport ready, the one which described me as a builder. Men in green uniforms treated everyone with an almost exaggerated gentleness. Were they police or army? I couldn't tell. I noticed how European they looked. Many were blond, positively Germanic. There was no difficulty. A customs man put his hand briefly into one of my boxes, then murmured: '*Listo*. Finished.' But there were posters on the walls. Photographs of weapons laid out on the ground; whole arsenals of rifles, grenades, machine guns and explosives. The message read: 'They were going to kill your son for not believing as they do.' Ironic propaganda. It would have done equally well for either side.

Then it was over, and I began the long descent to the Pan American Highway and Osorno.

It was a hell of a road; deep layers of loose stone, fine for cars, terrible for me, the worst of its kind since Ethiopia. I slid and slipped around the corners, brakes worse than useless, but even so I registered the dramatic change in appearance of everything on this side of the mountain. The vegetation looked sub-tropical. Big ferns and bamboos grew among the rocks. There were forests choked with creepers, the undergrowth was six feet high, with humid fat-leaved plants I did not expect so far south. Then, to my great relief, the road surface changed to tar and at the same time the country opened out into lush dairy land, carefully fenced and worked. Milk churns stood by the side of the road as they once did in England. I saw oxen pulling ploughs and carts. Just before six I arrived in Osorno.

'Don't bother with Osorno,' said Teddy. 'Go on to Pucatrihue. It's only another forty miles to the coast. There's a lovely little guest house you could stay at.'

I was in a quandary. I had no Chilean money and I had arrived too late for the banks. I had enough gas to get to the coast, though, and I had dollars and Argentine pesos. And I wanted to get to the Pacific. God, how I wanted that first glimpse of that ocean. To cross the Andes and reach the Pacific in one afternoon seemed fantastic. I couldn't resist it.

From Osorno the road was stone and dirt, not difficult but a road you had to keep an eye on. I counted without the sun. In Chile the setting sun is no modest red disc, no dying ember; it is hot and fierce and it slid down in front of me and blinded me. Whichever way I tried to tilt my head and helmet I couldn't keep the fire out of my eyes. In one hour I had scarcely done twenty miles, and at eight o'clock it was clear I would not reach the coast before nightfall. I resigned myself to sleeping out and, as usual, looked for a river and saw that the road would soon cross the Tranallaquin. I came to a wooden bridge and the loose planks clattered beneath me like a dud xylophone.

On the farther bank, to my right, I saw a spot where I thought I might sleep. A grassy path led to the river a little way downstream where there were small trees, clumps of reed and bamboo. It seemed sheltered and unobtrusive, although I could see that horses used it for watering. I wanted to keep out of sight. Some of my earlier nervousness must have remained, and yet, illogically, the first thing I did once the tent was up was to light a fire to cheer myself.

I ate steak and rice and drank well from my wineskin. The countryside was very quiet. Only two cars and a last bus rumbled across the bridge. The moon was out, and full. Ever since my first night on the sand dunes of Libya, the happiest parts of the journey had coincided with a full moon.

'Must be a lunatic enterprise,' I muttered to myself.

I slept easily on the soft grass. Didn't even undress, as I usually do; just wrapped the sleeping bag around me. At six I woke to a bright, clear sky. The air was warm already. I decided to get going and have breakfast when I arrived at the coast.

A horseman turned off the road and rode down as I was packing my things. He wore a trilby hat and a fog-coloured poncho. His stirrups were massive wooden things, impressively carved in the shape of a wild animal's head. He talked a difficult sing-song Spanish, different to the one I had become used to, but he had a speech defect which slowed him up, and I was able to follow it.

'Have you been here all night?' he asked. He seemed quite astonished to find me there, but he asked none of the usual questions about the bike and where I had come from. He asked whether I had seen a horse. I remembered hooves galloping away in the night and told him. The horse had not crossed the bridge, I pointed out.

'*Entonces,*' he said, 'it went the other way. *Gracias.*'

When he left he crossed the bridge, which I thought odd. I finished my packing and went on my way to the coast. With the sun rising behind me I took in the countryside and discovered that I was in yet another kind of paradise. Where yesterday I had been overwhelmed by grand vistas, here I was entranced by a purity of detail belonging to the pre-industrial age. This was not wild, untouched scenery. The hand of man was in evidence everywhere, in the hedgerows, the wooden fences, gates and barns, and among the cows, pigs and chickens they enclosed. The river tumbling past had cut a clean channel between level banks topped with thick, inviting turf and shaded conveniently here and there by trees. A rustic suspension bridge with a small gate at my end swung across the river to somebody's property, a garden path in flight. In the hedges were masses of flame-red flowers which made the green of the long fresh grass seem deeper and more vibrant even than it was. In the middle distance, green hills swelled and dipped, and far beyond them to the east rose a spectacular snow-streaked volcano with an insubstantial look, as though projected on the atmosphere.

Coloured birds sang to greet the sun under a deep sky. There was not a foot of concrete, not a pylon, not even a strand of barbed wire in sight. For a while, until the first car passed, the centuries dropped away and I fell with them into a romantic dream of pastoral perfection.

Eventually the river, and the road with it, sank into a cleft between headlands and issued into a small, sandy bay. I gazed out on the Pacific Ocean in quiet rapture and found the guest house perched among the rocks, a little further along the coast. It was eight in the morning as I walked up a steep pathway to the door. Two wolfhounds began to howl behind some chicken wire. A maid in cap and apron answered the howl. She was as round, neat and colourful as a Russian doll.

I said I wanted to spend a day and a night there. She looked a little suspicious and went back into the house, but returned smiling to invite me in.

Would I like some breakfast? I nodded enthusiastically. Then, as an afterthought I asked where there might be some gas, and added that I would need to change dollars or *pesos.* How I wished I had left well alone. When she returned it was without cups or jugs or breadbasket. Instead she said there was nothing they could do with my foreign money, since it was illegal to change it. There was no gas either, and certainly no breakfast.

Although the practical problems this raised seemed, for the moment, insoluble, it was the withdrawal of hospitality which hit me hardest. I sat looking at her in silence for a few minutes, hoping that she herself would find a way to cut the knot she had just tied, but she could suggest only that I see the police in the next bay. She was quite implacable in a way that I knew was unnatural to her. It was my first brush with the regime, and I was troubled by it.

Just south across the river was the next bay, Bahia Mansa. The police station, a small house with a garden, was neat and clean as a whistle. The policeman came to the door in a German-style field-green uniform, pressed and spotless. He himself was light-skinned and sandy-haired, tidy and shaven, with cheeks polished like apples. His grey eyes viewed me with uncritical candour. In all South America I had never seen a policeman like him.

I felt sure he would help if I gave him a chance, so I spun my story out, in execrable Spanish, trying to make it amusing and to give him time to get used to me.

"You were out all night?" he exclaimed, with the same surprised tone the horseman had used.

"You were very lucky. You could have been shot."

It took a moment for me to understand the Spanish for curfew.

"*Coberta fuego,*" he said. "After one in the morning nobody is allowed out. The soldiers can shoot strangers on sight. And they do. There are patrols everywhere, and the people are ordered to report anyone they see."

I could think of nothing to say. He took my jerry can and brought it back with five litres of gas, twice what I had asked for.

"I can do nothing with your money, but you could try the Germans in Mucolpue. Hotel Witmer."

My profuse thanks embarrassed him and he waved me off with a "God speed", so I rode along to the third and biggest of the bays. Here the ground rose behind the beach at an angle almost too steep for buildings, and the many brilliantly coloured clap-board houses stuck to the hillside seemed to defy perspective like a primitive painting.

The hotel consisted of three of these houses joined together. Herr Witmer was painting his doorway yellow. I asked him if I could speak German with him. He replied cheerfully, in Spanish, that it was all the same to him what we spoke. Anyway, he was not changing any dollars and he implied that the policeman must have lost his wits.

After a year on the road I had a beggar's instinct for a soft heart.

Normally I might have hoped for an invitation, a meal maybe or a bed, but behind his jocular manner I felt the same unnatural but implacable refusal I had been shown by the maid. It was as though a plague had passed through the land.

I looked out over the beach and the ocean in wistful frustration, breathing the strong, pure smell of the seaweed. A man was fishing the surf with a line wound round an oil can. Otherwise the beach was deserted. There were no sounds, no signs, no structures in any way extraneous to the life of the bay and the people who lived on it. Any holidaymaker who came here would have to live as they did, and fit in with what was there.

Once again I had the powerful feeling of having traveled back through time to an age just before the human miracle turned to madness. With a heavy heart, baffled by the ironies of my situation, I accepted that I might never see its like again.

Well, I thought, at least I can have my breakfast here. I had two eggs and a hunk of bread, and I set up my kitchen on the smooth black rocks just above the high-tide line of black kelp. I fried my eggs, made coffee. I would have spent the day and the night there, living off my stock of rice and taking a chance on being shot, but I already knew that the next day was a Bank Holiday, and after that came the weekend. I would have to survive four days and nights without money or food.

So I buried my eggshells, washed my dishes in the sea and slowly packed up for the ride back to Osorno. When I left, the fisherman had still caught nothing, but he went on smoothly casting his line as though he had all the time in the world.

Even on my way back inland I thought of getting my money and returning, but yet another obstacle arose to prevent it. A shock absorber failed and with the load I was carrying over this stony surface the other would be sure to go. By the time I got to Osorno I had convinced myself that I had woken from a dream, and that to try to re-enter it would be to invite a nightmare. Better leave the dream intact and go on to Santiago.

In Santiago I had friends of friends, and I was very fortunate with them. Roberto and Gloria were a gentle and generous middle-class couple who lived with their two young daughters in a small house in Nuñoa, a pleasant district full of gardens in flower and trees in blossom. They gave me their convertible couch to sleep on for five weeks, never failing to persuade me to stay as long as I could. They also gave me their lives and their stories, and remained a benchmark of normality against which to measure all the wild extremes I encountered as I roamed around the city.

He was a government employee who had voted for Allende, while she, who taught in a school for the poorest of the poor, had voted Conservative. He had been dismayed by the chaos and fever of the Allende government's last months, but could never condone the coup. She, on the other hand, had welcomed the army's action at first. Neither of them had anticipated the horrors to follow and it was clear that they were only just emerging from a state of shock. Like most others in their class, people of relatively mild opinion, they had shut their door on the world, knowing they could do nothing, and concentrated simply on survival.

An event had occurred only recently to cause Gloria to think again. She told me about it one evening, over a much-loved dish of stewed conger eel, a national favourite.

"Some government health workers came to the school one day and shaved the heads of many of our little girls because of the lice. Well, it was a harsh thing to do without warning, or telling the parents. The parents came next day – furious, naturally. They complained, but I said I had nothing to do with it, and they should complain to the Junta."

The country was run by a junta of military chiefs, headed by the Army General Pinochet, but at the local level too the military authorities were called juntas.

"Well, before long some soldiers came to the school. They came into my classroom, pointed a rifle at the back of my head, marched me out in front of the children and took me to the barracks. In front of the children," she repeated.

"God, weren't you scared?" I asked stupidly. She smiled. There was a strong, stubborn streak in Gloria.

"Yes, I was frightened. Well, they locked me in a room. Then I was taken to the colonel, still with the rifle pointed at me. And he accused me of inciting the people to revolt. So of course I denied it, but he went on blustering at me and then they locked me up again.

"*Bueno*, I was there for some hours, and they came back again with the rifle and took me back to the colonel. And he said I had to make a list of all the people I knew, friends and relations, with left-wing opinions. So I said I would be happy to do it if I could first give him a list of people I knew with right-wing opinions. So we argued a bit, but then he said 'Oh, get on with it.' The first person on my list was Pinochet."

It was pure luck. She was a distant relation of the Pinochet family, which had never been much to shout about before, but the colonel's mood changed dramatically and she was returned to the school with apologies. That incident finally turned her against the regime.

Her story affected me more profoundly than all the accounts of atrocities. It was proof that the poison was arbitrary, all pervasive and self-propagating. I determined to find out as much as I could about what was going on, although it never occurred to me that I could do anything to help.

My newspaper contact lived in the foothills on the south east edge of the city, and I rode out there to talk about things. One would never have imagined, riding through the capital on an early summer's day, that it was in an official 'state of siege'. Santiago was among the prettiest of South-American capitals, built on the older European model. There were few high buildings at that time, for the area is prone to earthquakes, and the scale of the houses and streets was humanely welcoming. Parks and trees appeared all around, along the river, even in the frantically busy center, and behind them everywhere stood the Andes, rising sheer to twenty thousand feet, as though painted on a backdrop which seemed at times to be only a stone's throw away.

It was a city made for a motorcycle. Fine weather, lovely avenues and the ever-present mountains made riding a joy. The people were civilized, hospitable, and, in their sense of isolation, anxious to entertain and question a stranger. And the women were undeniably attractive, as I had been promised time and time again on my way there. It was this contrast between, on the one hand, the visible beauty, the kindness and the well-being of Santiago and, on the other, the knowledge of the grotesque and barbaric deeds that were being perpetrated there at every moment, which gave a unique, shuddering vitality to every thought and emotion.

I arrived to be offered drinks and fascinating anecdotes by the poolside and I lapped them both up until a television journalist arrived to discuss a programme. We were introduced, perfunctorily, in Spanish when she came in. Her name escaped me, but not her face. She was quite beautiful in a Spanish way, but her personality was just as striking as her looks. The two were in equilibrium in a way that I found rare, neither having to accede to the other. She was poised, charming, intelligent, and her sense of humour was very evident. Even then, before my infatuation had overwhelmed me, I could find no fault with her, unless it was that she apparently spoke no English.

They excused themselves to sit at a table talking. I found that I could follow her conversation easily. She spoke a very lucid Spanish. I sat on a cushion watching her, finding her very exciting.

They were talking about women's independence, a hot subject in Chile. I composed a sentence in Spanish and launched it, nonchalantly, into a suitable gap.

'It appears to me that women feel themselves to be much more free in Chile than they do in Argentina.'

She turned to look at me in surprise. There was a slight pause of recognition.

'*Que barbara! Un gringo que habla Castellano.*'

She put everything into that one remark. It was a *coup de foudre*. Faint mockery, admiration, curiosity, an unmistakable challenge, and above all the direct warmth of those dark eyes.

The contract was drawn up right there. All we had to do was sign it.

The outward form of our relationship we devised that afternoon. Having traveled so much I must have formed impressions about the relative freedom of women in different countries. It would make a good interview, no?

I agreed, enthusiastically. We would meet and discuss it. She gave me an office telephone number.

"I will be there tomorrow, before lunch, if you are free?"

"Yes, I am free," I said. "But forgive me. I didn't catch your name."

"Elena Ortega," she said. "And you, how do you call yourself?"

"Ted Simon."

"Ah, *bueno*, Ted." She shook my hand. Her smile was just friendly now, and businesslike. "*Hasta mañana.*"

We met and lunched, and met again. Elena was as free as I, but she was also discreet. It would not necessarily be a good thing for her to be thought too intimate with a Gringo. She explained this honestly. Her family, for example, would not approve. She was a busy woman, and flattered me with the time she spent in my company, but it was never too much and I knew she was controlling it carefully.

We actually made the programme she had thought up so quickly at our first meeting. Eventually we also signed our own more personal contract, but there was some fine print which I did not look at too carefully. It read, so to speak 'I Elena Ortega do agree to fulfill wholeheartedly the terms of this agreement only provided that the said Ted Simon, also known as the "Gringo en Moto", will shortly continue his journey, at which time the contract expires and becomes void.'

It was a clause I had employed often enough myself on the way, but it was a new experience to have it used against me and when the time came I discovered how harsh it could be.

Santiago was an exciting and frightening city. Many times I rode back to Nuñoa from Elena's house just in time to beat the one o'clock curfew. Through dark, deserted streets, where only armed soldiers roamed, I raced along the complicated route, trusting to my memory and the accuracy of Elena's kitchen clock. Sometimes I heard gunfire to spur me on.

During the day the army was virtually invisible, but the police were a paramilitary force and had monstrous weapons slung over their shoulders. Even on the steps of the museums and art galleries they stood with their machine guns dangling.

I gathered information and personal stories wherever I could, determined to form my own opinion about the slaughter of democracy in Chile. I felt I was in an unusually good position to do so. During the year since the coup I had been fairly isolated from the propaganda and rhetoric surrounding the issue, but I had personal experience of the South American police state at work, and a good schooling in the Latin American personality, and its many variations. My Spanish was now adequate. I had good contacts with the rich through Elena, with the middle-class through the Duces and others, and with the poor through the priests to whom I had been directed by their brothers in Brazil.

Where my identity as a journalist was an obstacle the aura of the adventurer worked well. My experience made me equally at home in hovels and palaces. All in all, I was exceptionally well-placed.

There was no disputing the facts. Life before the coup had been increasingly chaotic. Some had found it exhilarating, many found it exasperating, and those with a lot to lose had naturally found it threatening. Those who enjoyed it most were the idealists and the opportunists. The latter exacerbated it, allowing the former to push harder and faster towards a fully-fledged Marxist state.

For the wealthy there had come a point where it was very clearly 'now or never'.

The belief that Chilean democracy and the Allende government could have survived was based on twin myths. One was the so-called traditional neutrality of the armed forces. The other was the conviction of the educated classes that the democratic idea had become an unalterable habit with the Chilean people. They called themselves 'the Switzerland of South America' and flaunted a rather arrogant political snobbery.

The army, which had in fact intervened once before in 1924, struck with terrible swiftness and brutality. Huge numbers were arrested, tortured, killed. Opinion-formers and militants in all the organizations of the peasantry and the urban poor were methodically jailed or butchered, unless they had fled into exile or sought asylum in the compounds of sympathetic embassies. The Italians, Mexicans and French were particularly hospitable, and their compounds were still packed with refugees when I arrived. After a year of confinement, the conditions there were miserable. The refusal of the government to allow their expatriation was only one of the scandals that sickened the world. The British, unfortunately, had made the complacent judgement that they could do more good by trying to influence the regime than by sheltering its opponents There is no evidence to suggest that they were right.

The reputation of the United States was tarnished beyond redemption. Almost everyone believed that the CIA had taken a hand in the coup. The sudden strike and the ensuing repression were managed with remarkable efficiency, and it was widely assumed that the Chilean military could not have pulled it off alone.

Two questions vexed me. One was whether or not the tragedy would have taken place without the connivance of the USA. The other was whether the generals themselves were of the kind to organize and condone the continuing obscenity of tortures and massacres, or whether they had become the creatures of the machine they had set in motion.

I was invited one Sunday afternoon to a small party in the garden of an architect's house. He was a plump, bearded man in his thirties, dressed rather ostentatiously in black, under a black-leather jacket. With him stood a vivacious woman in a summer dress and hat. He was telling us about his visit to New York and his feelings on coming back to Chile.

"I can't understand," I said, "why the Junta is turning on the middle classes now. Surely that is where they must look for most of their support. But now more and more of them are being arrested, interrogated, even tortured."

"Oh, you mustn't believe that," said the woman. "There are Marxists in every class, and they have to be found, but they don't torture innocent people. It's a lie."

"That's not what I've heard," I said.

"Well," said the man, "you have to be careful. The DINA have a simple method. Every person they arrest is asked to name all the people he knows. Then they arrest and question all those people. The net brings in everyone. I tell you frankly, I am a supporter of the army. But they arrested me and I was damned scared."

"What did they do to you?" I asked.

"I was kept in a cell for a week. Every time I was questioned I was blindfolded. I never saw a single one of my interrogators. I was not hurt because I didn't protest. I answered their questions. But what I heard was terrible. Terrible screams. But what do you expect? They are ruthless and so are the Marxists."

"Well," I said, "it sounds as if the Junta has just lost control."

"Are you writing articles for a newspaper?" asked the woman. Her curiosity seemed pointed.

"Sometimes," I replied. "But I write about my own personal experiences. Hardly ever anything political. Only what I know to be true at first hand. The *Sunday Times* is supporting me on my journey, and I send them things from time to time."

They kept me telling traveler's tales for a while, as the woman took me round the lawn introducing me. Before I left, she asked me whether I would be interested in meeting a member of the Junta.

"Well, of course I would," I replied, guardedly, "if I was under no particular obligation."

"I'll see what I can do," she said. "Maybe there's a chance."

She took my phone number.

"Come for lunch one day," she said. "Now I have to go. I have a family to feed."

I told Elena about it later.

"Oh, Perla," she said. "She writes for *Mercurio*. She does the social column. But she's very close to the editor. You never know . . ."

*El Mercurio* was the only daily paper of consequence still being published in Chile. Always an old-fashioned and conservative newspaper, it was now generally accepted to be the mouthpiece of the Junta. When the editor invited me for tea at his apartment I was certainly not predisposed to like him, but found it hard to withhold respect. Rene Silva Espejo was an old man, and evidently not well. He apologized at once for being unable to stand up to greet me, and remained on his sofa throughout the meeting, but his manner was considerate and his eyes lively and intelligent behind his spectacles. I found myself wanting to make excuses for him, guessing at the harrowing compromises one might be tempted into in his position.

For his part he showed an equal tolerance. I was wearing boots, jeans and a leather jacket, and my macho outfit must have jarred terribly with the venerable cabinetry, the expensive rugs, the rows of leatherbound volumes and the signed portraits of past presidents. They were the clothes I normally wore of necessity, and I had refused to bring out my only respectable shoes and trousers as a reminder to myself that I was not there to engage in any of the usual complicities which come so easily among journalists. If he thought my statement rather priggish he gave no sign of it. He spoke little English  but we conversed easily in French and he suggested that the Air Force General Gustavo Leigh Guzman might find it useful to talk to me. Only at the end did he smile, nod at my boots and wonder politely whether I would be wearing them for a meeting with the Junta.

'They might be thought a little shocking,' he said, and laughed. 'Although, God knows, you will see enough boots over there.'

I waited a long time before the general saw me. Twice meetings were arranged, then cancelled, but I was in no great hurry.

I was happy with Elena. We were spending more and more time together. She introduced me to Chilean literature, we went to the movies and to parties, and had lovely quiet dinners in her prettily decorated home. Gradually she became less cautious and reserved, and opened her heart more freely. It was marvellous then to see how easily she managed to combine a demanding professional life in the public eye with such natural femininity and warmth. It was made the more easy for her of course by a certain coziness that existed among the small professional classes in Chile restricted largely to a minority of educated people with private means. There was little of the bitter competitiveness with its accompanying anxieties and complexities which I was used to among the journalists of my own country. In the paternalistic society that Chile had once again become, Elena enjoyed a comfortable security that favoured her as a woman.

Naturally it troubled her conscience to be a member of this elite. Whenever possible she plunged with her cameras into the slums in order to highlight their growing misery, but the regime firmly limited her scope. She gave refuge too to people on the run from DINA, and on one occasion I met at her home a young man dodging desperately from house to house to keep ahead of the police. So that while we pursued our affair in luxury, it was spiced also by a hint of danger. In this heady atmosphere our feelings flourished until I was sure that we were well and truly in love.

Once I asked her whether she could imagine living anywhere outside Chile, but even in her attempt to consider the idea the impossibility of it became obvious. She loved the country passionately. She spoke of the mountains, the ocean, the people, with a love that seemed deeper than any personal feelings. To one as rootless as I felt, it was a shock to realize the heartbreak suffered by the thousands of refugees who had fled from Chile into exile. And, knowing that sooner or later I would have to leave too, I had a presentiment of the misery I would feel when we parted. I did my best to forget it. I dropped the subject and we did not speak of it again.

The meeting with Leigh was finally arranged. Perla asked me to come to her office and said that she would take me to the government building herself, no doubt to avoid, I thought to myself, the dread possibility of my turning up there on a motorcycle. On the appointed day I put on my fancy pants, cleaned and pressed in readiness, and went out to sup with the devil.

The old government palace, the Moneda, was still in ruins from the bombing attack ordered a year before by this same general I was now to meet. In the interim, the Junta had set up its headquarters in a modern glass-fronted building originally intended for a United Nations agency, UNCTAD. It was twenty storeys high, a rarity in Santiago, and helicopters clattered above, arriving and departing from the roof.

We waited outside on the pavement for Silva to arrive and take me in. Even that was a curious experience, as dangerous looking Carabinieri lined the street carrying the usual murderous weaponry and sporting the highly polished boots I had been promised. Then a limousine slid along beside us and stopped.

The driver helped Silva out, and I saw how frail he was. He could scarcely get one foot in front of the other, and seemed to have difficulty with his shoes. I respected him for taking the trouble to come. I guessed that he felt he was performing a duty.

Perla left us, and we walked at a snail's pace into the lobby, also heavily guarded. I was lightly searched and asked to open my camera case. Then a girl exchanged my passport for a piece of paper and we continued to the elevator. There were some steps to go down and Silva leaned heavily on me. On two occasions I had to save him from falling.

A guard traveled up with us and passed us on to another reception room. Then Silva went in to see Leigh alone for twenty minutes, before asking me to enter.

General Gustavo Leigh Guzman made no very strong impression on me at first. He was a short man with a faintly mottled complexion and dark hair slicked back. His smile had a lot of teeth in it. If you liked him you could say it was charming; if not, shark-like. He wore a plain uniform and, greeting me easily in Spanish, sat down opposite me at a table with Silva between us.

He asked me which countries I had visited, and I went through the list quickly and added, truthfully enough, how beautiful Chile was.

"And how do you find things here?'" he asked.

I said I was anxious first that he should know I was not required or expected to write anything, and that I would only do so if I thought it could be constructive, so that any opinions I gave him would be true ones and not simply what he might want to hear.

"Chile makes me nervous," I said. "I find that people here are very frightened of being carried off in the night."

We were talking in English now, which he spoke well. He made a long speech trying to convince me that Chile was the victim of a worldwide Communist conspiracy, that the military action and repression had been essential to prevent another Viet Nam in South America, and that Peru was now being armed by Russia to attack Chile. Meanwhile, he complained that the British were strangling his Air Force, by refusing to service his planes.

"It's your Communist unions. They have put a stranglehold on us. I am having to consider withdrawing our funds from England and transferring them to Washington. And perhaps then we will not be able to sell you any more copper."

Much of this was highly exaggerated. Some of it was absurd. There were no Communist unions in England in 1974. He spoke easily, without threatening or hectoring. I wasn't even sure that he expected me to believe any of it. As to the state of the trade in weapons and commodities, I knew too little to judge what was significant. I merely thought that he seemed strangely out of touch with world opinion.

"I wonder whether you realize," I said, politely, "the strength of the feeling that exists in Britain on the issue of human rights? One does not need to be a Communist to deny weapons to a country where thousands have been arrested, tortured and killed. Anyone who wanted to help Chile could not do so in face of the evidence.

"Surely," I went on, "after a year of repression you must have removed the threat to your internal security? Surely, you don't have to go on hunting people and throwing them into jail? Why don't you let some people go instead?"

He did not seem to be in the least surprised to hear this.

"Yes," he said. "The Marxists are defeated. There is no more an internal problem."

"Then you can put an end to your repressive measures?"

"Yes," again. "We must relax. I am going to talk to the other generals this month."

"And your prisoners?"

"We realize we must let them go."

I was astonished.

"How many prisoners do you say you have?" I asked.

"The numbers are much exaggerated. There are not more than 2,500 in prison. We have just signed the papers releasing the first hundred. But it is three months since Pinochet made his offer to release political prisoners if Russia and Cuba would do the same. Why didn't the world raise its arms and say, 'Yes. Good idea. That's the way to peace?'"

He seemed genuinely surprised that the world was reluctant to award Pinochet a peace prize. I asked him when he thought Chile might be restored to democracy. He got to his feet then and began to walk around, showing real agitation.

"We are tired of this work," he said, unexpectedly. "We were astonished to be called to power. We were compelled to take power. The majority of the people called us. If I could only leave this desk now and go home, I would be happy.

"They call us Fascists and Nazis. We want democracy. I want democracy. But if we hand over now to the politicians there will be a vacuum. We must first have a constitution which prevents any party from seizing absolute power."

He talked then about the good works which he said the Junta was carrying out, in the schools, the slums, the hospitals and the unions.

"So you see," he said proudly, "we are carrying out just the equalization programmes that were promised by Allende."

My friends the priests would have found that hard to swallow.

"And when then do you think Chile will be ready for democracy again?"

He smiled uneasily.

"Well, not around the corner. Maybe after the next block. But, you know, you should not be too critical of us. I have just been reading in the Economist that the army may take over in Britain too."

And that, I must admit, had me stupefied.

We talked for an hour and a half. Silva, now sitting farther away from us, said not a word. Then I shook hands with Leigh and Silva.

In French, Silva asked me: "Do you think you have something?"

"Yes, I think so," I replied.

"Good. Then, *au revoir.*"

I left the building trying to think just what it was I had got. A handful of sensational promises, but as far as I knew they had not been made before. Surely if they were printed large in the *Sunday Times* the Junta would have to make some of them good? Or maybe it would split the Junta. I was very excited at the thought that I might yet be able to do something useful. Even if it just got one extra man out of prison, that would be something.

I went back to Nuñoa and made something more orderly out of my hastily scribbled notes. Then I made the rounds of embassies and refugee organizations to see whether they already had indications that the Junta was planning to release prisoners. None of them had heard of any such promises.

One of my last calls was on a medium-ranking diplomat from the British Embassy whom I had already met casually. I visited him at his home in one of the wealthier parts of the city, where he lived in a degree of luxury which, he freely admitted, though with undue complacency, was quite out of proportion to his importance or to the state of the British economy at that time.

He put a drink in my hand and took me out to his verandah to survey the expensively plumbed lawn. A gardener, watering the roses, had accidentally sprayed the garden furniture and the diplomat said to him, with forced equanimity:

"You have wet the chairs."

The gardener smiled contentedly.

"*Si Senor,*" he said, and moved on to the rhododendrons.

We sat on the wet seats.

"They are only damp," he said, striving for conviction. It was an attitude which permeated his being. His clothes, his posture, his accent and probably, his morality all struggled towards a certain rectitude and failed by about three degrees to meet it, but this faint tilt away from the desired effect was glaringly evident and as troubling to the senses as a slightly crooked picture frame.

"Now, tell me about your meeting with Leigh," he said. "Didn't you find him pathological?"

"He has a prognathous jaw," I replied cautiously, already regretting my presence. Seeing no way out, I told him what Leigh had said. He made a steeple with his fingers, balanced his chin on it and assumed a grave expression.

"The Ambassador is away today, but I wish you would leave this with me. I'll talk to the First Secretary and we'll bring it to the Ambassador tomorrow."

I saw no harm in that, and agreed.

We met again two days later for tea. I had got no further with my own inquiries.

"We feel," he said, with a touch of majesty, "that it would be unwise to publish Leigh's proposals. We all agree that it's a plant. He simply wants to create a more favourable image but there is no reason to believe that they will release anyone. You would just be playing into his hands."

If I had been a reporter on an assignment I would have taken no notice. It would have been for the Foreign Office to address its homilies to my editor in London. But I had been away too long to think in those terms and had fallen into the habit of making my own independent judgements. What if they were right? The last thing I wanted to do was to make it easier for the Junta to win support.

I left, saying I would think about it. That evening I visited Elena. I was still undecided. As I saw it, my interview with Leigh would only serve any purpose if I could manage to make it seem of major importance. Sometimes a correspondent can do this. By making dramatic and expensive telephone calls to highly placed newspaper executives at inconvenient times, he can create an aura of urgency about a story which would never be accorded to the same information filed on a routine telex . There are obvious risks in this procedure. The reporter is playing double or quits with his credibility, but that was not my problem. I had a good relationship with the editor of the paper. Was this the right time to exploit it? Or would I simply be making wonderful propaganda for the Junta?

Elena was oddly unhelpful and my lack of resolution seemed to provoke her into impatience on a personal level. She became cool and distant, and I responded by trying in vain to win back from her the admiration I depended on.

At last she looked at me pointedly, and said:

'Perhaps you have been here too long.'

The accusation made me squirm. Nothing is more hurtful than to be shown a truth one has refused to recognize. The bravura of my first weeks with Elena was dissipated. We had reached the point where the practical realities of her life created new problems. Her work and her social life could only stretch so far to accommodate me. I was a bizarre phenomenon in her world. She called me her 'wild goose'. If we went on together much longer I would have to be accepted formally as a permanent element in her arrangements. This was impossible and she knew it, had known it from the start.

My meeting with Leigh had already maintained the excitement level between us beyond its normal span. Now, as I foundered in a morass of doubt about my role in that game – was I the knight or the pawn? – she saw with ruthless clarity that I had outlived my usefulness, both to her and to Chile. She was a woman of much warmth and compassion; I had seen that in her marvellously displayed. But those were not qualities to be exhausted in a fruitless affair like ours.

During the following days I prepared to leave, discovering as I did so how many ties I had created for myself in those five weeks. There were people everywhere I had grown fond of and wanted to see at least once more. As always when I stopped moving for any length of time my systems became dispersed. I traveled with a great array of objects that had all proved their usefulness again and again, and when packed on the motorcycle fell effortlessly into place in a pattern I had evolved and knew by heart. Now they were scattered far and wide through the house in Nuñoa, and getting them together again was hardly less difficult than ordering my own disturbed and scattered thoughts.

My idea of trying to launch Leigh's proposals into the mediasphere by dramatic calls to London began to seem childish and irresponsible. I had no confidence that my intervention would do any good, and I loathed the thought that I might be contributing to the survival of a regime I detested. I decided instead to write my story soberly and quietly and send it later as a background article on Chile.

During these days Elena was too busy to see me. She was involved in making a fashion programme with a German photographer called Siegfried. I had met Siegfried once, when Elena and I were still wonderfully sure of each other, and even then he had disturbed me. A tall, blond man with an autocratic manner, he projected a sense of his own power which I found overbearing and slightly offensive. At that time, with my own confidence intact, he seemed little more than another oddity on the scene, one of those men who sustain themselves on the humiliation of others, a psychological vampire drawn naturally to a society which reeked of power and bloodshed. Now, the thought of them working together sickened me, but my revulsion at least had the effect of making me all the more determined to get out.

I became aware, though, of another effect of my troubled state. For the first time I felt nervous and fearful for my own safety. It occurred to me that Leigh and his staff would be wondering why I had not sent my story. Wouldn't they be watching me? Was it safe for me to be visiting those whom I knew to be actively opposed to the regime? Would I even be allowed to leave until I had declared my hand? And if I left unscathed, would the DINA follow my departure with their own sinister visits on people I had grown to like and respect so much?

From thinking of myself as a knight errant I swung to the opposite extreme and imagined myself as the most reprehensible of all meddlers in the affairs of others, one who naively intrudes on matters too complex for his own understanding and departs ignorant of the pain and wreckage he leaves in his wake. If so, I thought, I have betrayed my journey, and done it in spades. The idea that even Roberto and Gloria might suffer for their abundant hospitality nauseated me, and I became unnaturally cautious and reserved, and all the more anxious to leave before more of this fancied damage could be done.

I chose to leave on a Monday. The day before, at Nuñoa, we had a farewell lunch. Roberto shopped for every Chilean delicacy I might have missed. A huge *centolla* crab sprawled in  the center of the table. We drank wonderful three-star wine from Santa Carolina and I drowned my fears for a while in the limitless warmth of their friendship.

"My dear Ted," said Roberto. "Are you sure you must leave? You can stay as long as you like. We will miss you so much. Our daughters will not know what to do."

The little girl I had nicknamed Mosquitito looked across at me with adoring eyes.

"I am only afraid that my staying here may still cause you some trouble," I ventured.

"What trouble?" scoffed Gloria. "Am I not related to Pinochet ?"

They laughed happily, and I found strength in their fearless generosity which was more potent than any wine.

Still, like a love-sick puppy, I could not abandon the chance of seeing Elena one more time. I called her, apologetically, to say I would be leaving the following day.

"You had better come over then," she said in a matter-of-fact tone.

I arrived to find that we were not alone. Siegfried was there, ostensibly to show fashion photographs he had taken at Vina de Mar. He projected them on to a screen and talked about them with assurance, as though lecturing on Rembrandt. Elena received them with little cries of "Oh" and "Ah" and "How enchanting."

Her praise of the photographs and her willingness to enter into analytical discussions with Siegfried about their excellence annoyed me. They had not seemed that good to me. I had to choose between finding fault with her taste or accepting that she had ulterior motives for flattering him. Either choice would be disagreeable, for it would diminish us both, but in my depressed state it was easier for me to imagine that she had already decided to transfer her favours to a new hero.

The signs read that I was overdue in Valhalla and if I insisted on hanging around I would have to suffer the inevitable humiliations. As always when I was unhappy with myself my command of languages was weakened. Siegfried, on the other hand, was in a triumphant mood. He talked, with all the fluency I had lost, about the exhilaration of living in Santiago among so much danger and death.

I felt that he was not only usurping my position but even a part of my charisma, and abusing it shamelessly to boot.

In an atmosphere of danger, he said, the key to a man's true nature is exposed. He may hide from the DINA but not from himself.

"It is as Heidegger says," he went on. "Every personality has a fixed point of reference which colours everything else about him. For example," and he turned his ruthless gaze on me, "your fixation, I suppose, is fear."

It was brilliantly done.

Numbed by the anxieties that had welled up in me during the past week and miserable at seeing Elena so comfortable in this company, I could find nothing convincing to say. Elena's inquiring gaze went through me like a skewer and I writhed in agony.

Eventually Siegfried left, only half an hour before curfew. I had waited desperately for this last chance to rescue something from Elena to take away with me. She was kind, but fatally withdrawn. I hoped for one last kiss, but she averted her face, and I left her with a peck on the cheek to run the gauntlet of the roadblocks one last time.

Leaving next day was more awkward and difficult than it had ever been. The bike, fully loaded, fell over in Roberto's front garden as I was trying to mount it. Twice more that day I dropped it in my clumsiness, a quite unprecedented happening. Even before I had left Santiago, the ignition failed on one cylinder and I had to unpack almost everything again to work on it. I took the wrong exit from Santiago, and added thirty five miles to my journey to the frontier. The landscape around me was first dull, then grim as I climbed among ugly, barren mountains.

The road led north, back to Argentina. The frontier was at Caracoles, ten thousand feet up, and there was one road across the mountain pass to Mendoza, but it was closed to traffic by the Chilean frontier guards. The only way through was by the railway tunnel. I waited for two hours, with a growing company of cars and trucks, until the oncoming train from Argentina had passed. Then I was sent in ahead of the four-wheeled traffic.

The tunnel was three kilometres long, an unlined hole through the living rock. Boards had been laid on either side of one rail, but I was warned to stay to the right, between the rail and the rock face. There was no lighting. The rocks dripped water on me and on the boards which were slippery with mud. I moved, painfully slow, through the gloom, aware of the car behind me which always seemed to be too close. Again and again I felt my rear wheel slip and slide out of control until at one point I was almost certain that the tyre was punctured, and I wondered how to choose between the twin horrors of risking an accident or trying to repair a tyre.

I went on and on, and on, interminably creeping through that foul hole until, at last, I saw a faint glimmer ahead.

Never have I been more glad to see the light at the end of a tunnel. I came out into a glorious valley and as I sped along beside a tumbling mountain stream it became ever more beautiful, ever more enticing. The valley broadened and deepened and my spirits, released from the dark tunnel, expanded and soared, and I was away and on the road and flying again.

# 25. Birth

The mention of hospital sent an icy dread through me. After all this time it had a ring of disaster about it. The optimism I had been struggling to maintain collapsed and drained away. I assumed that Francesca would be horrified. Her very words rang in my ears – "I've always hated hospitals" – and I felt terribly sorry for her and useless myself, unable to help. Her face betrayed no strong reaction. She seemed to be in a trance and I didn't want to talk to her while I was feeling so downcast.

The doctor and midwife took over in a very practical and determined way. I felt rejected, relieved of my functions as though I were in mild disgrace. It was entirely in my mind, but I couldn't help it. I had wanted so badly for Francesca's confidence to be rewarded.

There were things to pack, things that had been prepared as a formality, just to keep the doctor happy. Now I could hardly remember what they were. My weakness took me by surprise. I hadn't realized how much of myself I had expended during the day. However, I got the stuff together, remembered to bring the chicken too, and even found enough faith to bring the wine along.

Tee helped Francesca out of the house and down to the car. She was holding the IV bottle over Francesca's head, with the long, clear tube snaking down to a Bandaid on her arm, and they got into the back of the Valiant like that.

I was to drive and follow the doctor. He had a small Italian car, too small for such a big man, I thought irrelevantly. Then I saw that his number plate read FIFI. That forced a snort of laughter out of me. I told them in the back and they both laughed It was a relief to hear Francesca laughing. We kept the joke going most of the way, as the doctor dodged in and out of the traffic.

'Where's Fifi?' I kept asking. 'Don't let Fifi get away.'

But I was scared in spite of myself. It was such a bizarre trip. If we had just done what all the other normal people did, if we had not been so determined to be different, we would have made this same journey to hospital hours ago, comfortably and happily. Not like this, in a state of crisis.

Was it a crisis? I had no idea. The IV bottle gave it the flavour of emergency. I associated it with frantic dashes to the operating theatre, moments of life and death. My fears were suddenly dramatized around me. Police cars and an ambulance passed us on the highway, flashing red and blue light on our faces.

Tee's voice broke urgently into my thoughts.

"The blood's running back into the bottle. I can't get it high enough. What shall I do?' "

"Jesus," I said. "I don't know."

I looked over my shoulder and saw the tube black under the highway lights.

"Pull the needle out," I said. I couldn't think too well, trying to keep up with Fifi. I was worried I might miss the exit and lose him, because he wasn't taking the route I had rehearsed.

The needle slipped out easily from under the dressing, so that was all right.

"Are you okay?' I asked, and Francesca replied in a very matter of-fact way that she was. She was the calmest of the three of us, but I couldn't gauge what she was feeling. It was a weird journey, and all the time I was asking myself: Why, Why, Why?

As soon as we got through the hospital doors they had her in a wheelchair, with a tag crimped on to her wrist. We zoomed up to the fourth floor and when we got out they tagged her again. I only thought afterwards about all the mistakes that must have been made, for them to go to that kind of trouble.

We were taken to one of the rooms set aside for women in labor, and only then did my tenseness begin to ease. It was not a bad room – as homely as they could make it. There were curtains and patterned wallpaper, a sofa beneath the window, a reclining armchair and an almost ordinary bed. At least we weren't in one of the delivery rooms, which were really operating theatres, bathed in bright light and full of machinery. That disposed of my most obvious fear; an instant Caesarian.

Francesca put on her nightgown and got into bed, and we all relaxed. Then a hospital nurse joined us. She introduced herself to Francesca very nicely and, after talking to the doctor, suggested that she might like something to 'reduce the discomfort' and help her to save her strength for when she needed it. Francesca agreed without protests, and I was glad. This was a different game now, with different rules. They rigged up a new IV bottle, and slipped another needle into her arm.

"We're going to introduce Petosin intravenously," the nurse said. 'It will take a little while, and then you should be able to dilate nicely. So, now, try to take it easy. You've been having a busy time, I know."

"How long will it take to work?" I asked.

"Oh, an hour or two," said the nurse.

There was nothing for me to do any more. I sat down on the sofa, happy for Francesca, but hollow inside.

"Take the armchair," said the doctor, kindly. "Get some sleep. She'll need you later."

I was grateful for his words. They rescued me from my sense of total futility. I lay back in the chair next to the bed and held Francesca's hand. The nurse helped her through the contractions, and as they came and went she clasped my hand tightly. I was very much in love with her, and felt it strongly.

She'd had only the minimum dosage of pain killer and it wasn't effective, so they doubled the dose.

"Don't worry, my love," she said. "It's a great relief to be here. I feel much happier now."

Soon her pains softened under the drug. I closed my eyes.

Tee and the midwife were eating chicken and talking about windsurfing, music and cars, and their conversation penetrated my half-waking state with the incongruity of dreams.

"Well, I guess I'll go and write up my expenses in the office," said the midwife. "I never get the time for it."

I woke up at twenty minutes past midnight. There was a clock on the wall. I drank some coffee from a machine and ate some chicken. Francesca was sitting up now and the contractions were coming faster and harder. Tee was with her, talking her through them. The midwife came back. Then the nurse came in wheeling a trolley with an oscilloscope on it.

"What's that?" I asked, though I knew.

"This is a foetal monitor," she said. "Francesca is eight centimetres dilated so it won't be very long now. We'll be able to keep a good watch over the baby's progress."

The doctor had rubber gloves on now, and he introduced the lead and attached it to Iswas's scalp. I didn't like to ask how. The screen came to life, recording the baby's heartbeat and blood pressure. It was extraordinarily erratic and I got quite frightened, remembering the rock-steady beat I had once heard.

"Is there something wrong?" I asked, nervously. I was afraid they might be hiding some bad news, but they explained that it was the normal reaction of the foetus to the contractions of the womb, which were severe. The monitor helped to warn of those rare cases when the pressure stopped the heart altogether.

"God," I thought. "What must it be going through in there?"

The baby became real to me again then, and the atmosphere in the room began to tingle. Another doctor was observing us quietly from the corner, some matter of hospital protocol, so there were seven of us. It was impossible for anyone to be there and not feel involved. Francesca was working very hard now, gasping with the pain and the strain, but looking wonderfully alive and triumphant.

"Don't push," said the doctor. "Not yet. Hold on. Hold on. Look, you can see the baby's head."

It was true. A greyish circle of scalp was visible. They held a mirror between Francesca's legs so that she could see it too.

"I want to push," she said, very forcefully.

It was ama:zing to hear her speak with such authority about a sensation that she could never have known in her life before. Her true strength emerged very clearly then.

"No. Not yet," said the doctor. "Hold on. Nurse, I'll have to cut."

The nurse passed him a hypodermic and he plunged it in close to the baby's head.

"Hold on," he kept saying. "Not yet. Help her to hold on."

Then he had a pair of scissors, and cut deep into her flesh but, strangely, it meant nothing to me, and Francesca felt nothing either. Our normal reactions were completely suspended in the drama of this battle to give birth. She was consumed by the effort to dominate an irresistible force. It was utterly thrilling and awesome to watch.

"All right. I know you can't wait. Now go for it. Help her."

The midwife and I were on either side of her bed. We each had one arm under her thigh and the other round her back, and she pushed like a mad thing. Once. Twice. I saw the head emerge, face down. Thrice. And the baby tumbled out into the doctor's hands, too fast even to see. And with an elemental sigh of relief, the labor was done.

"It's a boy," said the doctor.

I hadn't even thought to look. But I looked now, and as I looked the boy cried out, unprompted, greedy for life, perfect in every detail.

There were other minor miracles. I was given the scissors and cut the cord myself. Then he lay quietly on his mother's breast for a moment.

"William Alexander," she said.

"Oh my goodness," I said to her. "Thank you."

The doctor produced the afterbirth and showed it to us, a little shyly. It was a wonder in itself, with a surface of polished purple marbled with the most intricate veins.

"We shall have to sew you up now," said the doctor. "You were in a hurry after all that waiting. You're a bit torn. So Ted gets to carry the baby."

"That'll be nice for you," she said to me. "I'm glad you'll have him. He's yours."

"Yes he is," I said. "He's ours and he's marvellous."

The nurse gave me the tiny baby wrapped in a receiving blanket and showed me how to let it suck on my little finger, to stimulate the reflex that would help it suck on the breast

"You'll be doing an important job," she said. "The sooner he starts sucking the better."

He took my little finger easily and contentedly, and I stood there and made a little speech over him. I hadn't meant to; it just came out of my feeling. I promised him all sorts of delights, a long life, full of love, excitement and knowledge, and many good friends. Then they took Francesca away to be stitched up.

So I had him for the first half hour of his life, and I don't suppose I will ever pass a more peaceful time with anyone. He sucked at my

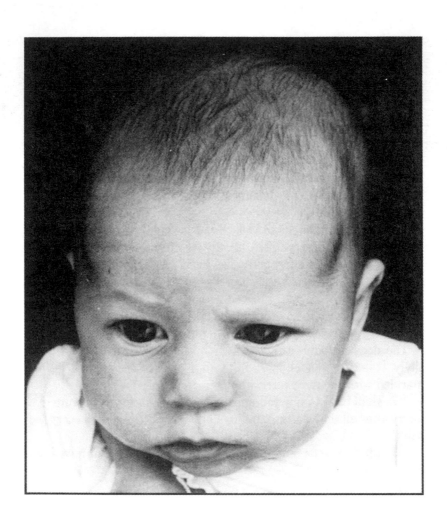

*Riding High*

finger gently all the while, and I looked down on him with a mind washed clean by the catharsis of his birth. No anxiety, no doubt, not a hint of regret, not a moment of self-examination entered my thoughts.

He had none of the blemishes we had been schooled to expect. In twenty-eight hours of labor he had had all the time he needed to prepare himself for the world. His skin was a healthy pink, the head only a little elongated. He had no hair on him anywhere, and I thought he looked happy. If he was as ugly as most new-born babies, I was quite blind to the fact.

Tee opened the bottle of wine and poured out a papercupful for each of us.

"He looks just great," she said. "He's a really good-looking kid. He'll be on his bike and away in no time."

I arrived home just before dawn. The room was in chaos, and the bed itself was devastated by the long and fruitless struggles. It was cold, and there was an aftertaste of despair. I cleared away some of the bundles of soiled linen, the unwashed dishes, the dirty cartons and the discarded paper thin rubber gloves pallid as embryos. The hospital, the excitement of the birth, the baby himself, all seemed far, far away in another world.

A terrible bleakness seized me, stretching from horizon to horizon.

Well, I thought, this is one you can't ride away from.

Can the pendulum really stop here?

What do we do now? Build a house? Plant a garden? Raise a child? And another? And another? Have a happy family?

But what have those things got to do with me? Where am I in all this? What do I know of such things?

I made some tea and wandered around the room sipping it.

Among some papers I found two scrawled sheets, written a long time before, when I had just returned from the journey; my first days back in the old house, bewildered, disoriented, not knowing what to do, what to say, how to stop moving.

Why was I rushing back from Istanbul? To my doom. Why did I rush away four years ago? From my doom. I had an appointment in Samara.

Doom is nameless dread, is lack of faith, is dried up springs, is childlessness? I feel fertile all of a sudden.

What is this place? A place to be in, or a place to have? Who will take it away from me? Have I circled the world to be set in cement?

I feel it loosening. Remember the feeling now? You were riding through Africa, you went through all that fear, that nameless dread. You put a name to it then.

There's no guilt, says Claude. It's a Judeo-Christian invention. Well, I'm Judeo-Christian all right, but the joke, the mystery of it is, I wasn't supposed to be. My mother was an Aryan atheist, my Dad disappeared, and they left me riddled with Judeo-Christian guilt. How is that possible! Is it in the blood? The toilet training? In the effort to escape?

The windows are open. I've shaved off my moustache. The breeze feels cool and promising and kisses my upper lip. I feel saved.

Where will salvation take me? To my typewriter? To California? To another round of the same?

How did I start? With a pain in the stomach like an ulcer, and a pain below my neck, and a rash of pain across my shoulders, and a terrible fear that I might not make it round the next bend. So what made me do it? Doom behind and nameless dread in front. But I said it was because I was curious about the world and wanted to see for myself. Because I never believed what I was told.

Did I ride all that way to know how far it was? Have I brought back anything more than a spear and a rug and a set of silver spoons from wherever the hell it was?

Let's be honest. None of it means anything to me now. None of it counts as much as my shaven upper lip. I had to do it all to shave my lip. How far must I go to shave my head?

Yes, I can find my way round Cape Town, and Cartagena and San Francisco, and who cares if I'm not there to do it. Can I find my way round here?

And have I proved how brave I am? Not to myself. How durable I am? I always knew that was my main fault. How young I am? I'm forty-six. How different I am? Not news. How it could be if . . . Ah, an echo of a living thought . . .

How it could be, if I could be the way I was that day in the desert, at the tea hut called the Crocodile's Mouth, . .

Then I remembered how, out of those ramblings, the journey had gradually become real to me again. I recalled how memories of the Sudanese desert had come to life, flickering gold in the bleakness. Before long I was able to begin writing, and from then on the book gathered strength all the way. So why couldn't I do that now? Images of our land in the valley formed before me, oak trees, a patch of green, driving the mists away.

I'll build a small cabin first, I thought, under the walnuts for shade, near the well, among the blackberries. I should be able to get that up in a couple of weeks, before the rain comes. I can do that. That will be a start. Then we can all move up there.

I saw myself at work, digging, sawing, hammering, and life came flooding back. That could be my salvation, keeping busy. As long as I was doing something, aiming for something I believed in, maybe it would be all right.

Road miles: 2970
By boat ------
By aeroplane ----

CARIBBEAN
SEA

Cartagena
TO
SAN ANDRÉS

Panama
City

PANAMA

Medellín

Bogotá

COLOMBIA

PACIFIC
OCEAN

Popayán

La Plata

Pasto

Quito

ECUADOR

Guayaquil

Talara
Paita

Chiclayo

P E R U

BRAZIL

N
W    E
S

Punta
Salinas

Lima

MILES
0          300
0          300
KM

# 26. Ecuador

I was riding alongside Bruno. It was a month since we had met, high up in the Andes on the Bolivian border. He was on his way from Paraguay, with his friend Antoine, and because we had enjoyed each other's company we had travelled together, loosely, to Lima. Antoine had flown back to Paris, but Bruno was going on to Mexico so we agreed to go on like that until our paths diverged.

He was in his battered white Renault van and I was on the Triumph. We were making our way lazily up the northern coast of Peru where it never rains. We were dried out by the sun and the arid winds, our skins salty from the ocean, and our belongings dusty with sand from the beaches. My mind was impregnated with images of complacent pelicans cruising above the waves, of oysters big as steaks, of bright red-and-blue fishing boats drawn up on the strand, of silver-painted pumps nodding tirelessly over oil wells among the deserted rocks. And I was thinking of the woman in the short black skirt and yellow jersey with the pink scarf tied round her head I had seen that morning, and of the three fishermen who were throwing her, fully clothed, into the sea, again and again, far away down the beach, too far for me to hear laughter or anger, like a silent film clip that was repeated every time I looked until it seemed that it was I who, by looking, set the inscrutable scene in motion every time.

We ate fish and drank tea and slept under the same stars each night and drifted north, not fast, not slow, but as though on the waves of time itself, to the border of Ecuador. There the change came so suddenly and unexpectedly that it gave no chance of easy adjustment. The coast swung away from the mountains, leaving

What is a journey without problems? We liked beaches but
Bruno's van did not. This was one of many  times he had to dig
himself out in Peru. And I got punctures. Not many, but enough to
get good at them. I blessed Meriden for the quick-detach wheel,
and Schrader for that clever pump of theirs. They saved me.

*Riding High*

room for great storm clouds to pile up and collapse thunderously over the land. From the crystalline desert we plunged abruptly into a steaming tropical broth.

Since it always is one damned thing after another, and it never rains but it pours, all kinds of unrelated problems appeared to hinder our progress. The immigration officer dawdled painfully through our papers. Changing money from *soles* to *sucres* was a costly nuisance. The jittery Ecuadorian army stopped us at six successive roadblocks, fearing that we might be forerunners of a Peruvian invasion force.

The road got worse as well as wet. On the motorcycle, of course, I felt it most: one day a lizard, the next day a frog. My waterproofs, ragged and improvised after eighteen months on the road, were stifling. Through misting goggles under a lowering sky I felt the world close in. Mud swirled across the road and spat from the tyres of passing trucks as the traffic became heavier. I felt the moisture seeping into my boots and leaking through seams into my crutch. I began to long for the end of that day, for our arrival somewhere dry and welcoming, and my mind took refuge from the discomfort in old fantasies of lordly hospitality, splendid meals and fine wines.

We were going towards Guayaquil, a lowland city and port of a million inhabitants or more, and it became certain that night would fall long before we got there. Hating to ride in the dark on wet and unreliable roads, hating even more to arrive in unfamiliar cities by night, I would have been glad to stop at any wayside hostel or even to set up my tent on the soggy ground, but the roadside was overrun now with poor shacks, fenced areas or impossibly thick vegetation, and the coast which had been so hospitable in Peru was now far from the road, marshy and inaccessible.

Our last hope, a crossroads town called El Triunfo, marked large on the map, turned out to be nothing more than a muddy morass of stalls and filling stations. By eight o'clock, two hours after dark, we crossed an immense bridge over the river Guayas and found our way to the central plazas. The good hotels were well beyond our means, and we settled for a shabby place, absurdly named after the Crillon in Paris.

It would be wrong to suggest that we were depressed by the day's difficulties. On the contrary, we were in quite a cheerful mood. Both of us, in our different ways, had endured far worse. Compared with the rivers I had fallen into on the Bolivian Altiplano, what was a wet night in Ecuador? And what did a few official pinpricks matter compared with my arrests in Egypt and jail in Brazil? I went through my usual big-city routine of manoeuvring the motorcycle into the hotel, unscrewing everything that might be unscrewed by others, and carrying my strange assortment of bags and boxes into the grubby bedroom. I found a pair of dry jeans, hung the wet ones over a chair, and went out with Bruno to find a beer and a hamburger, and to laugh at ourselves and the world. Nevertheless, my absurd fantasy of crisp clean sheets, a five-course dinner and a bottle of burgundy lingered on, however faintly, and made me just a little vulnerable.

When we returned to the hotel and switched on the bare overhead bulb in our shared room, the cockroaches fluttered into the shadows with a noise like creaking corsets. I took a shower and noticed that the plaster over my head had broken away to reveal the drain of the shower in the room above. The Sanyo Widemaster fan labored through the night at full speed, and we slept uneasily under a hot whirlwind of moist air where squadrons of mosquitoes fought for control.

My first business in the morning was with the bank. I was carrying a sheaf of traveler's checks, issued to me in Lima, which became a constant source of frustration. I had been forced to accept hundred dollar checks, and a hundred dollars was far more than I ever wanted to change at one time. The banks would only issue local currency, so I was obliged to carry many more *pesos,* or *soles* or *sucres* than I needed, and then to change them, always at a loss, at the borders. Dollar notes would have been far more flexible and economical but so far it had been impossible to buy them. Now, at the Banco del Discuento, a clerk told me he could change my checks for dollar notes. I was reluctant to believe him, but he insisted.

"Just countersign the checks," he said wearily, as though humoring an obstinate child.

"And you will give me dollars," I repeated.

"Yes, certainly. Of course."

I signed all eight hundred dollars' worth. He took them away and, after a long absence, came back with a bundle of Ecuadorian sucres. I became instantly and unwisely furious.

"*Esos no sirven por nada,*" I cried bitterly. "They are useless to me. You promised me dollars. Where are they? I must have dollars."

He looked at me with distaste.

"It is impossible," he said primly. "Government regulations. You can have sucres. Or I can give you back your checks."

"But now the checks are all countersigned. They are useless, and it's your foolishness. *Que tonteria! Que lata . . .*"

I saw him stiffen and tighten his lips. As I spluttered on in my rage I knew I was beaten. He would never admit his mistake, and I could not prove it.

It was one of the great disadvantages of traveling rough that one had no status with the business establishment of Latin America. In a well-pressed suit, a laundered shirt, polished shoes and, preferably, a discreet hat to top it all I might have fought my way through to the management of the bank and wrung out some sort of satisfaction. In jeans, boots and a wrinkled tee-shirt I had no chance. Disdain for the grubby Gringo and his pushy ways was written large over the clerk's smug countenance.

I took back my countersigned checks with very bad grace and stomped out of the building, knowing they would be an even bigger nuisance thereafter. In fact it was not until I got to Panama, months later, that I was able to get my dollars, and then only through the generous intervention of a high-ranking U S naval officer. It was like drawing teeth. They were Citibank checks, and I came to curse that bank with a similar but more excremental name.

Bruno, who had also hoped to see his own checks miraculously transmuted into real money, was only a bit less disappointed than I. We both felt a growing need for some thing to lift our spirits. However, there were unwritten rules which made the problem more difficult to solve.

Although I carried hundreds of dollars around with me, I was very strict about self-indulgences. There were usually two distinct standards one could live by in South America, the indigenous one and the imported one. At the indigenous level, where one consumed only what was locally produced and where one patronized only unpretentious establishments, life was spartan but wholesome, and very cheap indeed. The other level was the world of 'drinks', tablecloths, wine-lists, uniformed waiters, real coffee, laundries and taxis. These luxuries (with the exception of good wine, and coffee which was all sold abroad for hard currency) were available at bargain prices by normal Western criteria, but they would have inflated my own cost of living ten times, and since they were all luxuries that I enjoy enormously I had to practice an almost fanatical asceticism to root them out of my daily life. My method was to invest my journey with the sanctity of a religious crusade and to seek purity through simplicity and self-denial.

For the greater part of my journey, through the rural areas of the world, this attitude worked very well. For one thing, it is true that simplicity and austerity, practiced of one's own free will, do bring great rewards. For another, my virtue was more easily upheld because the sinful pleasures which I could not afford were usually not there to be had anyway. But in a dismal city like Guayaquil things appear differently. When rustic simplicity gives way to urban squalor, self-denial can lose its beauty and seem uncomfortably close to stupidity.

After the exasperating episode at the bank, in a damp and rat-ridden town which refused to yield even the slightest prospect of free enjoyment or interest, it would have been the most natural thing to slip into a bar and order, say, gin and campari on ice, and settle into a nice, rosy daydream. Since it was forbidden by the articles of my faith to spend money on such fripperies I did the next best thing. I applied myself to the task of getting them for free.

Before leaving England I had been to visit a friend who once won a silver medal at the Tokyo Olympics for sailing a Flying Dutchman. Such a famous sailor would be persona grata automatically with all the world's major yacht clubs. As a parting gift he had told me that if I ever cared to introduce myself as his friend and to mention modestly the incredible feat I was performing on my motorcycle, I would be received with warmth and compassion by his fellow sportsmen. All this flashed through my greedy mind when I noticed on my tattered tourist's plan of the city that Number 7, ringed on the riverbank, was listed below as the Yacht Clube.

It was after eleven in the morning. The club's members – I could almost see them – would be assembling at the richly polished mahogany bar. Waiters with white epaulettes and gloves would be gliding discreetly across the carpeted saloon, bringing trays of whisky, gin, amber sherries and glowing ruby aperitifs to the tables by the tall windows overlooking the estuary. Bronzed Ecuadorian yachtsmen would reminisce fondly over my friend's exploits at Tokyo, and there would surely be enough warmth and compassion to restore both Bruno and myself to our proper dignity.

The club was only a short walk away. As we approached it I became even more optimistic. The building was old colonial, white stucco, and looked rich.

'We're in luck,' I said. 'It's the real thing. Who knows, maybe lunch as well. Even lobster, perhaps . . .'

The lobster on this coast was acclaimed, but we had failed so far to find any.

'Wait. I will go first and introduce myself.'

I left Bruno on the embankment and walked across the gangway. The club was built on the riverbank itself, raised on piles. I thought it odd that there were no moorings around it, and certainly no boats. Also I began to sense a certain atmosphere of undue somnolence about the place. The door was locked, and it took the porter a long time to answer my knock. I announced in careful Spanish that I brought greetings from a famous British Olympic sailor and wanted to be introduced to some of the yachtsmen. He appeared to be puzzled by my request as much as by my appearance.

'There are no yachtsmen here, señor,' he said. 'The members are not yachtsmen. They come here only to drink.'

I could hardly admit that that had been my only true ambition also. Much disheartened, I turned on my heels and shuffled away. Really, I thought, this place is defeating me.

To Bruno, who had lived in South America longer than I, the idea of yachtsmen who would rather be wet inside than out was not strange. He was ready with another plan to wring satisfaction out of this sordid city, and we set off eastwards along the river to find the old quarter of Guayaquil at Las Peñas. The sun glared stickily through a humid haze as we sweated up and down a small hill looking for old-world charm. Perhaps my inner eye was already jaundiced; all I saw was an unattractive and dirty slum. Like the starving cats around us we foraged in a desultory way through the afternoon, and arrived back on one of the big avenues just before dusk. At a café table on the pavement we gave ourselves over to reviling Guayaquil as one of the true dumps of the world.

'You know why it's so bad,' I said. 'Because it isn't even bad

After Ecuador, Bruno and I continued into Colombia, until his van went terminal. In Pasto, he pictured me being interrogated by a typical crowd. And at San Agustin (below) we saw the bizarre stone figures excavated from the graves they had been guarding for 500 years. No two of them were alike.

enough to be interesting. That makes it truly awful.' I got wound up in my thesis. The heat was uncomfortable, but not uncommonly so. The humidity was just ordinarily oppressive. The food we had eaten was merely miserable. The buildings were mean but unromantic. The streets were filthy, but only with dull grime. The port was too far from the coast to be refreshed by the ocean, and too far again from the relief of the mountains. Even the cockroaches were not big enough to be extraordinary.

'Why,' I asked, 'are we here?' '

Bruno could not say. We sat drinking bad coffee, pestered by flies and shoeshine boys, unable to find a single redeeming quality in the place. Then a voice in my ear whispered: 'Dubonnet. '

As a rule there are a dozen drinks I would prefer, but in Guayaquil, at that moment, the mere suggestion of Dubonnet was electrifying. I turned to see a short and shabby man clutching nervously on a brown paper bag which revealed the outline of two bottles. He drew one bottle out by the neck and, before slipping it back quickly into the bag, turned it to give me a glimpse of the famous label as though it were extremely rude. Even at a glance, the label looked as worn and tired as the man himself.

"Dubonnet," he repeated. "One hundred and fifty *sucres.* "

To be fair to myself, I knew it was a fraud. In Ecuador, as in most South American countries, imported luxuries were exorbitantly expensive. In the rare shops which had such things, a bottle of good wine might sell for thirty dollars or more. Even for a smuggled bottle sold on the run, the five dollars he was asking was far too low as a starting price. I could have and should have ignored him, but the imagined taste of Dubonnet had already unseated my judgement. Such is the stuff that dreams are made on. Instead of sending him on his way I made a ridiculously low counter-offer, and hoped the temptation would just evaporate.

"Thirty *sucres,* " I said, contemptuously.

He accepted with such readiness that the odds against it being the real thing now soared into the billions. Unfortunately, the possibility of acquiring a bottle of Dubonnet for one dollar became correspondingly irresistible. I looked across at Bruno to see what he would make of it, but saw that he was bantering happily with a crowd of boys all pleading for a chance to polish his boots.

The sky was darkening, the lights were coming on in the street and the pavement was thick with people strolling, shopping and walking home from work, all swirling around our table. A perfect time, I thought, for an aperitif. I brought the three ten sucre notes from my shirt pocket and the man drew the bottle from his paper bag again.

"*Bien,*" I said. "All right. But first I am going to see what's in the bottle."

I took the bottle; he stretched out his palm and, unaccountably, I put the money in his hand.

I have thought long and hard since then to discover what prompted me to give him the money before I had opened the bottle. I would like to believe that it was a sense of justice and fair play, a nicely civilized desire to treat others as equals and bestow on them the benefit of the doubt. More probably, though, it was just a deep-seated fear of causing offence which disarms me at critical moments.

It was the work of a moment to break the forged seal, unscrew the cap and raise the bottle to my nose, but before the first acrid fumes of sour wine had wrinkled my nostrils the man had vanished into the crowd.

I sat back with a foolish grin on my face and told Bruno that we at last had vinegar for our salads. To my surprise, because I had thought him hardly aware of my transactions, he was outraged and sprang to his feet.

"*Putain,*" he cried. "I'll catch that son of a bitch," and darted up and down the street for a few moments, but without success. Then he turned to his small retinue of shoeshine boys.

"Ten *sucres* to the first one who finds him," he said. "Dead or alive."

They squealed with joy, and rushed off in all directions.

"Tell him we want to buy the other bottle," I yelled after them, warming to the project.

I took a sip from the bottle. It was cheap wine turned bad. I passed it across to Bruno who tried it and twisted his mouth in disgust.

"Truly, it is frightful," he said in French.

The fact that it was real wine made us both sadder. Red ink or sump oil I could have dismissed more easily. But to have a bottle of real wine and for it to be undrinkable, that was tragic.

The first of Bruno's scouts returned too soon, waving his arms and shouting: "He's there. I've seen him. Give me the money."

Then another boy arrived from the opposite direction with a more detailed and convincing story.

"I saw him with another man. He's up here, two blocks. I can show you."

Amid a babble of variations on the same theme, Bruno chose to go off with the second boy. My sense of my own stupidity prevented me from taking an active part. I found it hard to feel indignant, it was so clearly my own fault. Anyway, it was only a dollar. I thought back to my days of poverty in Paris long ago. What had we done then to revive bad wine? Perhaps heating it, with sugar and spices? *Mon dieu,* but the wine had never been this bad. Still, it was worth a try.

It was some time before Bruno returned. The boy had led him off the main avenue into a narrow side street, and then into the mouth of an alley. He had pointed out an extremely rough and ugly man standing in a doorway. The area was deserted.

"I waited for a while but no one came, and I could not see who else might be in the doorway." He shrugged. "I decided to leave it alone."

I applauded his logic, and we agreed that the least we deserved was a good dinner. We eventually spent much more on it than we had meant to, in an effort to compensate for our other disappointments. The main dish was lobster, but it was not what we had hoped for, and this further disappointment seemed to have been fore-ordained. When we returned to the hotel I still had with me the bottle of bad wine.

We left Guayaquil the next morning early, without regret. It was raining again from a heavy grey sky. Some of the bundles I usually tied on to the back of the motorcycle I asked Bruno to carry in his van. At the last moment I put the bottle of wine there as well. I could not have explained my attachment to it, I just knew that I had not finished with that incident yet. Bruno forbore to mention it, though he must have thought me quite eccentric.

We traveled over the big bridge and along the same road we had come by from Peru until we got back to the junction at El Triunfo, and then took the left turning for Riobamba. The road carried us past the wettest and lushest vegetation I had seen since Tanzania. The

With Bruno and Antoine I visited Macchu Piccu. The closest we could get by road was Cuzco, a romantic old town and one of the most beautiful in South America. From there we took a train. There were two choices: an expensive, comfortable tourist train that would take us to the foot of the mountain where Macchu Piccu is perched; or an unpredictable, slow, but very cheap train for the Indian population (who were not interested in going to Macchu Piccu). It used the same track but stopped two miles from our goal, at Aguas Calientes. Of course we chose the latter.

We planned to sleep at Aguas Calientes, and walk on early in the morning to be there before the tourists arrived, so we took our sleeping bags to the station. The entire area was covered by sleeping Indians, their livestock, and the bundles and baskets they were taking to market farther north. The train was supposed to leave at 1 pm. At 3 pm a false rumor of an approaching train stirred up a great commotion, but it subsided quickly. Then, at 3.30 a train was seen coming out of the shed.

The crowd rose as one and flung itself against the gates that guarded the platform. The gates held, but another set opened on the far platform. The crowd split in two and half of it rushed around the station, scattering stall-holders among their onions and bananas. Then our gates opened also, so we all collided on the tracks, as the train advanced slowly upon us. I scrambled aboard a moving carriage and, for one sweet moment, actually had a window seat, until an Indian matron with a dozen arms and legs sat on me and, with flailing limbs and flying breasts, wedged herself and her charming, filthy children between me and the window.

Opposite me, another harridan climbed over the back of a bench, forced herself, legs astride, behind the head of a seated Gringo, and slid down behind him until he toppled off, beaten by superior weight and conviction. It was class warfare, and it raged for fifteen minutes throughout the train. At the end there were no corpses in the aisles and, astonishingly, everybody had a seat.

The journey took four hours. We rose high above Cuzco, then descended alongside a wild river into dark canyons enclosed by steep 2000-foot mountainsides. At Aguas Calientes what little sky there was, was black. The ravine was so steep and narrow that there seemed only to be room for the track and a platform. We found a shack purporting to sell food. It was papered inside with magazine pages, and lit by an oil wick smoking under a portrait of the Madonna. As my eyes pierced the gloom, I perceived a myriad small children nestled like mice among sacks of beans and rice. Whatever item of food we asked for, they chorused joyously *"No hay,"* meaning "there isn't any." Finally we got the last six eggs, and found three iron frame beds for 50 cents each. Two Gringo climbers were sharing the fourth to save money.

We achieved our object, and had Macchu Piccu to ourselves for an hour next morning before the tourists, including the Iowa Farm Bureau, arrived. I found the ancient Inca ruins interesting, but most spectacular was the impossibly high and inaccessible site where they were built, and the perfectly conical mountain across the gorge. (see above). The railroad track can be seen meandering around at the bottom of the picture.

grasses were five and six feet tall, and among them, raised on stilts, stood simple wooden houses, dark-stained and dripping with moisture. And then the plantations, mile upon mile of banana trees, their great purple tongues lolling under the weight of the big bunches of ripening fruit. Then we began to rise at last into the Andes, to meet the cloud which turned to mist.

It felt fine to be in the mountains again, leaving the muggy heat below. The hills rose steep and green all around us, smoother than they had been in Peru with fewer rocky outcrops, more fertile, more thoroughly farmed, but still a wild, vast and open land. By mid-afternoon we had climbed over eight thousand feet and were looking for a place to spend the night.

Here and there I had seen farmhouses on the hillsides, shaded by trees in brilliant flower. The houses were white, with tiled roofs, verandas and balconies and looked quite grand. Their classical forms and seeming prosperity revived old dreams of being invited into some grand Spanish hacienda, but the houses had all been far off the road and with no obvious access. Then, when we had almost passed it, I looked over the embankment. Being higher up on the motorcycle and with an unrestricted view, I saw much more than Bruno could from his closed van. Down the hillside to my right was a similar house, quite close to the road.

I stopped, and when Bruno drew alongside I pointed the house out to him. We agreed it was worth a try, and turned off the road down a steeply sloping drive. It became obvious as we approached it that the house had none of the grandeur I had imagined, but by now I had become used to these deceptions and found them often more fruitful than disappointing.

We parked our vehicles and walked up to the house. It looked abandoned and untended. Only the song of birds and insects replaced the fading memory of engine noise in my ears. We knocked and called to no effect.

'It's not what I expected,' I said, 'but. . . well, let's have a look. '

I pushed the front door which was open, and walked in. The house was bare, no furniture, no floor coverings. Then a man, poorly dressed and wearing a grey trilby, came round the side of the house. He took off his hat and greeted us. In his place I think I would have been quite nervous of a sudden visit by strange foreigners, particularly one as outlandishly dressed and equipped as myself, and I admired him for the quiet, self-contained way in which he received us. He shook our hands and listened gravely as Bruno explained that we were hoping to find shelter for the night and asked what kind of house this was. Then, smiling, he said he was caretaker of a school, that there were no pupils there at present and that we were welcome to stay.

He showed us a room as bare as the rest of the house. The window frame was without windows. A cupboard without doors was built into the far corner of the room. On one of the shelves was some grass and four hen's eggs.

"Can we buy some food?" I asked. "Some eggs or, perhaps, a chicken?" I was thinking that he might be glad to sell something. At this point a woman, whom I took to be his wife, appeared. She was wearing the customary bowler hat we had become used to since Bolivia and, unlike the man who was dressed Western-style in shirt and pants, she wore an Indian blouse and voluminous skirts. Shyly gathered behind her were three children, a boy and two girls. The girls were dressed in miniature versions of their mother's clothes. Their bowler hats came down over their ears. The man and woman talked for a moment, then he directed us down the road we had just come up, to a neighbour who might sell us a chicken.

"*Cerquita,*" he said. "Not far."

We thanked them, and set about preparing ourselves for the night. It took some while to find a system for slinging our hammocks. Bruno solved the problem by uprooting a gatepost to wedge in the window frame. I thought the caretaker would object but, on the contrary, he seemed to enjoy the idea and helped Bruno pull it up. Then he collected the eggs from the cupboard and left us.

Later we walked down the hill together. The mist had burned away and the afternoon sun lapped the long emerald slopes of the mountains in a flood of translucent gold. In silence I let the landscape work its unfailing magic in me, an accumulation of joy that ached like the promise of paradise. I wanted only to exist disembodied among peaks and streams and rolling meadows, to become joined with the spirit that animates the rocks, trees and grasses and which tears at my heart. My journey changed its guise and purpose many times over the years, but among the green Andean mountains it always became a quest for peace and pastoral perfection.

Bruno had a more active idea of heaven. He was a small, light man with the build of a jockey, and had a passion for horses. He began to talk again about his dream.

"*Merde,*" he exclaimed suddenly. "I would like to sell that pig of a van, and buy a couple of horses. Just think how it would be to ride through these mountains. I must do it. Maybe in Colombia . . . or Guatemala. What an escapade! You can buy horses cheap here, good horses, used to the mountains. I tell you, it would be fantastic."

He snorted with delight, bubbling with plans, describing the route he would take, what he would carry, how long it would take, what it would cost.

"You must do it," I said. "Why don't you?"

"Yes. I must . . . somehow. We'll see." He sighed.

It was a long way, almost an hour's walk, before we found some huts by the road. The chickens were scratching in a backyard. There were three men and a woman who appeared to have an interest in them. At first they were dubious about selling one, then discussed at length which one to sacrifice. They offered us the cock but we thought it too expensive, and settled on a mottled hen for 50 *sucres.* We had a fine chase around the yard before we caught it, and I carried it up the hill, swinging it from my hand by its legs. I had never carried a hen like that before, and was amazed by its immobility after the frantic energy it had shown in eluding us. I had to keep examining its bright, darting eyes to make sure it was still alive.

At the house I tried to wring the bird's neck, as I had once seen a farmer do it, but I was cruelly unsuccessful, and we opted instead for a quick decapitation. I held the bird and Bruno wielded the machete. The family then plucked it, and I gutted and cut it up and boiled it over my small gas stove. It was a stringy creature but the legs were plump, and the family gave us a plate of pork as well, so that after all we had more than enough.

Then I turned my attention to the bad wine. Between us, on the van and the motorcycle, we ran a well-equipped kitchen. We had brown sugar, raisins and various spices. I warmed up a cupful of wine and gave it my tenderest care, determined somehow to turn that silly episode in Guayaquil to good account and to gain some virtue from my still-rankling stupidity. When I judged that the ingredients had had time to mingle and the brew was seething nicely over a low flame, I took a spoonful, blew on it and tasted it. It was disgusting.

Bruno concurred.

"Throw it away," he said. "Empty the bottle and get rid of it. *Ca ne vaut rien*. Don't torture yourself."

I could still not go so far as to throw the stuff away. I screwed the top on, stood it in the corner with the label towards the wall and decided to let it fade from my memory.

In the morning I was woken by the anxious clucking of a hen. It was pirouetting nervously on the window sill, confused. My hammock was slung between the window and the cupboard, and the hen wanted to get to its roost. It found courage finally to step out on to the hammock strings, trying to walk the tightrope. Halfway along the hammock it lost its balance, and the room was filled with squawking, flapping, feathery chaos.

Outside, the sun was golden, the sky blue, all the clouds gone. We packed up quickly to leave, and Bruno took his van up the steep slope to the road. His wheels lost their grip on the loose stones and he stalled, backed down, took a longer run, failed again, came even further back almost to the house, made one more frenzied assault and just managed to topple over the lip on to the asphalt surface.

I was waiting astride the bike and saw the caretaker, who had gone back into the house, come out again hastily, calling to me. He was waving the Dubonnet bottle in his hand.

"You have forgotten your wine," he cried.

"No," I said, "it is for you," and added rather lamely, "It is a poor wine, but if you wish it . . ."

He unscrewed the cap and put the bottle to his mouth. I waited sadly, expecting to see him struggle manfully to conceal his disappointment. Instead he beamed with unmistakable pleasure. He liked it. He thought it was delicious.

"*Muchas gracias*" he said. "*Muy bien*. Thank you. Very good. May you go with God."

The Dubonnet story illustrates rather well how I most wanted life to be. Times were good, then bad, then good again – and always interesting. I made my own decisions, imposed my own demands on myself and succeeded at what was most important. Every day was different. There was always something new to learn and enjoy, so that even the bad times became, in their way, enjoyable. The mistakes I made (there would always be mistakes – without them there could be no life, no evolution) were revealing, often amusing, but not tragic. I was making progress, in the most satisfying way I could imagine, towards the accomplishment of an objective which I, at least, considered quite grand: the mental and physical comprehension of the world. I was not unduly beholden to anyone, and I was free of guilt.

On the beaches of Peru, Bruno and I had talked about the future, his future usually. He was twenty-six years old and had been working in Paraguay for a year as an adviser to cotton farmers. There he had bought the Renault, already well used, and made his plan to drive it to Mexico City before flying home to Paris. It was a long journey, about seven thousand miles, and he had given himself four months to do it in. This seemed to him like a long time, the longest break he had ever made with the structured succession of school, university, career. We had been traveling alongside each other for some six weeks. I saw how well he had learned to appreciate the slow rhythm of our movement across the landscape, the importance of traveling at the pace which circumstance made comfortable, but at times he could not disguise his impatience. It ticked away inside him like an alarm clock and made him anxious. His prospects in Paris were far from appetizing. He would have to get a job, and it would probably be as a junior cog in some vast commercial machine or government bureaucracy. The idea of hurrying along here in South America, where one could dally so happily on a pittance, in order to return sooner to that kind of life appeared nonsensical; he freely admitted it, but he could not help himself. He was youthful and eager, and wanted to get on with Life. He knew that what we were doing was valuable, unique, and might never come his way again, but he was conditioned to believe that it could not be quite *serieux*. It was not Life. There was also some talk of a girl in Mexico City, but nothing much ever came of that anyway.

By the time we met I knew already that my journey, if I could finish it, would take at least three years, possibly four. To Bruno, as to almost everyone else, the thought of traveling for such an immense amount of time seemed extraordinary. When he and the others said 'I could never do that,' they tried to convey admiration, and there was, I knew, real respect for the extent of the commitment and the perseverance involved, but behind their words, more often than not, I sensed the tacit qualification '. . . because I would not want to.' It did not count as Life.

Whereas I had never known anything so much like life. It was not just that I never, even at the most uncomfortable moments, thought I would be better off somewhere else, doing a job or raising a family. It was more that the question never even arose in my mind. There could not imaginably be a more excellent and fruitful way of living than doing what I was doing.

At the time I was already almost halfway round the world. I had long ago left behind the fears and heartaches of departure, and I was too far away from returning to think about what that might mean. When I thought of the journey ending I thought of it only in terms of death. I had always to bear in mind that my method of traveling was potentially dangerous, and there were enough near misses to keep the thought usefully fresh. I had, in fact, come to accept a fatal accident as not altogether improbable, and I was quite clear about being content to take the risk. This thought passed through my mind often enough to create in me the general sense that my journey around the world might be the last thing I ever did. I did not find that knowledge morbid or depressing. Far from it, I was exultant. I knew the journey was supremely worth doing, and whatever came afterwards, if there was to be an afterwards, was not worth thinking about.

I had never been reconciled to death in this way before. Of course, I did not court it. I took precautions and did my best to survive, but only in order to continue what was essentially a dangerous course. My purpose in staying alive was to do what I was doing from day to day, and not to fulfill some distant ambition. In fact, without realizing it, I was obeying the most fundamental precepts for a good life, and my later affinity with Buddhism and the words of the *Bhagavad Gita* came naturally. I was unusually indifferent to material comforts. I was relatively free of the more cloying human attachments. I was concerned almost entirely with the present, rather than the future or the past, and I was living at a level of awareness unprecedented in my own experience. I was nearly reconciled to my own mortality, and I was deeply involved in a project which I felt held a growing spiritual significance, not only for myself but for others.

Small wonder that I found more peace and strength in myself than I had ever known or thought possible. It fluctuated, naturally, but at best it enabled me to approach others without ulterior motive and, consequently, without anxiety. Shyness, as the writer John Stewart Collis says, is truly a form of conceit, and demonstrates ignorance of human nature. I had been guilty of it once, but there was not a drop left. I found I could love my fellow human beings all the more for knowing that our time together would be short, and they in turn excelled themselves in the knowledge that they need only keep it up for a little while.

During the journey I became lighter physically than I had ever been as an adult, and I felt that lightness in every part of me, mentally and emotionally as well. It made me feel transparent, and seemed to give me the reciprocal power to see through others. Rightly or wrongly, I felt I could see other people's personalities and problems virtually laid out before me. As the hundreds of encounters became thousands, this unexpected access to strangers became, for me, almost miraculous; and the ability to make instant and intimate contact with all kinds of human being, regardless of language, class or nationality, gave me great spiritual satisfaction.

Only in one important respect did the future intrude on the present. I was a writer as well as a rider. It was impossible for me to live through the experiences of that journey, and to run such a gamut of emotions, without feeling an urgent need to write about them. I had already filled one notebook in Africa. Now I was halfway through another. During the long hours that I rode the empty roads, over barren mountains and beside deserted shores, the people I had come to know so briefly but so well swarmed upon my memory with rapturous encores of a hundred funny happenings and mysteries galore. If and when the journey ended I would have to write a book, but how and where this would happen, and with whom if anyone I would live I had no notion. Writing the book, I thought, would simply be a continuation of the journey, and it gave no clue to a future life.

In that journey I had found, while it lasted, a way of life that elated me. Why, then, should it ever end? Now that the traveling and the writing are long since over I can see more clearly that I was caught in a paradox. The beauty of that experience was inseparable from its being finite and unrepeatable. In this world the closer one comes to the ideal state, the shorter is its duration. Ecstasy lasts only a moment; great happiness will scarcely outlive the hour; contentment may endure uninterrupted for a day at best. To expect a generally satisfying way of life to last for several years is already asking a good deal. If I had not foreseen the end, it could not have lasted as long as it did. I was only able to content myself so deeply with the matters of the moment because I knew that, in its own good time, the end would come and I would never know this same experience again.

Most of the people I met on the way were less satisfied in their lives than I. The richer and more comfortable they were, the less their satisfaction. And the reason, as I saw it, was that they were generally frustrating themselves in pursuit of some imagined future idyll, and feared that an end might come arbitrarily to cut them off from their reward. They were not living with their fate, as I was, but against it. They were trying to win the game, while protecting themselves from life.

My whole purpose was to make myself as vulnerable as I dared to the unexpected, and to allow myself to be changed by it. It was the best way I could devise to experience the world's infinite variety.

'Glory be to God for dappled things -' said Gerard Manley Hopkins,

> 'For skies of couple-colour as a brinded cow;
> 'For rose-moles all in stipple upon trout that swim;
> 'Fresh-firecoal chestnut-falls; finches' wings;
> 'Landscape plotted and pieced - fold, fallow, and plough;
> 'And all trades, their gear and tackle and trim.
> 'All things counter, original, spare, strange;
> 'Whatever is fickle, freckled (who knows how?)
> 'With swift, slow; sweet, sour; adazzle, dim;
> 'He fathers-forth whose beauty is past change:
> 'Praise Him.'

I traveled the world to delight in its strangenesses, but also to find some measure of them in myself. It was not just fascination for oddities that kept me going, but a continuing effort to incorporate them into some scheme of understanding which might give me a glimpse of their source: 'the Father whose beauty is without change'. And in wanting this, I suppose, I was not very different from most thinking beings, except that I had chosen a very intense and deliberate way of going about it.

Obviously the journey was an allegory of life itself. During the best times, in Africa, South America and India, it flowed like a river to the sea. Whatever the eddies, obstructions and disturbances at the surface, it had a deep underlying momentum that carried it steadily forward to its natural end.

The cabin under the walnuts in Round Valley - after two weeks work.

# *Epilogue*

W e spent September together in Mill Valley – William Alexander, Francesca and I. Then I went up to camp on our place, and began to work feverishly at building the cabin before the rains came. First I fought with the berry bushes, then I set the foundation posts, six concrete footings buried in the ground. In three weeks the bare structure was up and roofed – a cabin sixteen feet by thirty two feet. I commuted a couple of times and at the beginning of November we all moved up to Round Valley, but we didn't have to live in that draughty shell because, by then, we had friends and neighbours, and the Wilson family took us in through a hard, cold winter, until the cabin was closed in and ready.

The house site worked out very well. In the hot summer, the canopy of walnut leaves, and the breeze, kept us cool. In the winter, our wood stove kept us cozy. We did many of the things I had always dreamed of. We kept pigs, and sheep and chickens. I built a barn and grew organic vegetables. Francesca did some weaving, but not enough. We had some wonderful times, but we had terrible times too. Things changed a lot through the years as WAS grew up to be the handsome young man that he is.

Sadly, there was never an IS. Francesca moved on, and of course we were not happy ever after. But then, tell me who is? And, after all, the journey, that long, wonderful journey, goes on.